AMERICAN HISTORY at SWT

Volume I

Second Edition

Department of History
Southwest Texas State University

KENDALL/HUNT PUBLISHING COMPANY
2460 Kerper Boulevard P.O. Box 539 Dubuque, Iowa 52004-0539

Billington, Ray Allen, "The Know-Nothing Uproar,", © 1959, by AMERICAN HERITAGE, a division of Forbes, Inc., February 1959, pp. 58–61, 94–97.

Carson, Gerald, "A Tax on Whiskey? Never," © 1963, by AMERICAN HERITAGE, a division of Forbes, Inc., August 1963, pp. 63–64, 101–105.

Catton, Bruce, "Hayfoot, Strawfoot," © 1957, by AMERICAN HERITAGE, a division of Forbes, Inc., April 1957, pp. 30–37.

Demos, John, "Entertaining Satan," © 1978, by AMERICAN HERITAGE, a division of Forbes, Inc., August 1978, pp. 14–23.

Haines, Francis, "How the Indian Got the Horse," © 1964, by AMERICAN HERITAGE, a division of Forbes, Inc., February 1964, pp. 17–18, 78–81.

Ketchum, Richard M., "England's Vietnam: the American Revolution," © 1971, by AMERICAN HERITAGE, a division of Forbes, Inc., June 1971, pp. 6–11, 81–83.

Koenig, Louis W., "The Rise of the Little Magician," © 1962, by AMERICAN HERITAGE, a division of Forbes, Inc., June 1962, pp. 29–31, 88–94.

Larkin, Jack. "The Secret Life of a Developing Country (Ours)," © 1988, by AMERICAN HERITAGE, a division of Forbes, Inc., September 1988, pp. 44–62.

McPherson, James M., "A War That Never Goes Away," © 1990, by AMERICAN HERITAGE, a division of Forbes, Inc., March, 1990, pp. 41–49.

Oates, Stephen B., "Children of Darkness," © 1973, by AMERICAN HERITAGE, a division of Forbes, Inc., October 1973, pp. 42–47, 89–91 .

Plumb, J. H., "America: Illusion and Reality," © 1976, by AMERICAN HERITAGE, a division of Forbes, Inc., August 1976, pp. 14–25.

Stewart, George R., "The Prairie Schooner Got Them There," © 1962, by AMERICAN HERITAGE, a division of Forbes, Inc., February 1962, pp. 4–17, 98–102.

Swan, Jon, "The Slave Who Sued for Freedom," © 1990, by AMERICAN HERITAGE, a division of Forbes, Inc., March 1990, pp. 51–55.

Weisberger, Bernard, "The Working Ladies of Lowell," © 1961, by AMERICAN HERITAGE, a division of Forbes, Inc., February 1961, pp. 42–45, 83–90.

Winston, Alexander, "Firebrand of the Revolution," © 1967, by AMERICAN HERITAGE, a division of Forbes, Inc., April 1967, pp. 61–64, 105–108.

Cover Illustration by Merry K. FitzPatrick

Contents

Part VI: Civil War and Reconstruction

Primary Documents

Part I:
Colonial America

America: Illusion and Reality

J. H. Plumb

merica was an experience man could only have once. Knowledge of China, knowledge of Africa, festooned as it was with the Spanish moss of myth and legend, had penetrated Europe from the days of Imperial Rome and beyond. When discovered, the animals of Australasia were stranger by far than America's, and the aborigines and the bushmen of Tasmania were more primitive, even more uniformly naked than the Caribs whose appearance was so startling to Columbus. By then the strangeness of the Americas had destroyed the sense of novelty. There could only be one New World.

When confronted by novelty, men try to domesticate what is strange and alien; they attempt to fit the exotic into their cherished intellectual schemes and to absorb it into their interpretation of the world and its past. They retain, as it were, a husk of strangeness in which to take delight, or to weave fantasies, or worse still to construct rationalizations of their own evil intentions. The discovery of America had all of these effects and more, for no event in the history of Western man provided so profound a shock to the imagination or to the mind. And yet one might argue that the most important results of this discovery were far more mundane—maize, tobacco, gold, fur—the never-ending abundance of the land that led to the rape of a continent which became a golden pasture for human locusts.

Columbus, amazed, unsure, reluctant to accept that he was *not* in the Indies, found it easier to fit the Caribs into the legend of the Golden Age. As Peter Martyr, the friend of Columbus, wrote in the early 1500's, they "seem to live in that golden world of which old writers speak so much, wherein men lived simply and innocently without enforcement of laws, without quarrelling, judges and libels, content only to satisfy nature." This was the beginning of that ever-lengthening legend of the innocence of America which shifts from island to the mainland, from Caribs to noble Indian chiefs. It took many centuries to die; indeed, it is hardly dead yet, for nowadays the innocence has been transferred to the wilderness, to the desert, to the primitive land still unscarred in the West.

The theory that the naked Caribs lived in innocent bliss was soon dispelled. The Spaniards learned with horror that the Caribs hung up the hams of men and women to cure in the sun like sides of bacon. They relished the taste of human flesh; for them it was a gourmet's revenge on an enemy. When the Spaniards began to root themselves inefficiently in Hispaniola, the denizens of the Golden Age rapidly became subhuman. The Spaniards stressed their cannibalism, their nakedness, their fornication, and their frequently deviant and public sexuality. This savage paganism made their salvation imperative and their servitude justifiable.

The Caribs wanted neither salvation nor servitude. Killed, hunted, tortured, beaten, and worked to death, they soon began to vanish, until genocide was virtually accomplished. Today scarcely any remain, but before they almost totally disappeared they had woven themselves into the imagination of Europe, as Hugh Honour has shown us in his recent book *The New Golden Land*, which is a brilliant discussion of the way the discovery of America haunted the European artistic imagination.

These Caribs, however, did more than stimulate the imagination. The brutal treatment accorded to them unleashed the passion of Bartolomé de Las Casas, whose bitter pen damned Spanish cruelty to a believing world of French, British, Germans, and Dutch—who, however, behaved no better themselves once they got a foothold in the New World. But Las Casas' fiery words and the undeniable truth of his tale of the brutalities, the killing, the torturing, and the wholesale destruction of primitive peoples started an enduring theme in America's history that still resonates in our own day. It is a long, bloody, bitter, and sad road that leads from Hispaniola to the slaughter at Wounded Knee or the atrocities in the forests of Brazil. Innocence and betrayal, fascination and disgust, illusion and reality, these have so often been the dual response of Europeans to the primitive peoples of America.

The discovery of America led to an appalling destruction of human life—probably over twenty million died in a half century—a fact all too rarely depicted in the artistic vision of America. It was the strangeness, the exotic nature of the people, the ornaments, their color that entranced the artist. They might pose them like classical heroes, but they dressed them in their own feather headdresses and feathered skirts or left them stark naked. For the first two decades these natives remained amorphous, exotic yet somewhat unreal, like strange Europeans. Many artists who painted them had never seen an Indian, although from Columbus' first voyage a few men and women had been ripped from their homes to be displayed as curiosities in the courts of Europe.

It was only quite late in the sixteenth century that Indians were depicted more accurately, placed in more exact settings, and their customs, dances, and villages shown with some appreciation of reality. John White's water colors of the Indians of Virginia, among whom he lived briefly in 1585–6, show greater precision and accuracy, even though he refrained from depicting the more primitive and savage of their customs. A Frenchman, Jacques Le Moyne, had been far more candid in his sketches of Florida Indians, but true realism had to wait until the seventeenth century, when two fine Dutch painters—Frans Post and Albert Eckhout—painted Brazilian landscapes and people exactly and vividly. And yet the art of fantasy in European paintings of Indians was not eradicated for centuries; even Delacroix in the early nineteenth century could paint Indians who looked like well-bred Europeans in fancy dress. The tradition of realism started by John White developed more slowly and only reached its apogee with Catlin, Bodmer, and Rosa Bonheur, just before the genocide of the Indians had begun in earnest.

It was not only the exoticism of the people that both entranced and horrified Europeans. Columbus had gone in search of riches, of the fabulous Cathay. The Spaniards wanted gold. And they found it, bountifully in Mexico and beyond their wildest hopes in Peru; and the gold in the end led to the mountains of silver in Potosí and Taxco. This success in the search for riches came slowly. There were very barren decades, so that every object that was rich and exotic to look at was valuable as propaganda in the courts of Europe, which had to finance the early voyages of exploration and colonization. So the splendors of Central and South American civilizations were soon on their way to Europe—the great golden disks, the brilliant feather-work cloaks, the terrifying death masks in jade and greenstone, works that when Albrecht Dürer saw them in Brussels made him marvel at "the subtle *ingenia* of men in foreign lands."

To the emperors they were indicators of riches to come, not works of art, and the golden vases, fountains, and animals that passed into the court of Charles V were quickly melted down for the money he always lacked. The feather cloaks were thrown away or left to rot in the attics of his palaces. Only a few men of taste or of obsessive curiosity found a home for them in their cabinets, and today only a handful of objects survive from the first century of European discovery.

Among the earliest collectors to appreciate the singularity and beauty of Mexican art were the emperor Ferdinand I (who died in 1564) and his two sons; the extraordinary Rudolph II, a patron of everything exotic; and not surprisingly, perhaps, the greatest family of art patrons in Italy—the Medici, who as early as 1539 had brought together, as Hugh Honour reminds us, forty-four pieces of feather-work as well as carved masks and animals in semiprecious stone. Perhaps the strangest fate of any American object in the sixteenth century was that of a Mexican obsidian disk that fell into the hands of John Dee, Queen Elizabeth I's astrologer and magician, who used it to conjure up spirits. It was, however, the common objects, novel to Europe yet totally adaptable, that were most quickly diffused—the first being the hammock, unknown to European gardens and ships until discovered in the West Indies; equally adaptable but later in time came the canoe of the American Indians and the kayak of the Eskimos.

Just as amazing to Columbus as the inhabitants of the West Indies were the flora and fauna of the New World. Some, of course, were easy to assimilate. The rather subdued colored parrots of Africa had been greatly prized possessions of the Europeans in the late Middle Ages, but the brilliant colored parrots of Brazil rapidly replaced them. These were represented as early as 1502 in Europe and appeared in a painting by Carpaccio, the Venetian artist, as early as 1507. Along with hummingbirds and Mexican quail, they were used as brilliant decorative motifs in the Loggetta of Raphael at the Vatican.

Hugh Honour has demonstrated the astonishing speed with which the artists of the Renaissance seized upon American birds and animals as well as Indians to use as dramatic motifs in their painting and sculpture. The turkey—now the all-pervasive Christmas dish of English families—reached Europe almost as quickly as the parrot. It was bred in Spain shortly after 1500, and the bird had reached Britain by 1525. Ironically, a hundred years after its discovery by Columbus the turkey had reached the East Indies. But it was the odder birds and animals that excited the most curiosity—the iguana, which was thought to be a dragon, discovered at last; the armadillo, whose true nature baffled scholars for decades; the opossum, which was the first marsupial known to Europeans; and the tapir and the llama, both of which defied description.

More important than the attempt to describe and to draw the birds, animals, and plants was the impact of their variety on the development of European botany and zoology. Knowledge of the new animals had reached Europe, along with specimens, from time to time. The rhinoceros had made a vivid impression on Europe, but Europeans had never been subjected to such a flood of wholly new birds, animals, fruits, vegetables, trees, and flowers as they were from the New World between 1500 and 1550. And it was this variety, its strangeness, and, at times, its marvelous adaptability and usefulness that led to the beginning of a scientifically precise observation—indeed, the beginning of botany and zoology as we know them.

The flora had a far greater impact than the birds and animals, so few of which could be domesticated. Maize, which could easily be grown in Europe, was exploited at once; within ten years of its discovery it was being cultivated in Italy, where it transformed Italian agriculture. Similarly, cassava, which reached West Africa very shortly after the Portuguese discovery of Brazil, had a like dramatic effect. The potato, which took far longer to establish itself as a crop rather than as a curiosity, ultimately had a more profound effect on European history than maize. The high nutritious quality of the potato enabled the European, particularly the Irish peasant, to maintain himself and his family on tinier and tinier garden plots. Millions of men and women depended on a single crop, and the disastrous potato blight of the nineteenth century destroyed the population in a monstrous famine in 1845 and, in an ironic twist of history, sent tens of thousands of starving Irish to find a new life and a new hope in America.

The contributions of the flora of the Americas to the enrichment of Europe is nearly endless; foods such as tomatoes, tapioca, chocolate, pineapples, avocados, runner beans, Jerusalem artichokes, passion fruit, and many more: flowers now common in Europe, such as morning-glory, nasturtium, dahlia, and the tobacco plant, the most dangerous and deadly of all the plants to reach not only Europe but the entire globe, certainly one of the greatest of all hazards to human health. It was thought oddly enough to be deadly and dangerous when first discovered, and no one damned it with greater vehemence than James I of England. But the habit of smoking proved contagious and the profit impossible to resist. The land of America was quickly ravaged by Europe's addiction to tobacco—and not only America but also Africa, whence came the slave labor needed for its intensive cultivation. What in 1570 was depicted as a delicately beautiful flower decoration of Albrecht V of Bavaria's prayer book became in less than fifty years a major export for America and a sweeping addiction with traumatic economic and social effects on Africa and Europe.

The potato and tobacco, along with maize, are perhaps the best known of the vegetables that changed the eating and social habits of Europe. What, perhaps, is not such common knowledge is that the great movement in landscape gardening that changed the face of the English countryside in the eighteenth century also owed a great deal to America, above all to Virginia. The Virginian oak was planted by the hundreds of thousands; so were a large number of American pines; and the *Magnolia grandiflora* became the prize possession of even small gardens. Without the influence of America the English landscape would look quite different today.

However, the mental image of America remained more powerful than the influence upon European artistic expression of its exotic people, plants, and animals, and surely matched even the influence of such exceptional material agents as maize, the potato, or tobacco. America remained for centuries the only New World. When the northern colonies established the first federal republic, at whose birth the liberties and rights of men were proclaimed as inalienable, another New World was born, as potent as that discovered by Columbus. A new political world had come into being, utterly distinct from anything Europe had known before—and one that created as entrancing an illusion as the civilizations the conquistadors had discovered.

To the poor and downtrodden peasants and workers of Europe it held out a new hope, a glittering image of riches and freedom. It is easy to forget the bitterness and brutalities of the ghettos of Europe or the starvation and deprivation that the wretched villagers of Greece and Italy suffered. It was their despair that eventually drove them to the coffin ships in which thousands died as they made the Atlantic crossing. The reality they found in America was harsher: hunger stalked on the Lower East Side; once more deprivation for many became part of their lot in life. And yet there *was* a reality in the illusion. There was more liberty, more social hope in America than in the lands they had quitted. There still is, in spite of the black ghettos and the long-enduring memory of slavery. The destruction of primitive peoples and slavery are the harsh realities of the American experience, for whose nakedness the Constitution, with its proud declaration of liberty, proved so pathetic a rag. So often illusion provided hope, reality the fate. And yet whatever the American experience might be, it remained for most Europeans an exotic continent.

After Buffalo Bill's fabulous success small boys in Riga, in Manchester, in Lyon, in Milan, played for generation after generation at cowboys and Indians; in the twentieth century Hollywood provided the dreams for the masses, and Disney captured the imagination of the child. No longer a fairyland of exotic peoples, animals, and plants, America has created a new world of fantasy.

In the lives of children, in the dream time of adolescents, even in the sexual expectations of the adult world, America still feeds Europe with its illusions. As with the illusions of the past, a harsher reality is always breaking in: the drugs, the dropouts, the divorces. Perhaps the tobacco plant with its vivid flowers, intoxicating scent, and deadly leaves should be the enduring symbol of that strange combination of illusion and reality with which America has continued to haunt Europe since its discovery.

How the Indian Got the Horse

Francis Haines

On Thursday, May 24, 1855, Lieutenant Lawrence Kip of the U.S. Army, stationed at Fort Walla Walla in what is now Washington, made this entry in his diary:

This has been an extremely interesting day, as about 2,500 of the Nez Percé tribe have arrived. It was our first specimen of this Prairie chivalry, and it certainly realized all our conceptions of these wild warriors of the plains. Their coming was announced about 10 o'clock, and going out on the plain to where a flag staff had been erected, we saw them approaching in one long line. They were almost entirely naked, gaudily painted and decorated with their wild trappings. Their plumes fluttered about them, while below, skins and trinkets of all kinds of fantastic embellishments flaunted in the sunshine. Trained from early childhood almost to live upon horseback, they sat upon their fine animals as if they were centaurs. Their horses, too, were arrayed in the most glaring finery. They were painted with such colors as formed the greatest contrast; the white being smeared with crimson in fantastic figures, and the dark colors streaked with white clay. Beads and fringes, of gaudy colors were hanging from the bridles, while the plumes of eagle feathers interwoven with the mane and tail, fluttered as the breeze swept over them, and completed their wild and fantastic appearance.

This image of the proud Indian on his splendid horse, both of them splashed with gaudy war paint and adorned with feathered devices, seems to personify the spirit of the old West in those far-off times before the buffalo herds were all slaughtered and barbed wire had enclosed the high plains. Very probably young Lieutenant Kip, like most white people of his day, accepted without question the idea that the Indians had always had horses. They were obviously an inseparable and essential element of Indian culture on the Great

Plains; and indeed, the first Anglo-Americans to reach those areas, in the latter part of the eighteenth century, had found the mounted Indians already in full force. Yet in 1855 less than 150 years had passed since the first Nez Percé ever to mount a horse had taken his first daring ride.

The fossil discoveries of the later nineteenth century made it clear that, although prehistoric horses had roamed the western plains in large numbers for a million years, some odd, selective catastrophe wiped them out, along with camels, perhaps 15,000 years ago. Hence, when the Spanish explorers of the sixteenth century rode their horses into the Southwest, the Indians gazed with wonder at the strange beasts. The process by which the native tribes adopted the animal, and consequently were able to hold the land against all intruders until the destruction of the buffalo herds starved them into submission, has been the subject of much speculation and dispute.

Until recent years historians and anthropologists accepted rather casually the theory that horses lost from early Spanish expeditions had, by natural increase, stocked the western ranges with wild bands that supplied the various Indian tribes with their animals. The favored choice for the supposed source of the breeding stock was either the expedition of Hernando de Soto or that of Francisco Vásquez de Coronado, both of which reached the plains of Texas in 1541–42.

De Soto, after conquering Peru, had returned to Spain, married, and secured the governorship of Cuba, with the privilege of exploring and conquering Florida and the land to the north and west. His quest ended when he died of fever on the shore of the Mississippi River in May, 1542. The remnants of his forces, led by Luis Moscoso, travelled west and south to Texas in a vain attempt to reach Mexico overland. Failing in this, they returned to the Mississippi and built a fleet of seven brigantines on which they embarked with 22 horses, all that were left of their original 243.

As the Spaniards sailed down the river they killed the horses one by one for food, until only five or six of the best were left. These they turned loose in a small, grassy meadow near the mouth of the river. Legend would have it that these horses remembered the plains of Texas and wished to return there. They swam the river, splashed through a hundred miles of swamps and marshes, and finally reached open country with abundant grass. Here, supposedly, they settled down and reproduced at a prodigious rate. Soon their offspring covered the Texas plains and attracted the attention of the local

Indians, who knew how to catch and train them from having seen the Spanish ride by on such animals years ago.

Stubborn facts undermine this pretty tale. First, one of the Spaniards in Moscoso's party said later that Indians came out of the bushes and shot the liberated horses full of arrows even before the Spanish boats had passed beyond the next bend. Second, even if they had survived, the route to the west was impassable for horses, which in any case had no way of knowing the direction to take to reach Texas. Third, and finally, these war horses were all stallions. The Spanish rode no other kind to battle. For these reasons it is obvious that de Soto's animals could not have stocked the western plains with horses, wild or tame.

The other candidate, Francisco Coronado, approached Texas from the west. He started from Mexico City, mustered his expedition at Compostela, and marched north to Arizona, then east to New Mexico and on to Texas. In 1541 he approached the Plains with a force estimated at 1,500 people, 1,000 horses, 500 cattle, and 5,000 sheep. He spent more than five months on the Plains, where he lost many horses. Some were gored by buffalo, some fell into a ravine during a buffalo chase. A few might have strayed away without their loss being noted by the chronicler, and it is conceivable that a stallion and a mare might have strayed off together. The muster rolls of the expedition list two mares starting out from Compostela, and there might have been a few more not listed.

Assume, then, that such a pair escaped in northern Texas, adjusted to the range conditions, and produced offspring, all of whom survived. It is mathematically possible that in sixty years or so the resulting herd would number several thousand. They would have ranged the plains for hundreds of miles, leaving their spoor at every water hole. Yet Spanish explorers and buffalo hunters from the later Sante Fe settlements found no wild horses of any kind in this area before 1700. It seems reasonable, then, that any such strays were wiped out by bad water, storms, accidents, and predators such as the wolf and cougar. These hazards to the foals should not be discounted; in 1719 the Paducahs reported that they had not been able to raise any colts, but had to obtain all their horses by barter—and they had owned horses for several years by that time.

Nor could even the most intelligent Indian hope to learn the art of catching, breaking, and training wild horses just from watching the Spanish ride by on tame ones. For a primitive people to learn such a complex pattern in a short space of time, they must have skilled horsemen for teachers and gentle, well-trained horses to handle. Even under these conditions such learning is sometimes difficult.

For example, according to Flathead tradition, their tribe secured a gentle horse in western Montana around 1700, and some of them attempted to ride it. One man would lead the horse slowly along while the rider attempted to balance himself with the aid of two long sticks, one in each hand, reaching to the ground like crutches. When one of the young men finally managed to ride unaided at a trot, he was the hero of the whole band.

The simplest and most effective way for the Indians of the Southwest to learn how to break, train, and care for horses was for them to work for the Spaniards. Such an opportunity was forced on the Pueblo Indians of New Mexico in the seventeenth century.

In 1595 Philip II of Spain commissioned Juan de Oñate, a wealthy citizen of Zacatecas, to conquer and settle the upper valley of the Rio Grande del Norte, where the Pueblo Indians lived in their farming villages. Early in the spring of 1598 Oñate led forth his caravan of soldiers and settlers, with their families and slaves, both Indian and Negro. Franciscan friars accompanied the caravan to care for the spiritual needs of the settlers and to convert the heathen.

They travelled north across Chihuahua and through the great gap in the mountains, El Paso del Norte. There they crossed the Rio Grande and swung east and north to avoid the river canyon. Finally they reached the upper valley with its Indian settlements and took possession of all the land, forcing the Pueblos to work as serfs in the fields they had once owned.

The Spanish brought herds of sheep, cattle, and horses to pasture on the desert ranges. Herding these animals was an endless task, for there were no fences of any kind on the pasture lands and no adequate material for building them until the invention of barbed wire some two and a half centuries later. Even the cultivated fields in the alluvial soil along the valley floor went unfenced from lack of material. Hence herdsmen were needed day and night to keep the flocks and herds from straying, to protect the animals from predators, and to keep them out of the growing crops.

Indian herdsmen proved adept at managing the sheep and goats, moving them to fresh pastures and holding them away from the fields. This they could do on foot; but the half-wild range cattle could be handled only by skilled *vaqueros* mounted on fleet, well-trained horses. Spain, in her colonial regulations, had decreed that no Indian should be permitted to own or ride a horse. Thus all the arduous work of handling the range cattle and range horses devolved on the Spanish men.

Each *vaquero* needed a riding string of twelve to fifteen horses to handle his job properly. These animals were not shod, and seldom tasted grain. A *vaquero's* mount needed several days of rest after each day of work, to regain his strength and to allow his hoofs to grow. Each Spanish family also needed several horses for transportation, for there were no carriage roads on the frontier. Many additional horses were needed for military patrols, and for exploring expeditions or the pursuit of raiding Indians. A large herd of breeding stock was necessary to supply all these animals.

The care of these thousands of horses required a good deal of menial labor, furnished, of course, by the Indians. Indian boys brought fresh horses in for their masters to use, and returned the tired ones to the corrals. They did the saddling, unsaddling, and rubbing down. They fed and watered the animals, and cleaned the stables and corrals. Sometimes a rancher, careless of the regulations forbidding an Indian to ride, would send a boy to help drive in a herd from the hills; sometimes, leaving on an extended journey, he would choose two or three Indians to ride with him—to look after the spare mounts and to handle the camp chores. In the face of emergencies the decrees of King Philip of Spain carried little weight on the frontier, far from the eyes of the nearest government official. So, in one way or another, the stable boys learned how to ride and how to handle horses.

Most of the Pueblo Indians resigned themselves to servitude under the Spanish. They had no place to run, no place to hide. But for a stable boy there was one avenue of escape if conditions became too harsh or masters too domineering; and his work with the horses seemed to breed in him more spirit than showed in the field hand. By watching for a favorable opportunity, the stable boy could slip away some dark evening with two or three of the best horses, and be off to an independent tribe, safe from effective pursuit. He might risk death or further enslavement, but there was always a good chance that the tribe would accept him and his horses. Then he could teach them the art of horsemanship, and could help his hosts secure more horses from the ranches.

With such a teacher, and some tame, well-trained horses to work with, the wild tribe could rapidly learn how to use this wonderful new mode of transport. Soon they would want more horses and would take their goods off to trade with the Spanish, as they had been doing for years. But the Spanish were reluctant to trade horses to the Indians: such trading took place in towns, under the eyes of Spanish colonial officials.

When the Spanish refused to exchange horses for dried meat and tanned robes, the Indians sought other articles of trade, and found one so valuable to the Spanish that the laws would be suspended in special cases. The Indians traded men.

The Spanish, in an effort to discourage the escape of Pueblo Indians, offered cloth and weapons for any runaways the wild tribes could capture. But the Indians soon learned that the Spanish would pay higher prices for mission Indians, and still higher prices to ransom Spaniards captured by the tribes. They demanded horses for such captives, and the priests argued with the civil authorities that it was better to bend the law a little than to leave Christians in heathen hands.

Thus, year by year, the tribes adjacent to the Spanish settlements learned to use horses, and slowly increased their herds. The first documentary evidence of the use of horses by Indians in the American West comes sixty-one years after the arrival of Oñate's colony: In 1659 the governor at Sante Fe sent to Mexico City an official report of a raid from the northwest by a band of mounted Navaho Apaches.

Finally, in 1680, the Pueblo Indians rose up against their masters. They resented the brutal treatment, the forced labor, and, above all, the strict laws against their ancient religious ceremonies. A deposed medicine man, Popé, organized a widespread revolt, and on the appointed day the Pueblos attacked at many points in northern New Mexico, killing over 400 Spanish in the first attack. The 2,500 survivors withdrew to El Paso to wait for reinforcements from Mexico; but they had lost their homes, their farms, and all their herds to the Indians.

The Pueblo Indians found the horse herds an embarrassment of riches. They were hard to manage on the range, and they ate the grass needed for sheep. Moreover, the Pueblos had no use for as many horses as the Spanish had abandoned. They were willing to trade large numbers of them to the Plains tribes to the northeast, and to the Navahos and Utes to the northwest. The Pueblos also lacked the organization to patrol the ranges as the Spanish had done, and lost more horses to enemy raiders.

All through the Plains regions each band had friendly trade relations with two or three of its neighbors. A farming village would customarily trade with a hunting band to the south and another to the north. Each of these hunting bands in turn would trade with another farming village, the hunters in each case offering dried meat and buffalo robes for corn and squash. This helps to explain the rapid spread of horses to all the Plains tribes. The result was a basic pattern of horse culture, borrowed from the Spanish and common to all the western tribes using horses.

Typically, this trading pattern would provide each tribe at first with a few older, gentler horses. Nez Percé tradition, handed down by word of mouth to early white frontiersmen, gives an account of such an event. According to this story they got their first animal, a gentle white mare, from the Shoshone in the Boise Valley. Day after day the curious Nez Percés gathered from all around to watch the mare crop grass near the village. They learned how a horse acted: how it fed, how it exercised, how it rested. In a few weeks the mare dropped a foal, and the crowds increased. Soon other villages sent south for horses of their own, to be treasured as curiosities and pets. At The Dalles, Oregon, some two hundred miles down river from the Nez Percé, the first few horses were led around at festivals and were shown at the big dances. Later they were used as pack animals, and finally as riding horses.

Although details of the first contacts with horses among the Plains tribes have been lost, they must have followed the Nez Percé pattern. In each case it would take a tribe only about ten to fifteen years to learn how to use the great innovation, and to build up a substantial herd.

Horses made life far easier, richer, and more exciting for the Plains tribes. One good horseman in a morning hunt could kill enough buffalo to supply his family with meat for weeks, and robes for a year. Now tepees could be much larger, for a horse could carry a lodge-covering weighing 200 to 300 pounds, and drag the many long tepee poles needed to support it. The whole band now had more leisure time, and more chance to develop the special Plains culture which was in full flower by 1800.

As for the impact of the horse on Indian warfare, it would be difficult to exaggerate. With the tremendous increase in mobility and speed, the Plains warrior became a truly formidable foe. General Randolph B. Marcy, a Regular Army officer with many years of experience in the West, wrote this impression of the mounted Indian in his memoirs:

> His only ambition consists in being able to cope successfully with his enemy in war and in managing his steed with unfailing adroitness. He is in the saddle from boyhood to old age, and his favorite horse is his constant companion. It is when mounted that the prairie warrior exhibits himself to the best advantage; here he is at home, and his skill in various maneuvers which he makes available in battle—such as throwing himself entirely upon one side of his horse and discharging his arrows with great rapidity toward the opposite side from beneath the animal's neck while he is at full speed—is truly astonishing. . . . Every warrior has his war-horse, which is the fleetest that can be obtained, and he prizes him more highly than anything else in his possession, and it is seldom that he can be induced to part with him at any price.

Farming tribes along the borders of the Plains found the horses almost as valuable as did their brothers to the west. They began to range farther from home in a seminomadic state for several months of each year, subsisting more on meat and less on corn. Added mobility increased their trading area and gave them a greater variety of goods. Some of them even gave up their old ways entirely and became true nomads of the Plains.

Chief among these wanderers were the Sioux. They are usually considered the typical Indian tribe of the northern Plains, yet as late as 1766 at least one large band of Sioux still lived in the lake and swamp district of Minnesota. They used bark huts for shelter and canoes for transportation; wild rice furnished most of their food. Within the next decade they gave up their canoes for horses, and their wild rice for buffalo. They moved out to the grasslands of North Dakota and developed spectacular riding costumes topped with the famous Sioux war bonnet.

This late acquisition of horses by the Yankton Sioux emphasizes the relatively slow northward movement of the horse frontier on the Great Plains. Many thousands of animals were needed to fill those vast grazing lands and to supply the numerous large tribes. Winter storms and fierce wolves took heavy toll of the colts, so most of the increase of the herds depended on fresh stock from the New Mexico ranches.

West of the Continental Divide the horse moved northward more rapidly. Here the Indians were few in number, and in the central areas their small valleys furnished scant pasture; hence within thirty years or so, the horses had moved north of Great Salt Lake to the fine stock ranges of the upper Snake Valley, where they multiplied rapidly. Here they had ample protection from the winter storms and predators were less of a problem than on the Plains. Even the desert plateau furnished ample forage in the winter when storms filled the water holes. This was the country of the western Shoshone, who in time furnished stock to all their neighbors, especially to the Crows, Blackfeet, and Nez Percé.

Once the Nez Percé secured some breeding stock they found that their country was even better for raising range horses than the upper Snake Valley. With excellent grass, ample water, and both summer and winter ranges, it cost them little effort to raise more horses than they could use. They learned to geld some of their poorer stallions, and this practice, combined with their fine range land, produced horses of superior quality.

Up to this time the Nez Percé had been a fishing tribe, living in about fifty small, permanent villages along the Snake River and its tributaries, the Clearwater and the Salmon. Once they learned to use horses, they became more adventurous. They opened a trail along the timbered ridges of the Bitterroot Range to reach the buffalo herds of Montana more than a hundred miles away. In Montana they soon met the Crows and Blackfeet, and later the Sioux. From each they borrowed items of Plains culture, until they had more in common with the Plains Indians than they did with their old neighbors in the fishing villages to the west.

From their ample herds the Nez Percé eventually supplied horses to all their neighbors—at a price, of course. Each year they would ride out to the various intertribal trading grounds with some of their excess stock. One such center was a hundred miles north of the Snake River, on the small plain where the Little Spokane River joins the main stream a few miles below the falls. Since the Spokanes and the Nez Percé were of different language groups, the bartering had to be carried on principally by signs. Each usual article of trade, including the average horse, had an established value, yet the trading was a leisurely process.

The Nez Percé lined up on one side, each man holding the lead rope of his "trading" horse. Each Spokane came forward and placed his pile of trade goods in front of the horse he liked. If the Nez Percé was satisfied, he handed over the lead rope and took the goods. If not, he might try for an extra article, or he might lead his horse to some other pile which interested him. It might take all of a pleasant summer day to trade forty horses, but this seemed to worry nobody.

The Nez Percé also traded horses as far west as The Dalles, and as far east as the Crow country in southern Montana. Later they traded mounts to the fur companies, and to travellers on the Oregon Trail.

George Catlin, the great painter of Indians in the early West, made an entry in his journal in 1834 that epitomizes what the horse did for the Indian. The artist had just encountered his first Comanches, and he soon concluded that they were the most extraordinary horsemen in the world. Dismounted, he wrote, they were "heavy and ungraceful . . . one of the most unattractive and slovenly-looking races of Indians that I have ever seen; but the moment they mount their horses, they seem at once metamorphosed, and surprise the spectator with the ease and elegance of their movements. A Camanchee on his feet is out of his element, and comparatively almost as awkward as a monkey on the ground, without a limb or a branch to cling to; but the moment he lays his hand upon his horse, his *face*, even, becomes handsome, and he gracefully flies away like a different being."

One of the Spanish conquistadors, in the sixteenth century, had observed confidently: "Horses are what the Indians dread most, and by means of which they will be overcome." He failed to foresee that the Indians would make the horse their own, and that thereby their native culture would not only be tremendously enhanced, but would flourish for over a hundred years before their warriors would be crushed by the advancing Anglo-Americans.

A Model of Christian Charity (1630)

John Winthrop

G od Almighty, in His most holy and wise providence, hath so disposed of the condition of mankind, as in all times some must be rich, some poor, some high and eminent in power and dignity, others mean and in subjection.

THE REASON HEREOF

First, to hold conformity with the rest of His works. Being delighted to show forth the glory of His wisdom in the variety and difference of the creatures; and the glory of His power, in ordering all these differences for the preservation and good of the whole; . . .

Secondly, that He might have the more occasion to manifest the work of His Spirit. . . .

Thirdly, that every man might have need of other, and from hence they might be all knit more nearly together in the bond of brotherly affection. From hence it appears plainly that no man is made more honorable than another, or more wealthy etc., out of any particular and singular respect to himself, but for the glory of his creator and the common good of the creature, man. . . .

It rests now to make some application of this discourse by the present design, which gave the occasion of writing of it. Herein are four things to be propounded: first, the persons; secondly, the work; thirdly, the end; fourthly, the means.

First, for the persons. We are a company professing ourselves fellow members of Christ, in which respect only, though were absent

From *The Winthrop Papers in Five Volumes*, Volume 2 pp. 282–295. Published and copyrighted by the Massachusetts Historical Society. Reprinted by permission from each other many miles, and had our employments as far distant, yet we ought to account ourselves knit together by this bond of love, and live in the exercise of it, if we would have comfort of our being in Christ. This was notorious in the practice of the Christians in former times; . . .

Secondly, for the work we have in hand. It is by a mutual consent, through a special overvaluing providence and a more than an ordinary approbation of the churches of Christ, to seek out a place of cohabitation and consortship under a due form of government both civil and ecclesiastical. In such cases as this, the care of the public must oversway all private respects, by which not only conscience, but mere civil policy, doth bind us. For it is a true rule that particular estates cannot subsist in the ruin of the public.

Thirdly, the end is to improve our lives to do more service to the Lord, the comfort and increase of the body of Christ whereof we are members, that ourselves and posterity may be the better preserved from the common corruptions of this evil world, to serve the Lord and work out our salvation under the power and purity of his holy ordinances.

Fourthly, for the means whereby this must be effected. They are twofold: a conformity with the work and end we aim at; these we see are extraordinary, therefore we must not content ourselves with usual ordinary means. Whatsoever we did, or ought to have done, when we lived in England, the same must we do, and more also, where we go. That which the most in their churches maintain as a truth in profession only, we must bring into familiar and constant practice, as in this duty of love. We must love brotherly without dissimulation, we must love one another with a pure heart fervently, we must bear one another's burdens, we must not look only on our own things, but also on the things of our brethren. Neither must we think that the Lord will bear with such failings at our hands as He doth from those among whom we have lived, and that for three reasons.

First, in regard of the more near bond of marriage between Him and us, wherein He hath taken us to be His after a most strict and peculiar manner, which will make Him the more jealous of our love and obedience. So He tells the people of Israel, you only have I known of all the families of the earth, therefore will I punish you for your transgressions. Secondly, because the Lord will be sanctified in them that come near Him. We know that there were many that corrupted the service of the Lord, some setting up altars before

His own, others offering both strange fire and strange sacrifices also; yet there came no fire from heaven or other sudden judgment upon them, as did upon Nadab and Abihu, who yet we may think did not sin presumptuously. Thirdly, when God gives a special commission He looks to have it strictly observed in every article. When He gave Saul a commission to destroy Amalek, He indented with him upon certain articles, and because he failed in one of the least, and that upon a fair pretense, it lost him the kingdom which should have been his reward if he had observed his commission.

Thus stands the cause between God and us. We are entered into covenant with Him for this work; we have taken out a commission, the Lord hath given us leave to draw our own articles. We have professed to enterprise these actions upon these and those ends; we have hereupon besought Him of favor and blessing. Now if the Lord shall please to hear us, and bring us in peace to the place we desire, then hath He ratified this covenant and sealed our commission, [and] will expect a strict performance of the articles contained in it. But if we shall neglect the observation of these articles, which are the ends we have propounded, and dissembling with our God, shall fall to embrace this present world and prosecute our carnal intentions, seeking great things for ourselves and our posterity, the Lord will surely break out in wrath against us, be revenged of such a perjured people, and make us know the price of the breach of such a covenant.

Now the only way to avoid this shipwreck, and to provide for our posterity, is to follow the counsel of Micah: to do justly, to love mercy, to walk humbly with our God. For this end, we must be knit together in this work as one man. We must entertain each other in brotherly affection; we must be willing to abridge ourselves of our superfluities for the supply of others' necessities; we must uphold a familiar commerce together in all meekness, gentleness, patience and liberality. We must delight in each other, make others' conditions our own, rejoice together, mourn together, labor and suffer together, always having before our eyes our commission and community in the work, our community as members of the same body. So shall we keep the unity of the spirit in the bond of peace. The Lord will be our God, and delight to dwell among us as His own people, and will command a blessing upon us in all our ways, so that we shall see much more of His wisdom, powers goodness and truth, than formerly we have been acquainted with. We shall find that the God of Israel is among us, when ten of us shall be able to resist a thousand of our enemies, when he shall make us a praise and glory, that men shall say of succeeding plantations: "the Lord make it like that of NEW ENGLAND." For we must consider that we shall be as a city upon a hill: The eyes of all people are upon us, so that if we shall deal falsely with our God in this work we have undertaken, and so cause Him to withdraw His present help from us, we shall be made a story and a by-word through the world; we shall open the mouths of enemies to speak evil of the ways of God and all professors for God's sake. We shall shame the faces of many of God's worthy servants, and cause their prayers to be turned into curses upon us, till we be consumed out of the good land whither we are going.

And to shut up this discourse with that exhortation of Moses, that faithful servant of the Lord, in his last farewell to Israel, Deuteronomy, 30: beloved, there is now set before us life and good, death and evil, in that we are commanded this day to love the Lord our God, and to love one another, to walk in His ways and to keep His commandments and His ordinance and His laws, and the articles of our covenant with Him, that we may live and be multiplied, and that the Lord our God may bless us in the land whither we go to possess it. But if our hearts shall turn away, so that we will not obey, but shall be seduced, and worhip other Gods—our pleasures and profits—and serve *them*, it is propounded unto us this day, we shall surely perish out of the good land whither we pass over this vast sea to possess it:

Therefore let us choose life,
that we and our seed
may live by obeying His
voice and cleaving to Him,
for He is our life, and
our prosperity.

Entertaining Satan

What sorts of activities and set of circumstances would get a person accused of witchcraft according to this article?

John Demos

It seems Demos has omitted one crucial criteria. To what I am referring? Can you surmise?

The place is the fledgling community of Windsor, Connecticut: the time, an autumn day in the year 1651. A group of local militiamen has assembled for training exercises. They drill in their usual manner through the morning, then pause for rest and refreshment. Several of the younger recruits begin a moment's horseplay; one of these—a certain Thomas Allen—cocks his musket and inadvertently knocks it against a tree. The weapon fires, and a few yards away a bystander falls heavily to the ground. The unfortunate victim is an older man, also a trainee, Henry Stiles by name. Quickly, the group converges on Stiles, and bears him to the house of the local physician. But the bullet has fatally pierced his heart.

One month later the "particular court" of the Connecticut colony meets in regular session. On its agenda is an indictment of Thomas Allen: "that . . . [thou] didst suddenly, negligently, carelessly cock thy piece, and carry the piece . . . which piece being charged and going off in thine hand, slew thy neighbor, to the great dishonor of God, breach of the peace, and loss of a member of this commonwealth." Allen confesses the fact, and is found guilty of "homicide by misadventure." For his "sinful neglect and careless carriages" the court orders him to pay a fine of twenty pounds sterling. In addition he is bound to good behavior for the ensuing year, with the special proviso "that he shall not bear arms for the same term."

But this is not the end of the matter. Stiles's death remains a topic of local conversation, and three years later it yields a more drastic result. In November, 1654, the court meets in special session to try a case of witchcraft—against a woman, Lydia Gilbert, also of Windsor: "Lydia Gilbert, thou art here indicted . . . that not having the fear of God before thine eyes, thou hast of late years or still dost give entertainment to Satan, the great enemy of God and mankind, and by his help hast killed the body of Henry Stiles, besides other witchcrafts, for which according to the law of God and the established law of this commonwealth thou deservest to die." The court, in effect, is considering a complicated question: did Lydia Gilbert's witchcraft *cause* Thomas Allen's gun to go off, so as to kill Henry Stiles? Evidence is taken on various points deemed relevant. Henry Stiles was a boarder in the Gilbert household for some while before his death. The arrangement was not a happy one; neighbors could recall the rounds of frequent quarreling. From time to time Stiles loaned money and property to his landlord, but this served only to heighten the tension. Goodwife Gilbert, in particular, violated her Christian obligation of charitable and peaceable behavior. A naturally assertive sort, she did not conceal her sense of grievance against Goodman Stiles. In fact, her local reputation has long encompassed some unfavorable elements: disapproval of her quick temper, envy of her success in besting personal antagonists, suspicion that she is not above invoking the "Devil's means." The jury weighs the evidence and reaches its verdict—guilty as charged. The magistrates hand down the prescribed sentence of death by hanging. A few days thereafter the sentence is carried out.

On the next succeeding Sabbath day, and with solemn forewarning, the pastor of the Windsor church climbs to the pulpit to deliver his sermon. Directly he faces the questions that are weighing heavily in the minds of his parishioners. Why has this terrible scourge of witchcraft been visited on their little community? What has created the opportunity which the Devil and his legions have so untimely seized? For what reason has God Almighty condoned such a tragic intrusion on the life of Windsor? The pastors answer to these questions is neither surprising nor pleasant for his audience to hear, but it carries a purgative force. The Windsor townsfolk are themselves at least partially to blame. For too long they have strayed from the paths of virtue: overvaluing secular interests while neglecting religious ones, tippling in alehouses, "nightwalking," and— worst of all—engaging one another in repeated strife. In such circumstances the Devil always finds an opening; to such communities God brings retribution. Thus the recent witchcraft episode is a lesson to the people of Windsor, and a warning to mend their ways.

Lydia Gilbert was not the first witch to have lived at Windsor, nor would she be the last. For so-called Puritans, the happenstance of everyday life was part of a struggle of cosmic dimensions, a struggle in which witchcraft played a logical part. The ultimate triumph of Almighty God was assured. But in particular times and places Satan might achieve some temporary success—and claim important victims. Indeed he was continually adding earthly recruits to his nefarious cause. Tempted by bribes and blandishments, or frightened by threats of torture, weak-willed persons signed the "Devil's Book" and enrolled as witches. Thereafter they were armed with his power and obliged to do his bidding. God, meanwhile, opposed this onslaught of evil—and yet He also permitted it. For errant men and women there was no more effective means of "chastening."

In a sense, therefore, witchcraft was part of God's own intention. And the element of intention was absolutely central, in the minds of the human actors. When a man lay dead from a violent accident on a training field, his fellow townspeople would carefully investigate how events had proceeded to such an end. But they sought, in addition, to understand the *why* of it all—the motives, whether human or supernatural (or both), which lay behind the events. The same was true for other forms of everyday mischance. When cows took strangely ill, when a boat capsized in a sudden storm, when bread failed to rise in the oven or beer went bad in the barrel, there was cause for careful reflection. Witchcraft would not necessarily provide the best explanation, but it was always a possibility—and sometimes a most convenient one. To discover an unseen hand at work in one's life was to dispel mystery, to explain misfortune, to excuse incompetence. Belief in witchcraft was rooted in the practical experience no less than the theology of the time.

A single shocking episode—the Salem "hysteria" of 1692—has dominated the lore of this subject ever since. Yet the Salem trials were distinctive only in a quantitative sense—that is, in the sheer numbers of the accused. Between the late 1630's and 1700 dozens of New England towns supported proceedings against witchcraft; some did so on repeated occasions. The total of cases was over a hundred (and this includes only actual trials from which some record survives today). At least forty of the defendants were put to death; the rest were acquitted or convicted of a lesser charge. Numerous additional cases went unrecorded because they did not reach a court of law; nonetheless they generated much excitement—and distress. "Witches" were suspected, accused informally, and condemned in unofficial ways. Gossip and rumor about such people constituted a staple part of the local culture.

The typical witch was a woman of middle age. Like Lydia Gilbert, she was married, had children, and lived as a settled member of her community. (However, widows and childless women were also suspected, perhaps to an extent disproportionate to their numbers in the population at large.) Some of the accused were quite poor and a few were given to begging; but taken altogether they spanned the entire social spectrum. (One was the wife of a leading magistrate in the Massachusetts Bay Colony.) Most seemed conspicuous in their personal behavior: they were cantankerous, feisty, quick to take offense, and free in their expression of anger. As such they matched the prevalent stereotype of a witch, with its emphasis on strife and malice and vengeance. It was no accident, in a culture which valued "peaceableness" above all things, that suspected witches were persons much given to conflict. Like deviant figures everywhere, they served to mark the accepted boundaries between Good and Evil.

Their alleged victims, and actual accusers, are much harder to categorize. Children were sometimes centrally involved—notoriously so at Salem—but witchcraft evidence came from people of both sexes and all ages. The young had their "fits"; older witnesses had other things of which to complain. Illness, injury, and the loss of property loomed largest in such testimony; but there were reports, too, of strange sights and sounds, of portents and omens, of mutterings and curses—all attributable in some way to the supposed witch. The chances for conviction were greatest when the range of this evidence was wide and the sources numerous. In some cases whole neighborhoods joined the ranks of the accusers.

Usually a trial involved only a single witch, or perhaps two; the events at issue were purely local. A finding of guilt would remove the defendant forever from her community. An acquittal would send her back, but with a clear warning to watch her step. Either way tension was lowered.

Occasionally the situation became more complicated. In Connecticut, during the years from 1662 to 1665, the courts heard a long sequence of witchcraft cases—perhaps as many as a dozen. Some of the accused were eventually executed; others fled for their lives to neighboring colonies. Almost none of the legal evidence has survived; it is known, however, that Connecticut was then experiencing severe problems of religious factionalism. The witch trials may well have been a direct result.

The context for the other wide-scale outbreak is much clearer. Salem, in the closing decades of the seventeenth century, was a town notorious for internal contention. An old guard of village farmers was arrayed against newly prosperous merchants and townsmen. For years, indeed decades, local governance was disrupted: town meetings broke up with important issues unresolved, ministers came and left (out of favor with one side or the other), lawsuits filled the court dockets. Thus when the first sparks of witchcraft were fanned, in a small group of troubled girls, they acted like tinder on a dried-out woodpile. Suspicion led immediately to new suspicion, and accusation to accusation—with results that every schoolchild knows. Soon the conflagration burst the boundaries of Salem itself; eventually it claimed victims throughout eastern Massachusetts. By the time cooler heads prevailed—especially that of the new governor, Sir William Phips—twenty witches had been executed and dozens more were languishing in local jails.

But the Salem trials—to repeat—were highly unusual in their sheer scope: witch-hunting gone wild. In the more typical case, events moved slowly, even carefully, within a limited and intensely personal framework. This dimension of the witchcraft story also deserves close attention.

October, 1688. A cart stops by the roadside in the south part of Boston. A tall man alights and hurries along a pathway toward a small house. A door opens to admit him and quickly closes again. The visitor is Rev. Cotton Mather, a young but already eminent clergyman of the town. The house is occupied by the family of a mason named John Goodwin.

Immediately upon entering, Mather becomes witness to an extraordinary scene. On the parlor floor in front of him two small human forms are thrashing about. A girl of thirteen (named Martha) and a boy of eleven (John, Jr.) are caught in the throes of agonizing fits. Their bodies contort into strange, distended shapes. Their eyes bulge. Their mouths snap open and shut. They shriek uncontrollably. From time to time they affect the postures of animals, and crawl about the room, barking like dogs or bellowing like frightened cows. Their father and several neighbors look on in horror, and try by turns to prevent serious damage to persons or property.

Mather waits for a moment's lull; then he opens a Bible, kneels, and begins to pray. Immediately the children stop their ears and resume their shrieking. "They say we must not listen," cries the girl, while hurling herself toward the fireplace. Her father manages to block the way; briefly he catches her in an awkward embrace. But she reels off and falls heavily on her brother.

Soon it is time for supper. The children quiet temporarily, and come to the table with their elders. However, when food is offered them, their teeth are set as if to lock their mouths shut. Later there are new troubles. The children need assistance in preparing for bed, and they tear their nightclothes fearfully. At last they quiet and pass into a deep sleep.

Mather sits by the fireside and reviews the history of their affliction with the distraught parents. The family is a religious one, and until the preceding summer the children were unfailingly pious and well behaved. Martha's fits had begun first, John's soon thereafter; indeed, two still younger children in the family have also been affected from time to time. A physician had been summoned, but he could discover no "natural maladies" at work.

The parents recall an episode that had directly preceded the onset of Martha's fits. The girl was sent to retrieve some family linen from a laundress who lived nearby. Several items had disappeared, and Martha complained—intimating theft. The laundress angrily denied the charges, and was joined in this by her own mother, an Irishwoman named Glover.

Goodwife Glover was already a feared presence in the neighborhood; her late husband, on his deathbed, had accused her of practicing witchcraft. Now she poured out her retaliative anger on young Martha Goodwin. The girl has not been the same since.

Late in the evening, having listened with care to the entire story, Mather prepares to leave. John Goodwin explains that several neighbors have been urging the use of "tricks"—countermagic—to end his children's difficulties. But Goodwin prefers a strategy based on orthodox Christian principles.

In this Cotton Mather is eager to cooperate. He returns to the Goodwin house each day for a week, and on one particular afternoon he is joined by his fellow clergymen from all parts of Boston. Eventually he invites Martha Goodwin into his own home for a period of intensive pastoral care. (Martha's younger brother is taken, at the same time, into the home of the minister at Watertown.) Their afflictions continue, though with lessened severity.

Meanwhile the courts intervene and Goodwife Glover is put on trial for her alleged crimes. She has difficulty answering the prose-

cutor's questions; she can speak only in her native tongue (Gaelic),
so the proceedings must involve interpreters. Her house is searched,
and "puppets" are discovered—small images, made of rags, believed
to be instrumental in the perpetration of witchcraft. Eventually she
confesses guilt and raves wildly in court about her dealings with the
Devil. The judges appoint six physicians to assess her sanity; they
find her compos mentis. The court orders her execution.

On her way to the gallows Goodwife Glover declares bitterly
that the children will not be cured after her death, for "others had a
hand in it as well." And in fact, the fits suffered by Martha and young
John increase immediately thereafter. Winter begins, and suspicion
shifts to another woman of the neighborhood. However, the new
suspect dies suddenly, and under strange circumstances, before she
can be brought to trial. At last the children show marked improvement, and by spring they are virtually their former selves. Meanwhile a relieved, and triumphant, Cotton Mather is spending long
days in his study, completing a new book that will soon be published
under the title *Memorable Providences, Relating to Witchcraft and
Possessions*. A central chapter deals at length with selected "examples," and includes the events in which Mather himself has so
recently participated. The Goodwin children will be leading characters in a local best seller.

Goodwife Glover was relatively rare, among those accused of
witchcraft in early New England, in confessing guilt. Only at Salem
did any considerable number choose to convict themselves—and
there, it seemed, confession was the strategy of choice if one wished
to avoid the gallows. Were Goody Glover's admissions, in effect,
forced out of her? Was she perhaps seriously deranged (the opinion
of the court-appointed physicians notwithstanding)? Did she truly
believe herself guilty? Had she, in fact, sought to invoke the power
of the Devil, by stroking poppets with her spittle—or whatever?

We have no way now to answer such questions; the evidence
comes to us entirely through persons who believed—and prosecuted—the case against her. It does seem likely, in a community
where virtually everyone accepted the reality of witchcraft, that at
least a few would have tried to practice it. In a sense, however, it no
longer matters whether specific individuals were guilty as charged.
What does matter is that many of them were believed guilty—and
that this belief was itself efficacious. As anthropologists have observed in cultures around the world, people who regard themselves

as objects of witchcraft are vulnerable to all manner of mischance. They blunder into "accidents," they lose their effectiveness in work and social relations, they occasionally sicken and die.

No less was true in early New England. The victims of witchcraft—whatever the variety of their particular afflictions—had this in common: they believed *beforehand* that they had been marked as targets for attack. Their fearful expectation became, at some point, incapacitating—and yielded its own directly feared result. Thus the idea of witchcraft served both as the *ad hoc* cause of the victim's troubles and as the *post hoc* explanation. The process was neatly circular, for each explanation created a further cause—which, in turn, required additional explanation. In the language of modern medicine, these episodes were "symptoms," and their basis was "psychogenic."

The seizures of the afflicted children were but the extreme end of the symptomatic continuum. When Martha Goodwin had been drawn into a bitter exchange with a suspected witch, she was left deeply unsettled. She feared retaliation; she wished to retaliate herself; she felt acutely uncomfortable with the anger she had already expressed. Henceforth an anguished "victim" of witchcraft, she was, in effect, punished for her own vengeful impulse. Yet, too, she *had* her revenge, for her accusations led straight to the trial and conviction of her antagonist. The same inner processes, and a similar blend of wish and fear, served to energize fits in victims of witchcraft all across New England.

But fits could be explained in other ways—hence the requirement that all such victims be examined by medical doctors. Only when natural causes had been ruled out was a diagnosis of witchcraft clearly justified. Normally, beyond this point, clergymen would assume control of the proceedings, for they were "healers of the soul" and experts in the struggle against Evil. Long sessions of prayer, earnest conversation with the afflicted, occasional periods of fasting and humiliation—these were the preferred methods of treatment.

At least they were the *Christian* methods. For—much to the chagrin of the clergy—there were other ways of combating witchcraft. From obscure sources in the folk culture of pre-Christian times the New Englanders had inherited a rich lore of counter-magic—including, for example, the tricks which John Goodwin refused to try. Thus a family might decide to lay branches of "sweet bays" under their threshold. ("It would keep a witch from coming in.") Or a woman tending a sick child would perform elaborate rituals of protection. ("She smote the back of her hands together sundry times, and spat in the fire; then she . . . rubbed [herbs] in her hand and strewed them about the hearth.") Or a man would hurl a pudding into a fire in order to draw a suspect to the scene of his alleged crimes. ("To get hay was no true cause of his coming thither, but rather the spirit that bewitched the pudding brought him.") All this was of a piece with other strands of belief and custom in seventeenth-century New England: fortunetelling, astrology, healing charms, love potions and powders—to mention a few. Witchcraft, in short, belonged to a large and complex world of interest in the supernatural.

Beyond the tricks against witches, besides the efficacy of prayer, there was always legal recourse. Witchcraft was a capital crime in every one of the New England colonies, and thus was a particularly solemn responsibility of the courts. Procedure was scrupulously observed: indictment by a grand jury, depositions from qualified witnesses, verdict by a jury of trials, sentencing by the magistrates. Some features of witchcraft trials seem highly repugnant today—for example, the elaborate and intimate body searches of defendants suspected of having "witch's teats" (nipplelike growths through which the witch or wizard was believed to give suck to Satan). But in the context of the times, such procedures were not extraordinary. Contrary to popular belief, physical torture was *not* used to obtain evidence. Testimony was taken on both sides, and character references favorable to the defendant were not uncommon. Guilt was never a foregone conclusion; most trials ended in acquittal. Perhaps *because* the crime was a capital one, many juries seemed reluctant to convict. Some returned verdicts like the following. "[We find her] not legally guilty according to indictment, but [there is] just ground of vehement suspicion of her having had familiarity with the Devil."

At Salem, to be sure, such caution was thrown to the winds. The creation of special courts, the admission of "spectral evidence" (supplied by "shapes" visible only to the afflicted victims), the strong momentum favoring conviction—all this marked a decided tilt in the legal process. But it brought, in time, its own reaction. Magistrates, clergymen, and ordinary participants eventually would see the enormity of what they had done at Salem in the name of law and religion. And they would not make the same mistakes again.

Thus the eighteenth century, in New England, was essentially free of *legal* action against witchcraft. However, the belief which had sustained such action did not evaporate so quickly.

Hampton, New Hampshire: March 26,1769. The finest house in the town, a mansion by any standard, is destroyed in a spectacular fire. The owner is General Jonathan Moulton—scion of an old family, frequent town officer, commander of the local forces in various Indian wars, businessman of extraordinary skill and energy. Yet despite these marks of eminence, Moulton is no favorite of his fellow townsmen. To them he seems ruthless, crafty, altogether a "sharp dealer." Indeed, the local gossips have long suggested that Moulton is in league with the Devil. There is no easier way to explain, among other things, his truly prodigious wealth.

The ashes of Moulton's house are barely cold when a new story circulates in the town: the fire was set by the Devil, because the General had cheated him in a bargain. The details are told as follows. Mouton had pledged his soul to the Devil, in exchange for regular payments of gold and silver coins. The payments were delivered down his chimney and into his boot, which was hung there precisely for this purpose. The arrangement went smoothly for awhile, but then came a time when the boot took far more coins than usual. The Devil was perplexed, and decided to go down the chimney to see what was wrong. He found that the General had cut off the foot of the boot, the room was so full of money that there was scarcely air to breathe.

The fire—and this account of it—notwithstanding, Moulton quickly recoups. He builds a new mansion even more grand than the first one. His business enterprises yield ever greater profit. He serves with distinction in the Revolutionary War and also in the convention which draws up the constitution of the state of New Hampshire. Yet his local reputation shows little change with the passage of years. When he dies, in 1788, the news is carried to the haymakers on the Hampton marsh: "General Moulton is dead!" they call to one another in tones of evident satisfaction. And there is one final peculiarity about his passing. His body, prepared for burial, is suddenly missing from the coffin. The people of Hampton are not surprised. "The Devil," they whisper knowingly to one another, "has got his own at last."

Similar stories are preserved in the lore of many New England towns. Through them we can trace an enduring interest in the idea of witchcraft and also an unmistakable change. The figure of the witch gradually lost its power to inspire fear. In many towns, for many generations, there were one or two persons suspected of practicing the black arts, but the effects of such practice were discounted. Witches were associated more and more with simple mischief—and less with death and destruction. There was even, as the Moulton story shows, an element of humor in the later lore of witchcraft.

In our own time the wheel has turned full circle. There are many new witches among us—self-proclaimed, and proud of the fact. They haunt our television talk-shows and write syndicated columns for our newspapers. Their witchcraft is entirely constructive—so they assure us—and we are all invited to join in their celebration of things occult. Meanwhile some of the old witches have been rehabilitated.

Hampton, New Hampshire: March 8,1938. A town meeting considers the case of a certain Eunice Cole, whose witchcraft was locally notorious three centuries before. The following motion is made: "*Resolved*, that we, the citizens . . . of Hampton . . . do hereby declare that we believe that Eunice (Goody) Cole was unjustly accused of witchcraft and familiarity with the Devil in the seventeenth century, and we do hereby restore to the said Eunice (Goody) Cole her rightful place as a citizen of the town of Hampton." The resolution is passed unanimously. In fact, the legend of Goody Cole has become a cherished part of the local culture. A bronze urn in the town hall holds material purported to be her earthly remains. A stone memorial on the village green affirms her twentieth-century rehabilitation. There are exhibits on her life at the local historical society. There are even some *new* tales in which she plays a ghostly, though harmless part: an aged figure, in tattered shawl, seen walking late at night along a deserted road, or stopping in the early dawn to peer at gravestones by the edge of the green.

And now an author's poscript:

Hampton, New Hampshire: October, 1972. The living room in a comfortable house abutting the main street. A stranger has come there, to examine a venerable manuscript held in this family through many generations. Laboriously his eyes move across the page, straining to unravel the cramped and irregular script of a bygone era. Two girls, aged nine or ten, arrive home from school; after a brief greeting they move off into an alcove and begin to play. Awash in the sounds of their game, the stranger looks up from his work and listens. "I'll be Goody Cole!" cries one of the girls. "Yes," responds the other, "and I'll be the one who gives you a whipping—you mean old witch!"

It is a long way from their time to ours, but at least a few of the early New England witches have made the whole journey.

Part II: Revolutionary America

Firebrand of the Revolution

Alexander Winston

embers of the British Parliament who voted approval of the Stamp Act late one night in 1765 and went yawning off to bed had never heard, it would seem, of Boston's "Man of the Town Meeting," Samuel Adams. It was a fatal lapse. From that moment until the Declaration of Independence, Sam Adams pounced on Britain every time she moved to impose her will on the colonies. He made politics his only profession and rebellion his only business. He drove two royal governors out of Massachusetts and goaded the British government into open war. New England Tories branded him the "grand Incendiary," the "all-in-all" of colonial turmoil, and neatly capsuled Boston resistance as "Adams' conspiracy." In the opinion of his astute cousin John Adams, Sam was "born and tempered a wedge of steel to split the knot of *lignum vitae* that tied America to England."

"Born and tempered," as Cousin John put it, was more than rhetorical flourish. Sam's father—also named Samuel—made an avocation of politics, and was suspected of republican leanings. The boy got a taste for public affairs almost with his milk; while he was but a toddler his father was deep in the Caucus Club, the same radical brotherhood that Sam was to use with such adroitness. Sam senior clashed with the royal governors, and in 1741 saw his Land Bank venture—an effort to aid debtors by putting negotiable paper money into circulation—outlawed by Parliament. Father and son shared the bitter conviction that Britain's colonial policy was both arbitrary and unjust.

From his parents Sam also inherited a strenuous Calvinism that was to make his vision of the conflict with Britain resemble a huge and murky illustration for *Paradise Lost*. The American patriots, Sam was sure, were children of light who fought England's sons of Belial in a struggle decisive for the future of mankind. Everyone knew where God stood on that. Sam saw England through a glass, darkly: her government venal, her manners effeminate and corrupt, her religion popish. In saving the colonies from her tyranny Sam hoped to save their manly virtues as well, and make of Boston a "Christian Sparta"—chaste, austere, godly. By 1765 three dominant strains were firmly fixed in his character: puritanism, political acumen, and hatred of British rule. He laced them together tight as a bull whip and, as Parliament was to discover, twice as deadly.

Any calm appraisal of his life up to that point, however, would surely have rated him among those least likely to succeed. After Harvard (M.A., 1743) he had dabbled at the study of law and later spent a few fruitless months as apprentice in a countinghouse. His father loaned him a thousand pounds to make a try at business—any business. The money ran through his fingers like water. Appointed Boston's tax collector in 1756, he combined softheartedness and negligence so ably that he ended at least four thousand pounds in arrears and faced court action. The prosperous little malt works that his father had left the family fell to ruins. The sheriff threatened to sell his house for debts. When the Stamp Act was passed in 1765, Sam was forty-two; he looked prematurely old, his hands trembled, his head shook with a palsied tremor.

But while his private affairs were in perpetual state of collapse, Sam was making himself the gray eminence of Boston politics. The base of his power was the Caucus Club, a judicious mixture of shipyard laborers ("mechanics") and uptown intellectuals. They met in a garret to drink punch, turn the air blue with pipe smoke, and plot the next political move. Their decisions were passed quietly along to other radical cells—the Merchants' Club (which met in the more genteel Boston Coffee House), the contentious Monday Night Club, the Masons, the Sons of Liberty. With tactics mapped out and support solidified, the action was rammed—or finessed, if need be—through town meeting. Nothing was left to chance; Sam and his tight coterie of patriots simply outworked, outmaneuvered, and, on occasion, outlasted the opposition.

At first rumor of the Stamp Act, Sam cried that "a deep-laid and desperate plan of imperial despotism has been laid, and partly executed, for the extinction of all civil liberty." But Parliament considered its act perfectly just. England's recent conquest of Canada, which had removed an armed threat to the colonies from the French, had also run up a burdensome debt. Obviously the colonies, who had benefited most from the costly Canadian expedition, should not mind paying part of the bill. Passed in the spring of 1765, the Stamp Act required that after November 1 of that year validating stamps be bought from government offices and affixed to all legal documents, customs papers, newssheets, and pamphlets. To enforce the act Parliament decreed that offenders be tried in admiralty courts, where there were no juries, and pay their fines in silver coin, which was hard to get.

Sam rolled out his artillery months before the act went into effect. The instructions from the Boston town meeting to its representatives in the Massachusetts House constituted one of the first formal protests made in the colonies against the act, and one of the first appeals for united resistance. Sam declared that since the act imposed taxation by a body in which the taxed were not represented it flouted the Massachusetts charter, violated the established rights of British subjects, and was therefore null and void.

On the morning of August 14, 1765, the effigy of old Andrew Oliver, Boston distributor of stamps, hung from the Liberty Tree, a great oak in Hanover Square. Sam inspected the stuffed figure with care and wondered aloud how it got there. That night a mob knocked down the frame of the stamp office and built a fire of the debris in front of Oliver's house. After burning the decapitated effigy, they made the real Oliver swear to resign at the Liberty Tree—which he did, finally, under the added humiliation of a driving December rainstorm.

Sam was pleased. The event, he announced, "ought to be forever remembered in America," for on that day "the People shouted; and their shout was heard to the distant end of this Continent." Two weeks later rioters sacked and gutted the mansion of Lieutenant Governor Thomas Hutchinson, emptying his wine cellar and scattering his papers in the street.

On November 1, 1765, the day the Stamp Act went into effect, church bells tolled as for the dead. Flags hung at half-mast; from the harbor rolled the dull boom of minute guns. For the next six weeks the people of Boston refused to buy stamps. Port business came to a halt, law courts tried no cases. Sam had warned the farmers: "If our Trade may be taxed why not our Lands? Why not the Produce of our Lands and in short everything we possess or make use of?" He doubly damned the stamp revenue by prophesying that it would be used to fasten an episcopacy on puritan New England. In the provincial House, to which he had been elected in September, Sam had a gallery installed to bring waverers under the accusing eye of his patriots. He and his colleague James Otis published a black list of those House members whose antagonism to the act lacked proper vigor. Frightened stamp officials fled for protection to Castle William in the harbor. Enforcement collapsed, and early in the next year Parliament repealed the act. But Sam did not join in Boston's celebration. Why rejoice, he grimly demanded, when Parliament has only granted us our just due?

The defeat of the Stamp Act suggested that no one in the colonies could hatch and execute a scheme with half Sam's cunning. His strategy was to let Britain make all the moves and then give her a bloody nose. "It is a good maxim in Politicks as well as War," he counselled, "to put and keep the enemy in the wrong." Britain soon obliged again. In May, 1767, Parliament launched a series of colonial bills named for their sponsor, Charles Townshend, Chancellor of the Exchequer. The Townshend Acts placed import duties on painters' colors, glass, lead, paper, and tea. At the same time they set up Commissioners of Customs with broad powers, authorized search warrants, and specified that the revenue would be used to pay Crown officials previously salaried (and therefore in part controlled) by the colonies.

Sam worked hard at nonimportation as the chief weapon against the Townshend Acts. By 1769 all the colonies had joined in the boycott. Sam revelled in their unity: "The *tighter* the cord of unconstitutional power is drawn round this bundle of arrows, the firmer it will be."

To enforce the boycott in Boston, gangs ranged outside the homes of Tory merchants by night, and small boys pelted their customers with dirt and dung by day. One shopkeeper, more obstinate than the rest, was ridden out of town to the gallows and loosed only when he swore never to return. Tories slept with loaded pistols by their beds. Governor Francis Bernard pleaded for military protection, and in September of 1768 two regiments of soldiers sailed in from Halifax. They set up guardposts, and levelled a pair of cannon at the town hall.

Overnight Governor Bernard became the most hated man in Massachusetts. The House demanded his removal; at Harvard, students slashed his portrait. Sam denounced him as "a Scourge to this Province, a curse to North America, and a Plague on the whole Empire." Recalled to England, Bernard sailed at the end of July, 1769, leaving Hutchinson to act as governor in his place. Despite

Sam's outraged cry that Boston was now an occupied town, the troops remained, and he began sending a periodic *Journal of Events* to other colonies, accusing the redcoats of beating defenseless boys and raping women.

Early in March, 1770, a soldier was injured in a scuffle with dockmen. One morning soon after, the town was plastered with forged notices, allegedly signed by redcoats, promising a broad-scale attack on the townspeople. That night, March 5, as a bright moon shone on the late snow, a crowd gathered in front of the Custom House. It began to taunt the nine-man guard; snowballs and brickbats flew, the guard fired, and five citizens were left dead or dying.

The town was in a frenzy of anger. On the following afternoon an immense rally of excited citizens massed in and around Old South Church. Hutchinson told a committee of protest that he was willing to send the one offending regiment to the fort at Castle William but that he had no military authority to send the other as well. At dusk Sam came to the State House to deliver his ultimatum: "If you . . . have the power to remove *one* regiment you have the power to remove *both*. It is at your peril if you refuse. The meeting is composed of three thousand people. They are become impatient. A thousand men are already arrived from the neighborhood, and the whole country is in motion. Night is approaching. An immediate answer is expected. Both regiments or none!" Hutchinson caved in and ordered the two regiments out of town.

Sam relished his moment of triumph. "If Fancy deceive me not," he reported, "I observ'd his Knees to tremble. I thought I saw his face grow pale (and I enjoy'd the Sight)." Copley's fine portrait catches Sam at the moment of confrontation: broad forehead, heavy eyebrows, steady blue-gray eyes, nose like the prow of a ship, stubborn mouth, a chin you could plow with.

Sam wanted the soldiers who had fired the fatal shots to be tried immediately, while indignation still flamed white-hot, but the judges put it off for six months. He acquiesced when two patriots, his cousin John and Josiah Quincy, volunteered to be defense attorneys, sure that they would not press too hard on prosecution witnesses. The two proved more honorable than he had counted on; they argued their case ably and the sentence was light—a pair of soldiers were branded on the thumb. Sam was disgusted. He retried the case in the Boston *Gazette*, over the signature "Vindex," the avenger.

After that, to Sam's chagrin, things quieted down. The blood of the "massacre" had washed away with the melting snow. In England a liberal government had assumed power and in April it repealed the Townshend Acts, except for the duty on tea. A majority of the colonists were tired of agitation, and the radical patriots temporarily lost control of the Massachusetts House. John Hancock courted the royalists; John Adams shook the dust of politics from his shoes and went back to pastoral Braintree. James Otis, who had been bludgeoned in a brawl, sank into recurrent fits of dementia.

Only Sam never let up. "Where there is a Spark of patriotick fire," he vowed, "we will enkindle it." Between August, 1770, and December, 1772, he wrote more than forty articles for the *Gazette*. Night after night, a lamp burned late in the study off his bedroom. Friends, passing in the small hours, could look up at the yellow square of window light and comfort themselves that Sam Adams was busily at work against the Tories. Sam alternately stated the fundamentals of colonial liberty (based on the charter, British law, and, finally, natural right) and whiplashed the British for transgressing it. His style in this period was at times severely reasoned, more often impassioned; the content was unfailingly polemical, partisan, and, on occasion, willfully inaccurate. As the conflict with Britain deepened, his accusations became more violent. "Every dip of his pen," Governor Bernard had once said, "stung like a horned snake." As clerk of the House (to which office he had been elected in 1765) Sam poured out a stream of remonstrances, resolves, and letters to the colony's London agent; but beyond their effect as propaganda he expected them to do little good. When his daughter expressed awe that a petition to the King might be touched by the royal hand, he growled that it would more likely be spurned by the royal foot.

In November, 1772, Sam managed to set up a Boston Committee of Correspondence to link the Massachusetts towns. Within a few months other towns had followed suit, and he had a taut organization poised to act at his command. A discerning Tory declared it the "foulest, subtlest, and most venomous serpent ever issued from the egg of sedition."

In fact, everything Sam did for a decade smacked of sedition. As early as 1768 Hutchinson had secretly sent depositions to England to see if there might be grounds for his arrest. Parliament dusted off a neglected statute of Henry VIII that would bring all treasonable cases to London for trial. Tories were sure that Sam would now end on the gibbet, where he belonged. They gloated that he "shuddered at the sight of hemp." A Londoner wrote jubilantly to Hutchinson: "The talk is strong of bringing them over and trying them by impeachment. Do you write me word of their being seized, and I will send you an account of their being hanged." But the British solicitor general took a long look at the evidence and decided that it was not sufficient—yet.

Meanwhile Sam was out to ruin Hutchinson, and didn't care how he did it. To beat the devil any stick would do. The chance came in 1772 when Ben Franklin, then in London as an agent for the Massachusetts House, laid hands on a bundle of letters written by Hutchinson and Andrew Oliver to correspondents in England. Franklin sent them to Boston with instructions to share them among the trusted inner circle of patriots and return them uncopied and unpublished. Whether he meant these instructions to be strictly obeyed, or issued them for his self-protection, we do not know. The patriots brooded over the letters for several months; then Sam announced that "a most shocking scene would soon open," and that a vicious plot against American liberties would be disclosed.

Expectation of horrifying news was raised to a fever pitch. In June, 1773, Sam ordered the House galleries cleared. He told the members in grave tones that he had letters vital to their concern, but that they must first swear neither to copy them nor make them public. At this Hancock rose to say that someone unknown to him had thrust copies of letters into his hand on the street. Might they be the same as those held by Mr. Adams? If so, were the letters not already abroad? Yes, to be sure, they were the same, obviously they were abroad. The House decided that the letters should no longer be concealed.

Hutchinson's correspondence was really fairly mild, and said little that he had not already stated openly, but Sam managed to put it in the worst possible light. When the letters were published, passages had been slyly snipped from their context, and an outraged commentary had been so mixed with the text that the unwary reader was easily led to see an evil purpose when none was intended. Other letters in the packet were more damaging than Hutchinson's, but he was neatly smeared with their brush. He suffered great discredit even in the rural villages, where most of his conservative support lay. The House petitioned the King, asking that Hutchinson be removed from office.

Now the storm was gathering. Alone of the revenue acts, the duty on tea remained. For years Boston matrons had boycotted the rich English brew, and instead had concocted somewhat unsavory beverages of catnip and mint. Prompted by the desperate straits of the East India Company, Parliament tried in 1773 to help the company unload its embarrassing stockpile of tea on the colonies. Boston patriots decided that the flesh should not be so tempted. While ships bearing 342 chests of tea lay at the wharfs, Sam gave the signal and a band of his mechanics disguised as Mohawk Indians whooped off toward the harbor. As every schoolboy knows, they dumped the whole cargo into Massachusetts Bay. "Sam Adams is in his glory," said Hutchinson; and he was.

Parliament retaliated in a rage. In March, 1774, it ordered the port of Boston clamped shut. It decreed that after August 1 the Provincial Council, which formerly had been elected by the House, would be named by the governor, as would the higher judges. The royal sheriff would select all juries; town meetings throughout the province would assemble only with the governor's consent, and discuss only what he authorized. General Thomas Gage, commander in chief of His Majesty's forces in America, supplanted Hutchinson as governor. By June, four regiments of redcoats were encamped on the Common. This was the showdown; it was knuckle under or risk war.

Sam knew that to pit Boston (population 17,000) against British power was to place the mouse beneath the lion's paw. "I wish we could arouse the continent," he had written to a fellow patriot the year before. Now, in the spring of 1774, the continent was awakening: a Continental Congress was in the making. How could this matter be discussed and delegates elected before Gage got wind of it and prorogued the Massachusetts legislature? He already had moved the House temporarily from troublesome Boston to the Tory stronghold of Salem; the town swarmed with redcoats.

For ten days the House dispatched routine business with disarming amiability while Sam lined up votes behind the scenes. On June 17, when all was ready, he suddenly ordered the doors of the meeting hall locked. Sensing a plot, one Tory member slipped past the doorkeeper and hurried away to alert Gage. Sam put the key in his pocket and presented a slate of delegates (of which he was one) to attend the Congress, set for Philadelphia in September. Gage scratched off a hurried order to dissolve the House, but the messenger beat on the door in vain. Inside, the House leisurely elected the delegates and assessed the towns for their expenses.

For the first time in his life Sam Adams was to leave the shores of Massachusetts Bay. He still lived in the crumbling ancestral home on Purchase Street, with land running down to the harbor, where he had a small dock. The household consisted of his second wife, Elizabeth Wells Adams (his first wife had died in 1757), a son and a daughter by his earlier marriage, a servant girl, and a shaggy dog famed for biting redcoats. Elizabeth Adams was devoted and above all frugal, for since their marriage his only earnings had been the meager allowance granted him as clerk of the House of Representatives. Fortunately he had few personal wants, and would live on bread and milk and dress in threadbare clothes, if the cause of liberty were thereby served. "He says he never looked forward in his Life," recorded Cousin John, with Yankee amazement at such carelessness, "never planned, laid a scheme, or formed a design of laying up any Thing for himself or others after him."

Friends put together the money to outfit him for the journey to Philadelphia. He was resplendent in new suit, wig, hose, shoes, and cocked hat; he swung a gold-topped cane, and in his pocket there was a much-needed purse of money. On August 10, 1774, the delegation—John Adams, Sam Adams, Thomas Cushing, and Robert Treat Paine—rolled out of Boston in full array—coach, coachmen, and mounted servants.

They were received with great honor along the route, but friendly patriots in Philadelphia advised them that the other colonies were suspicious of Boston's hot-headed radicals. John Adams summed up their warning: "You must not utter the word independence, nor give the least hint or insinuation of the idea, either in Congress, or any private conversation; if you do, you are undone, for independence is as unpopular in all the Middle and South as the Stamp Act itself. No man dares speak of it. . . ."

During the seven-week session the Massachusetts delegation stayed discreetly in the background. When Sam urged that an Anglican clergyman be permitted to open the sessions with prayer, southerners decided that the dour Calvinist might have some good in him after all. But he was bold in opposing any concessions to Britain: "I should advise persisting in our struggle for liberty, though it was revealed from heaven that nine hundred and ninety-nine should perish, and only one of a thousand survive and retain his liberty. One such freeman must possess more virtue and enjoy more happiness than a thousand slaves; and let him propagate his like, and transmit to them what he hath so nobly preserved."

From 1774 to 1781 Sam Adams' public life was bound up with successive Congresses. He brought to them the same stubborn energy and forehandedness that had worked so well in Boston. "He was constantly holding caucuses of distinguished men," Jefferson recalled, ". . . at which the generality of the measures pursued were previously determined on, and at which the parts were assigned to the different actors who afterwards appeared in them." His name bobs up almost daily in the congressional journal. Joseph Galloway, leader of the conciliatory wing in the Congress, recognized him as one to keep a wary eye on, "a man who, though by no means remarkable for brilliant abilities, yet is equal to most men in popular intrigue and the management of a faction. He eats little, drinks little, sleeps little, thinks much, and is most decisive and indefatigable in the pursuit of his objects. It was this man, who, by his superior application, managed at once the faction in Congress at Philadelphia and the factions in New England."

Sam was ready for independence when most Congress members still clung to compromise. Philadelphia Quakers were for leaving the issue to Providence; he tartly replied that Providence had already decided for liberty. To James Warren in Plymouth he wrote during the spring of 1776: "The Child Independence is now struggling for Birth. I trust that in a short time it will be brought forth, and, in Spite of Pharaoh, all America will hail the dignified Stranger."

In July he signed the Declaration of Independence, and with that stroke of the pen signed away his real vocation. Success put him out of business. America no longer needed an agitator; now it had to defeat an army in the field and build a new nation.

Sam admitted that he was unfit for "founding Empires," and in various ways he proved it. In Congress he favored a citizen militia until forced to concede that the war could be fought only with a more permanent army and a unified command. Frankly critical of Washington's Fabian tactics, Sam was widely accused of involvement in a cabal to replace him, but there is no evidence to support the charge. He disapproved of any social gaiety in so grave an hour, and had Congress pass rules forbidding members to attend balls or entertainments. They voted the rules, and diligently ignored them. His weakness for government by committee led the French minister to lament over the man "whose obstinate, resolute character was so useful to the Revolution at its origin, but who shows himself so ill-suited to the conduct of affairs in an organized government."

Yet Sam worked with his old doggedness through the dark years of war. Jefferson considered him "more than any other member, the *fountain* of our more important measures." At the low ebb of American fortunes in October, 1777, he was one of only twenty members who stuck with Congress. "Though the smallest," Sam remarked, "it was the truest Congress we ever had." He was on the committee that framed the Articles of Confederation in 1777. Four years later, when Congress celebrated their ratification with a keg of wine and some biscuits, Sam alone remained of the original drafters. In April, 1781, he went home and never crossed the borders of Massachusetts again.

He returned, like Ulysses, to find his hall full of strangers—the young, the new postwar merchants: unfamiliar faces, other times. John Hancock, who had been elected first governor of independent Massachusetts, led Boston a merry romp of feasts and revels; it was far from the "Christian Sparta" of which Sam still dreamed. The old radical was elected to the state Senate and became its president, but he was no longer invincible. In 1783 and again in 1787 he lost the race for the rather empty and unsalaried office of lieutenant governor; in 1788 a youngster defeated him for the first Congress under the federal Constitution. But in 1789, when he teamed with Hancock to become lieutenant governor, some enthusiasts wrote his name on their ballots in gold. At Hancock's death in 1793 he succeeded to the governor's chair, and was re-elected by solid majorities for three more one-year terms.

Changing times even forced the revolutionary into the camp of reaction. As president of the Senate, which under the state constitution required its members to have an estate of four hundred pounds, he headed a body designed to check the democratic excesses of the House. Some Bostonians thought the town's growth warranted a change to representative government; Sam reported for his committee that the town-meeting system had no defects in it. Debtors in the western counties who in 1786, under a Revolutionary War veteran named Daniel Shays, resorted to mob violence discovered in the former rebel an implacable foe. He branded them "banditti" and urged the execution of their leaders. Popular opinion was more merciful; Hancock commuted the death penalty. As governor, Sam vetoed a bill to permit stage performances, and Bostonians howled that he was robbing them of their natural rights. Toward the dispossessed Tories, others softened, but Sam's hatred burned with its old fierceness. He would not have a British subject left on American soil nor, indeed, admitted by naturalization.

But Sam had not really changed at all, and that was his misfortune. He earned the lasting enmity of Federalists by his opposition to the new federal Constitution proposed in 1787. Shocked to discover that it would set up "a National Government instead of a Federal Union of Sovereign States," he declared himself "open & decided" against it. But he also insisted that the state convention called in 1788 to ratify the federal Constitution give the document the careful paragraph-by-paragraph discussion that it deserved. Antifederalists who wanted a quick vote while their hostile majority was intact pleaded financial inability to stay for a long session. Sam dryly remarked that if they were so pressed he would dig up funds for their living expenses.

Very likely some of the fight went out of him with the death of his doctor-son while the convention was going on. According to one story, the Federalists finally swung him around by a shrewd move. They staged a meeting of Sam's beloved mechanics at the Green Dragon Inn, where resolutions were passed urging ratification. Daniel Webster wrote a dramatized account of how Paul Revere brought Sam the news:

" 'How many mechanics,' said Mr. Adams, 'were at the Green Dragon when the resolutions were passed?'

" 'More, sir,' was the reply, 'than the Green Dragon could hold.'

" 'And where were the rest, Mr. Revere?'

" 'In the streets sir.'

" 'And how many were in the streets?'

" 'More, sir, than there are stars in the sky.' "

Sam, Webster tells us, thought that over a while. To him, the voice of the common man was as close to the voice of God as one could get. "Well," he mused, "if they must have it, they must have it."

He retired from public life in 1797, and lived six years more in a yellow frame house on Winter Street. Its parlor was hung with engravings of the great champions of liberty. He liked to sit on the doorstep or wander in the little garden, talking about old times. Death came on October 2, 1803, when he was 81 years of age.

The Federalist regime in Massachusetts was embarrassed about full burial honors for its political foe. The governor was absent; no subordinate dared risk a misstep, and the first suggestion was a modest cortege of school children. Aroused at this, friends rallied a fitting processional of state and town officials, dressed out with a muster of cadets. But eulogies delivered in the Massachusetts House were whittled down for public consumption. In Congress no member from Sam's state rose to memorialize him. It fell to Virginia's John Randolph of Roanoke to remind the House that a great patriot had died. With these small honors "The Father of the Revolution" went to his last sleep in the soil of a free and independent America.

Resolutions of the Stamp Act Congress (1765)

The members of this Congress, sincerely devoted with the warmest sentiments of affection and duty to His Majesty's person and Government, inviolably attached to the present happy establishment of the Protestant secession, and with minds deeply impressed by a sense of the present and impending misfortunes of the British colonies on this continent; having considered as maturely as time will permit the circumstances of the said colonies, esteem it our indispensable duty to make the following declarations of our humble opinion respecting the most essential rights and liberties of the colonists, and of the grievances under which they labour, by reason of the several late Acts of Parliament.

I. That His Majesty's Subjects in these colonies owe the same allegiance to the Crown of Great Britain that is owning from his subjects born within the realm, and all due subordination to that august body of the Parliament of Great Britain.

II. That His Majesty's liege subjects in these colonies are intitled to all the inherent rights and liberties of his natural born subjects within the kingdom of Great Britain.

III. That it is inseparably essential to the freedom of a people, and the undoubted right of Englishmen, that no taxes be imposed on them but with their own consent, given personally or by their representatives.

IV. That the people of the colonies are not, and from their local circumstances cannot be, represented in the House of Commons in Great Britain.

V. That the only representatives of the people of these colonies are persons chosen therein by themselves, and that no taxes ever have been, or can be constitutionally imposed on them, but by their respective legislatures.

VI. That all supplies to the Crown being free gifts of the people, it is unreasonable and inconsistent with the principles and spirit of the British Constitution, for the people of Great Britain to grant to His Majesty the property of the colonists.

VII. That trial by jury is the inherent and invaluable right of every British subject in these colonies.

VIII. That the late Act of Parliament, [the Stamp Act], by imposing taxes on the inhabitants of these colonies; and the said Act, and several other Acts, by extending the jurisdiction of the courts of Admiralty beyond its ancient limits, have a manifest tendency to subvert the rights and liberties of the colonists.

IX. That the duties imposed by several late Acts of Parliament, from the peculiar circumstances of these colonies, will be extremely burthensome and grievous; and from the scarcity of specie, the payment of them absolutely impracticable.

X. That as the profits of the trade of these colonies ultimately center in Great Britain, to pay for the manufactures which they are obliged to take from thence, they eventually contribute very largely to all supplies granted there to the Crown.

XI. That the restrictions imposed by several late Acts of Parliament on the trade of these colonies will render them unable to purchase the manufactures of Great Britain.

XII. That the increase, prosperity, and happiness of these colonies depend on the full and free enjoyments of their rights and liberties, and an intercourse with Great Britain mutually affectionate and advantageous.

XIII. That it is the right of the British subjects in these colonies to petition the King or either House of Parliament.

Lastly, that it is the indispensable duty of these colonies to the best of sovereigns, to the mother country, and to themselves, to endeavor by a loyal and dutiful address to His Majesty, and humble applications to both Houses of Parliament, to procure repeal of the Act for granting and applying certain stamp duties, of all clauses of any other Acts of Parliament whereby the jurisdiction of the admiralty is extended as aforesaid, and of the other late Acts for the restriction of American commerce.

The Declaratory Act
(1766)

Whereas several of the houses of representatives in his Majesty's colonies and plantations in America have of late, against law, claimed to themselves, or to the general assemblies of the same, the sole and exclusive right of imposing duties or taxes upon his Majesty's subjects in the said colonies and plantations; and have, in pursuance of such claim, passed certain votes, resolutions, and orders, derogatory to the legislative authority of parliament, and inconsistent with the dependency of said colonies and plantations upon the crown of Great Britain: . . . be it declared . . . That the said colonies ought to be subordinate unto and dependent upon the imperial crown and parliament of Great Britain; and that the King's majesty, by and with the advice and consent of the lords spiritual and temporal, and commons of Great Britain in parliament assembled, had, hath, and of right ought to have full power and authority to make laws and statutes of sufficient force and validity to bind the colonies and people of America, subjects of the crown of Great Britain, in all cases whatsoever.

England's Vietnam: The American Revolution

Richard M. Ketchum

I f it is true that those who cannot remember the past are condemned to repeat it, America's last three Presidents might have profited by examining the ghostly footsteps of America's last king before pursuing their adventure in Vietnam. As the United States concludes a decade of war in Southeast Asia, it is worth recalling the time, two centuries ago, when Britain faced the same agonizing problems in America that we have met in Vietnam. History seldom repeats itself exactly, and it would be a mistake to try to equate the ideologies or the motivating factors involved; but enough disturbing parallels may be drawn between those two distant events to make one wonder if the Messrs. Kennedy, Johnson, and Nixon had their ears closed while the class was studying the American Revolution.

Britain, on the eve of that war, was the greatest empire since Rome. Never before had she known such wealth and power; never had the future seemed so bright, the prospects so glowing. All, that is, except the spreading sore of discontent in the American colonies that, after festering for a decade and more, finally erupted in violence at Lexington and Concord on April 19, 1775. When news of the subsequent battle for Bunker Hill reached England that summer, George III and his ministers concluded that there was no alternative to using force to put down the insurrection. In the King's mind, at least, there was no longer any hope of reconciliation—nor did the idea appeal to him. He was determined to teach the rebellious colonials a lesson, and no doubts troubled him as to the righteousness of the course he had chosen. "I am not sorry that the line of conduct seems now chalked out," he had said even before fighting began; later he told his prime minister, Lord North, "I know I am doing my Duty and I can never wish to retract." And then, making acceptance of the war a matter of personal loyalty, "I wish nothing but good," he said, "therefore anyone who does not agree with me is a traitor and a scoundrel." Filled with high moral purpose and confidence, he was certain that "when once these rebels have felt a smart blow, they will submit. . . ."

In British political and military circles there was general agreement that the war would be quickly and easily won. "Shall we be told," asked one of the King's men in Commons, "that [the Americans] can resist the powerful efforts of this nation?" Major John Pitcairn, writing home from Boston in March, 1775, said, "I am satisfied that one active campaign, a smart action, and burning two or three of their towns, will set everything to rights." The man who would direct the British navy during seven years of war, the unprincipled, inefficient Earl of Sandwich, rose in the House of Lords to express his opinion of the provincial fighting man. "Suppose the Colonies do abound in men," the First Lord of the Admiralty asked, "what does that signify? They are raw, undisciplined, cowardly men. I wish instead of forty or fifty thousand of these *brave* fellows they would produce in the field at least two hundred thousand; the more the better, the easier would be the conquest; if they did not run away, they would starve themselves into compliance with our measures. . . ." And General James Murray, who had succeeded the great Wolfe in 1749 as commander in North America, called the native American "a very effeminate thing, very unfit for and very impatient of war." Between these estimates of the colonial militiamen and a belief that the might of Great Britain was invincible, there was a kind of arrogant optimism in official quarters when the conflict began. "As there is not common sense in protracting a war of this sort," wrote Lord George Germain, the secretary for the American colonies, in September, 1775, "I should be for exerting the utmost force of this Kingdom to finish the rebellion in one campaign."

Optimism bred more optimism, arrogance more arrogance. One armchair strategist in the House of Commons, William Innes, outlined for the other members an elaborate scheme he had devised for the conduct of the war. First, he would remove the British troops from Boston, since that place was poorly situated for defense. Then, while the people of the Massachusetts Bay Colony were treated like the madmen they were and shut up by the navy, the army would move to one of the southern colonies, fortify itself in an impregnable position, and let the provincials attack if they pleased. The British could sally forth from this and other defensive enclaves at will, and eventually "success against one-half of America will pave the way to the conquest of the whole. . . ." What was more, Innes went on, it was "more than probable you may find men to recruit your army in America." There was a good possibility, in other words, that the British regulars would be replaced after a while by Americans who were loyal to their king, so that the army fighting the rebels would be Americanized, so to speak, and the Irish and English lads sent home. General James Robertson also believed that success lay in this scheme of Americanizing the combat force: "I never had an idea of subduing the Americans," he said, "I meant to assist the good Americans to subdue the bad."

This notion was important not only from the standpoint of the fighting, but in terms of administering the colonies once they were beaten; loyalists would take over the reins of government when the British pulled out, and loyalist militiamen would preserve order in the pacified colonies. No one knew, of course, how many "good" Americans there were; some thought they might make up half or more of the population. Shortly after arriving in the colonies in 1775, General William Howe, for one, was convinced that "the insurgents are very few, in comparison with the whole of the people."

Before taking the final steps into full-scale war, however, the King and his ministers had to be certain about one vitally important matter: they had to be able to count on the support of the English people. On several occasions in 1775 they were able to read the public pulse (that part of it, at least, that mattered) by observing certain important votes in Parliament. The King's address to both Houses on October 26, in which he announced plans to suppress the uprising in America, was followed by weeks of angry debate; but when the votes were counted, the North ministry's majority was overwhelming. Each vote indicated the full tide of anger that influenced the independent members, the country gentlemen who agreed that the colonials must be put in their place and taught a lesson. A bit out of touch with the news, highly principled, and content in the belief that the King and the ministry must be right, none of them seem to have asked what would be best for the empire; they simply went along with the vindictive measures that were being set in motion. Eloquent voices—those of Edmund Burke, Charles James Fox, the Earl of Chatham, John Wilkes, among others—were raised in opposition to the policies of the Crown, but as Burke said, ". . . it was almost in vain to contend, for the country gentlemen had abandoned their duty, and placed an implicit confidence in the Minister."

The words of sanity and moderation went unheeded because the men who spoke them were out of power and out of public favor; and each time the votes were tallied, the strong, silent, unquestioning majority prevailed. No one in any position of power in the government proposed, after the Battle of Bunker Hill, to halt the fighting in order to settle the differences; no one seriously contemplated conversations that might have led to peace. Instead the government—like so many governments before and since—took what appeared to be the easy way out and settled for war.

George III was determined to maintain his empire, intact and undiminished, and his greatest fear was that the loss of the American colonies would set off a reaction like a line of dominoes failing. Writing to Lord North in 1779, he called the contest with America "the most serious in which any country was ever engaged. It contains such a train of consequences that they must be examined to feel its real weight. . . . Independence is [the Americans'] object, which every man not willing to sacrifice every object to a momentary and inglorious peace must concur with me in thinking this country can never submit to. Should America succeed in that, the West Indies must follow, not in independence, but for their own interest they must become dependent on America. Ireland would soon follow, and this island reduced to itself, would be a poor island indeed."

Despite George's unalterable determination, strengthened by his domino theory; despite the wealth and might of the British empire; despite all the odds favoring a quick triumph, the problems facing the King and his ministers and the armed forces were formidable ones indeed. Surpassing all others in sheer magnitude was the immense distance between the mother country and the rebellious colonies. As Edmund Burke described the situation in his last, most eloquent appeal for conciliation, "Three thousand miles of ocean lie between you and them. No contrivance can prevent the effect of this distance in weakening government. Seas roll, and months pass, between the order and the execution; and the want of a speedy explanation of a single point is enough to defeat a whole system." Often the westerly passage took three months, and every soldier, every weapon, every button and gaiter and musket ball, every article of clothing and great quantities of food and even fuel, had to be shipped across those three thousand miles of the Atlantic. It was not only immensely costly and time consuming, but there was a terrifying wastefulness to it. Ships sank or were blown hundreds of miles off course, supplies spoiled, animals died en route. Worse yet, men died, and in substantial numbers: returns from regiments sent from the British Isles to the West Indies between 1776 and 1780 reveal that an average of 11 percent of the troops was lost on these crossings.

Beyond the water lay the North American land mass, and it was an article of faith on the part of many a British military man that certain ruin lay in fighting an enemy on any large scale in that savage wilderness. In the House of Lords in November, 1775, the Duke of Richmond warned the peers to consult their geographies before turning their backs on a peaceful settlement. There was, he said, "one insuperable difficulty with which an army would have to struggle"—America abounded in vast rivers that provided natural barriers to the progress of troops; it was a country in which every bush might conceal an enemy, a land whose cultivated parts would be laid waste, so that "the army (if any army could march or subsist) would be obliged to draw all its provisions from Europe, and all its fresh meat from Smithfield market." The French, the mortal enemies of Great Britain, who had seen a good deal more of the North American wilds than the English had, were already laying plans to capitalize on the situation when the British army was bogged down there. In Paris, watchfully eyeing his adversary's every move, France's foreign minister, the Comte de Vergennes, predicted in July, 1775, that "it will be vain for the English to multiply their forces" in the colonies; "no longer can they bring that vast continent back to dependence by force of arms." Seven years later, as the war drew to a close, one of Rochambeau's aides told a friend of Charles James Fox: "No opinion was clearer than that though the people of America might be conquered by well disciplined European troops, the country of America was unconquerable."

Yet even in 1775 some thoughtful Englishmen doubted if the American people or their army could be defeated. Before the news of Bunker Hill arrived in London, the adjutant general declared that a plan to defeat the colonials militarily was "as wild an idea as ever controverted common sense," and the secretary-at-war, Lord Barrington, had similar reservations. As early as 1774 Barrington ventured the opinion that a war in the wilderness of North America would cost Britain far more than she could ever gain from it; that the size of the country and the colonials' familiarity with firearms would make victory questionable—or at best achievable only at the cost of enormous suffering; and finally, even if Britain should win such a contest, Barrington believed that the cost of maintaining the colonies in any state of subjection would be staggering. John Wilkes, taunting Lord North on this matter of military conquest, suggested that North—even if he rode out at the head of the entire English cavalry—would not venture ten miles into the countryside for fear of guerrilla fighters. "The Americans," Wilkes promised, "will dispute every inch of territory with you, every narrow pass, every strong defile, every Thermopylae, every Bunker's Hill."

It was left to the great William Pitt to provide the most stirring warning against fighting the Americans. Now Earl of Chatham, he was so crippled in mind and body that he rarely appeared in the House of Lords, but in May, 1777, he made the supreme effort, determined to raise his voice once again in behalf of conciliation. Supported on canes, his eyes flashing with the old fire and his beaklike face thrust forward belligerently, he warned the peers: "You cannot conquer the Americans. You talk of your numerous friends to annihilate the Congress, and of your powerful forces to disperse their army, but I might as well talk of driving them before me with this crutch. . . . You have been three years teaching them the art of war, and they are apt scholars. I will venture to tell your lordships that the American gentry will make officers enough fit to command the troops of all the European powers. What you have sent there are too many to make peace, too few to make war. You cannot make them respect you. You cannot make them wear your cloth. You will plant an invincible hatred in their breast against you. . ."

"My lords," he went on, "you have been the aggressors from the beginning. I say again, this country has been the aggressor. You have made descents upon their coasts. You have burnt their towns, plundered their country, made war upon the inhabitants, confiscated their property, proscribed and imprisoned their persons. . . . The people of America look upon Parliament as the authors of their miseries. Their affections are estranged from their sovereign. Let, then, reparation come from the hands that inflicted the injuries. Let concilation succeed chastisement. . . ." But there was no persuading the majority; Chatham's appeal was rejected and the war went on unabated.

It began to appear, however, that destruction of the Continental Army—even if that goal could be achieved—might not be conclusive. After the disastrous campaign around Manhattan in 1776, George Washington had determined not to risk his army in a major engagement, and he began moving away from the European battle style in which two armies confronted each other head to head. His tactical method became that of the small, outweighed prizefighter who depends on his legs to keep him out of range of his opponent and who, when the bigger man begins to tire, darts in quickly to throw a quick punch, then retreats again. It was an approach to fighting described by Nathanael Greene, writing of the campaign in the South in 1780: "We fight, get beat, rise, and fight again." In fact, between January and September of the following year, Greene, short of money, troops, and supplies, won a major campaign without ever really winning a battle. The battle at Guilford Courthouse, which was won by the British, was typical of the results. As Horace Walpole observed, "Lord Cornwallis has conquered his troops out of shoes and provisions and himself out of troops."

There was, in the colonies, no great political center like Paris or London, whose loss might have been demoralizing to the Americans; indeed, Boston, New York, and Philadelphia, the seat of government, were all held at one time or another by the British without irreparable damage to the rebel cause. The fragmented political and military structure of the colonies was often a help to the rebels, rather than a hindrance, for it meant that there was almost no chance of the enemy striking a single crushing blow. The difficulty, as General Frederick Haldimand, who succeeded Carleton in Canada, saw it, was the seemingly unending availability of colonial militiamen who rose up out of nowhere to fight in support of the nucleus of regular troops called the Continental Army. "It is not the number of troops Mr Washington can spare from his army that is to be apprehended," Haldimand wrote, "it is the multitude of militia and men in arms ready to turn out at an hour's notice at the shew of a single regiment of Continental Troops. . . ." So long as the British were able to split up their forces and fan out over the countryside in relatively small units, they were fairly successful in putting down the irregulars' activities and cutting off their supplies; but the moment they had to concentrate again to fight the Continentals, guerrilla warfare burst out like so many small brush fires on their flank and rear. No British regular could tell if an American was friend or foe, for loyalty to King George was easy to attest; and the man who was a farmer or merchant when a British battalion marched by his home was a militiaman as soon as it had passed by, ready to shoulder his musket when an emergency or an opportunity to confound the enemy arose.

Against an unnumberable supply of irregular forces the British could bring to bear only a fixed quantity of troops—however many, that is, they happened to have on the western side of the Atlantic Ocean at any given moment. Early in the war General James Murray had foreseen the difficulties that would undoubtedly arise. Writing to Lord Barrington, he warned that military conquest was no real answer. If the war proved to be a long one, their advantage in numbers would heavily favor the rebels, who could replace their losses while the British could not. Not only did every musket and grain of powder have to be shipped across the ocean; but if a man was killed or wounded, the only way to replace him was to send another man in full kit across the Atlantic. And troop transports were slow and small: three or four were required to move a single battalion.

During the summer of 1775 recruiting went badly in England and Ireland, for the war was not popular with a lot of the people who would have to fight it, and there were jobs to be had. It was evident that the only means of assembling a force large enough to suppress the rebellion in the one massive stroke that had been determined upon was to hire foreign troops. And immediately this word was out, the rapacious petty princes of Brunswick, Hesse-Cassel, and Waldeck, and the Margrave of Anspach-Bayreuth, generously offered up a number of their subjects—at a price—fully equipped and ready for duty, to serve His Majesty George III. Frederick the Great of Prussia, seeing the plan for what it was, announced that he would "make all the Hessian troops, marching through his dominions to America, pay the usual cattle tax, because, although human beings, they had been sold as beasts." But George III and the princes regarded it as a business deal, in the manner of such dubious alliances ever since: each foot soldier and trooper supplied by the Duke of Brunswick, for instance, was to be worth seven pounds, four shillings, fourpence halfpenny in levy money to his Most Serene Highness. Three wounded men were to count as one killed in action, and it was stipulated that a soldier killed in combat would be paid for at the same rate as levy money. In other words the life of a subject was worth precisely seven pounds, four shillings, fourpence halfpenny to the Duke.

As it turned out, the large army that was assembled in 1776 to strike a quick, overpowering blow that would put a sudden end to the rebellion proved—when that decisive victory never came to pass—to be a distinct liability, a hideously expensive and at times vulnerable weapon. In the indecisive hands of men like William Howe and Henry Clinton, who never seemed absolutely certain about what they should do or how they should do it, the great army rarely had an opportunity to realize its potential; yet, it remained a ponderous and insatiable consumer of supplies, food, and money.

The loyalists, on whom many Englishmen had placed such high hopes, proved a will-o'-the-wisp. Largely ignored by the policy makers early in the war despite their pleas for assistance, the loyalists were numerous enough but were neither well organized nor evenly distributed throughout the colonies. Where the optimists in Britain went wrong in thinking that loyalist strength would be an important factor was to imagine that anything like a majority of Americans *could* remain loyal to the Crown if they were not continuously supported and sustained by the mother country. Especially as the war went on, as opinions hardened, and as the possibility increased that the new government in America might actually survive, it was a very difficult matter to retain one's loyalty to the King unless friends and neighbors were of like mind and unless there was British force nearby to safeguard such a belief. Furthermore, it proved almost impossible for the British command to satisfy the loyalists, who were bitterly angry over the persecution and physical violence and robbery they had to endure and who charged constantly that the British generals were too lax in their treatment of rebels.

While the problems of fighting the war in distant America mounted, Britain found herself unhappily confronted with the combination of circumstances the Foreign Office dreaded most: with her armies tied down, the great European maritime powers—France and Spain—vengeful and adventurous and undistracted by war in the Old World, formed a coalition against her. When the American war began, the risk of foreign intervention was regarded as minimal, and the decision to fight was made on the premise that victory would be early and complete and that the armed forces would be released before any threatening European power could take advantage of the situation. But as the war continued without any definite signs of American collapse, France and Spain seized the chance to embarrass and perhaps humiliate their old antagonist. At first they supported the rebels surreptitiously with shipments of weapons and other supplies; then, when the situation appeared more auspicious, France in particular furnished active support in the form of an army and a navy, with catastrophic results for Great Britain.

One fascinating might-have-been is what would have happened had the Opposition in Parliament been more powerful politically. It consisted, after all, of some of the most forceful and eloquent orators imaginable, men whose words still have the power to send shivers up the spine. Not simply vocal, they were highly intelligent men whose concern went beyond the injustice and inhumanity of war. They were quick to see that the personal liberty of the King's subjects was as much an issue in London as it was in the colonies, and they foresaw irreparable damage to the empire if the government followed its unthinking policy of coercion. Given a stronger power base, they might have headed off war or the ultimate disaster; had the government been in the hands of men like Chatham or Burke or their followers, some accommodation with America might conceivably have evolved from the various proposals for reconciliation. But the King and North had the votes in their pockets, and the antiwar Opposition failed because a majority that was largely indifferent to reason supported the North ministry until the bitter end came with Cornwallis' surrender. Time and again a member of the Opposition would rise to speak out against the war for one reason or another: "This country," the Earl of Shelburne protested, "already burdened much beyond its abilities, is now on the eve of groaning under new taxes, for the purpose of carrying on this cruel and destructive war." Or, from Dr. Franklin's friend David Hartley: "Every proposition for reconciliation has so constantly and uniformly been crushed by Administration, that I think they seem not even to wish for the appearance of justice. The law of force is that which they appeal to. . . ." Or, from Sir James Lowther, when he learned that the King had rejected an "Olive Branch Petition" from the provincials: "Why have we not peace with a people who, it is evident, desire peace with us?" Or this, from General Henry Seymour Conway, inviting Lord North to inform members of the House of Commons about his overall program: "I do not desire the detail; let us have general outline, to be able to judge of the probability of its success. It is indecent not to lay before the House some plan, or the outlines of a plan. . . . If [the] plan is conciliation, let us see it, that we may form some opinion of it; if it be hostility and coercion,

I do repeat, that we have no cause for a minute's consideration; for I can with confidence pronounce, that the present military armament will never succeed." But all unavailing, year after year, as each appeal to reason and humanity fell on ears deafened by self-righteousness and minds hardened against change.

Although it might be said that the arguments raised by the Opposition did not change the course of the war, they nevertheless affected the manner in which it was conducted, which in turn led to the ultimate British defeat. Whether Lord North was uncertain of that silent majority's loyalty is difficult to determine, but it seems clear that he was sufficiently nervous about public support to decide that a bold policy which risked defeats was not for him. As a result the war of the American Revolution was a limited war—limited from the standpoint of its objectives and the force with which Britain waged it.

In some respects the aspect of the struggle that may have had the greatest influence on the outcome was an intangible one. Until the outbreak of hostilities in 1775 no more than a small minority of the colonials had seriously contemplated independence, but after a year of war the situation was radically different. Now the mood was reflected in words such as these—instructions prepared by the county of Buckingham, in Virginia, for its delegates to a General Convention in Williamsburg: ". . . as far as your voices are admitted, you [will] cause a free and happy Constitution to be established, with a renunciation of the old, and so much thereof as has been found inconvenient and oppressive." That simple and powerful idea—renunciation of the old and its replacement with something new, independently conceived—was destined to sweep all obstacles before it. In Boston, James Warren was writing the news of home to John Adams in Philadelphia and told him: "Your Declaration of Independence came on Saturday and diffused a general joy. Every one of us feels more important than ever; we now congratulate each other as Freemen." Such winds of change were strong, and by contrast all Britain had to offer was a return to the status quo. Indeed, it was difficult for the average Englishman to comprehend the appeal that personal freedom and independence held for a growing number of Americans. As William Innes put it in a debate in Commons, all the government had to do to put an end to the nonsense in the colonies was to "convince the lower class of those infatuated people that the imaginary liberty they are so eagerly pursuing is not by any means to be compared to that which the Constitution of this happy country already permits them to enjoy."

With everything to gain from victory and everything to lose by defeat, the Americans could follow Livy's advice, that "in desperate matters the boldest counsels are the safest." Frequently beaten and disheartened, inadequately trained and fed and clothed, they fought on against unreasonably long odds because of that slim hope of attaining a distant goal. And as they fought on, increasing with each passing year the possibility that independence might be achieved, the people of Britain finally lost the will to keep going.

In England the goal had not been high enough, while the cost was too high. There was nothing compelling about the limited objective of bringing the colonies back into the empire, nothing inspiring about punishing the rebels, nothing noble in proving that retribution awaited those who would change the nature of things.

After the war had been lost and the treaty of peace signed, Lord North looked back on the whole affair and sadly informed the members of the House of Commons where, in his opinion, the fault lay. With a few minor changes, it was a message as appropriate to America in 1971 as to Britain in 1783: "The American war," he said, "has been suggested to have been the war of the Crown, contrary to the wishes of the people. I deny it. It was the war of Parliament. There was not a step taken in it that had not the sanction of Parliament. It was the war of the people, for it was undertaken for the express purpose of maintaining the just rights of Parliament, or, in other words, of the people of Great Britain, over the dependencies of the empire. For this reason, it was popular at its commencement, and eagerly embraced by the people and Parliament. . . . Nor did it ever cease to be popular until a series of unparalleled disasters and calamities caused the people, wearied out with almost uninterrupted ill-success and misfortune, to call out as loudly for peace as they had formerly done for war."

The Slave Who Sued
For Freedom

Jon Swan

Early during the year 1781, having heard a lot of talk about the "rights of man," a slave woman named Mum Bett walked out of her master's house in western Massachusetts to tell a lawyer that she wanted to sue for her freedom. After asking her what had put such an extraordinary idea into her head and being satisfied by her reply, the lawyer agreed to represent her. The case is a reminder of the fact that slavery existed even in the cradle of abolitionism, and it is a testament to the hopes inspired by revolutionary rhetoric. But it is most fascinating, perhaps, for the glimpse it yields of a singular woman who was determined to be free.

Bett and a younger sister, Lizzie, grew up as slave children in Claverack, New York, about twenty miles south of Albany. Their owner was a Dutchman, Pieter Hogeboom. In 1735 his youngest child, Hannah, married John Ashley, the son of one of the original proprietors permitted by the General Court of Massachusetts to organize settlements along the Housatonic River.

The Ashleys had four children. Exactly when they acquired Bett and Lizzie is not known, but Hannah's father died in 1758, when Bett was about fourteen.

By this time John Ashley had become an important figure in Sheffield, Massachusetts, the largest settlement in the western slice of Massachusetts that would later be called Berkshire County. In 1761 he was appointed judge of the Court of Common Pleas, a post he voluntarily resigned twenty years later, when his servant Bett's case came before that court. Col. John Ashley was an honorable man.

Described as "patriarchal of appearance, of middling size," according to an early biographical sketch, Ashley was also a cautious man. As a member of the Massachusetts Assembly, he signed a letter drafted by Samuel Adams in 1768 objecting to the "several acts of Parliament, imposing Duties & Taxes on the American colonys"; but, along with only a few of his colleagues, he subsequently bowed to the governor's demand for a disavowal of the letter.

A town meeting held in Great Barrington, one of the three Berkshire County towns that Ashley represented, denounced him for repudiating the "highly approved circular letter." Nevertheless, in the next election he was again chosen to represent the area, and when, in 1773, Sheffield appointed a committee "to take into consideration the grievances which Americans in general and Inhabitants of this Province in particular labor under," Colonel Ashley was appointed chairman.

The meeting of that committee, held in Colonel Ashley's home in early January of 1773, very probably was a turning point in the life of Mum Bett. She was now almost thirty years old. The committee's clerk, Theodore Sedgwick, was the lawyer who would ultimately take her case. Sedgwick was only twenty-six. He had been expelled from Yale for unspecified "boyish gaities" but then studied law in Great Barrington and set up practice in downtown Sheffield. The meeting lasted for several hours, and Mum Bett presumably served refreshments—and perhaps listened in—as the men discussed the evening's business in the pine-paneled study on the second floor of the Ashley house.

The result of that discussion was a document called the Sheffield Declaration. While duly respectful of the crown, it contained a resolution that read: "Resolved that Mankind in a State of Nature are equal, free and independent of each other, and have a right to the undisturbed Enjoyment of their lives, their liberty and Property." Clearly somebody there had read John Locke. Mum Bett had not— she never learned to read or even to write her name—but she seems to have taken the philosopher's message more directly to heart than anyone else in the room.

The Sheffield Declaration, the first of its kind, was subsequently "twice Reade distinctly" at the Sheffield town meeting and unanimously approved. The following year—no doubt to the colonel's consternation—the townspeople of Great Barrington, where Ashley sat as a judge, packed the courthouse so that no further business could be carried out until a state constitution had been drawn up and approved. Thereafter the so-called Berkshire Constitutionalists shut down courts throughout the county until 1780, the year Massachusetts finally approved its constitution.

The first article of the Declaration of Rights of the new constitution stated that "all men are born free and equal, and have certain natural, essential, and inalienable rights. . . ." Thus the sentiments expressed by the Sheffield Declaration and the Declaration of Independence were now the law of the state and county in which Mum Bett lived and worked.

A single, but dramatic, domestic scene apparently made her decide that the time had come to put those high-sounding words to the test. In "The Practicability of the Abolition of Slavery," a lecture delivered fifty years after the event, Henry Dwight Sedgwick, one of Theodore Sedgwick's ten children, recalled the episode.

"Slavery in New-York and New-England," he first explained, "was so masked, that but a slight difference could be perceived in the condition of slaves and hired servants. . . . The younger slaves not only ate and drank, but played with the children. They thus became familiar companions with each other. The black women were cooks and nurses, and as such assisted by their mistresses. . . . In this state of familiar intercourse, instances of cruelty were uncommon, and . . . caused a degree of indignation not much less than if committed upon a freeman.

"Under this condition of society, while Mum Bett resided in the family of Col. Ashley, she received a severe wound in a generous attempt to shield her sister. Her mistress in a fit of passion [had] resorted to a degree and mode of violence very uncommon in this country: she struck at the weak and timid [Lizzie] with a heated kitchen shovel: Mum Bett interposed her arm, and received the blow; and she bore the honorable scar it left to the day of her death."

After this incident, according to the lawyer's son, Mum Bett set off to consult Theodore Sedgwick. By now Bett was about thirty-seven years old; Sedgwick was thirty-four. He had seen action in the Revolutionary War and in 1780 had been elected to the first General Court held under the new state constitution. The conversation between the slave and the lawyer was preserved by Harriet Martineau, a novelist with strong abolitionist views who visited the Berkshires a couple of years after Mum Bett's death in 1829 and who was, for a time, a close friend of the Sedgwicks. According to her account, when the lawyer asked the slave how she had learned "the doctrine and facts on which she proceeded, she replied, 'By keepin' still and mindin' things.'" And when pressed to explain to what things she had paid mind, she replied that, "for instance, when she was waiting at table, she heard gentlemen talking over the Bill of Rights and the new constitution of Massachusetts; and in all they said she never heard but that all people were born free and equal, and she thought long about it, and resolved she would try whether she did not come in among them."

"By keepin' still and mindin' things" sounds authentic. So does a long sentence recollected by Theodore Sedgwick's daughter Catharine: "Anytime, anytime while I was a slave, if one minute's freedom had been offered to me, and I had been told I must die at the end of that minute, I would have taken it—just to stand one minute, I would have taken it just to stand one minute on God's earth a free woman—I would."

In 1781 it seemed to her that she could hope for more than just a single minute of freedom—if Sedgwick would consent to take her case. Just why he agreed to do so, given his close friendship with Colonel Ashley, whose generally conservative views he shared, remains something of a mystery. The historian Arthur Zilversmit has speculated that some Berkshire County residents seized upon the case as a means of testing the constitutionality of slavery in Massachusetts.

What effect Sedgwick's acceptance of the suit had on his friendship with the Ashleys is unknown. If Colonel Ashley was, as Catharine Sedgwick described him, "the gentlest, most benign of men," while his wife was "a shrew untamable" and "the most despotic of mistresses," it would seem likely that he viewed the whole matter more philosophically than she did—as an interesting case, an important case, which just happened to involve a woman whom his wife may have regarded as a valuable part of her inheritance.

Nor do we know why a co-plaintiff—another Sheffield slave, a man named Brom—came to be involved in the case. A surviving record of the case calls it *Brom & Bett* v. *J. Ashley Esq.* Brom is described simply as "a Negro Man . . . of Sheffield" and a "Labourer"; Bett, as "a Negro Woman . . . of Sheffield" and a "Spinster." And that's all we learn about Brom.

The case was set in motion when Sedgwick obtained a writ of replevin—a form of action taken for the recovery of property—from the Berkshire County Court of Common Pleas. The property in this case was two humans who claimed they were being illegally detained. At least two such writs were sent to the colonel and also to his son, John Ashley, Jr. (in whose household Brom may have been employed). After the Ashleys refused to release the two slaves, the court ordered the sheriff to issue a summons to both father and son to appear at its next session. The case was heard in Great Barrington on August 21, 1781.

Both sides brought in prominent counsel. Sedgwick had enlisted the assistance of Tapping Reeve, of Litchfield, Connecticut, who later founded the Litchfield Law School; the Ashleys were represented by David Noble, who subsequently became a judge, and John Canfield, a respected lawyer from Sharon, Connecticut.

Noble and Canfield argued that "the said Brom and Bett, are and were at the time of Issuing the original Writ [or replevin], the legal Negro Servants of the said John Ashley during their Lives" and that this could be proved; thus the suit should be dismissed. Sedgwick and Reeve countered by insisting that the plaintiffs were not the servants of John Ashley "during their Lives," but on what legal ground they based this assertion the record does not make clear.

However, the duc de la Rochefoucauld-Liancourt, who visited Sedgwick in Stockbridge, provided in his *Travels* an outline of the argument that Sedgwick and Reeve presented. They pleaded, he wrote: "(1) That no antecedent law had established slavery, and that the laws which seemed to suppose it were the offspring of error in the legislators . . ." and "(2) That such laws, even if they had existed, were annulled by the new Constitution."

In any event, the jury was persuaded. Not only did "Jonathan Holcomb Foreman & His Fellows" find that Brom and Bett "are not and were not at the time of the purchase of the original Writ the legal Negro Servants of him the said John Ashley during life," but they ordered Ashley to pay thirty shillings' damages and the cost of the suit—five pounds, fourteen shillings, and four pence.

Ashley appealed, but then a few months later he dropped the appeal. Moreover, as Zilversmit has pointed out, "he confessed judgment—that is, he assented to the lower court ruling that Brom and Bett were not slaves." Why? Because, in the intervening months, the state's supreme court had ruled, in another case, that slavery was unconstitutional in Massachusetts. That decision, in *Caldwell* v. *Jennison*, was a murky one, and some have argued that because no legislation banned slavery in the state, it was strictly legal until 1866—though not practiced.

Mum Bett changed her name to Elizabeth Freeman, and for the rest of her working life she served as a paid domestic in the household of Theodore Sedgwick and his second wife, Pamela—first in Sheffield and then in Stockbridge, where the family moved in 1785.

Mum Bett was "the main pillar of the household," according to Pamela's lastborn daughter, Catharine Maria. Pamela slipped into severe depression, and Mum Bett was "the only person who could tranquilize my mother when her mind was disordered. . . . She treated her with the same respect she did when she was sane . . . her superior instincts hit upon the mode of treatment that science has since adopted."

When, in the winter of 1785, followers of Shays' Rebellion broke into the house demanding the family silver, Mum Bett faced them down. With Theodore Sedgwick away, she had hid the silver in her own chest of drawers; after leading the untidy men from room to room she shamed them out of looking in her chest by urging them to do so. "Oh, you had better search that—an old nigger's as you call me." Thus she saved the family silver.

At what age Mum Bett retired is unknown. But she did have enough money to buy herself a home—a "little hut," Catharine Sedgwick called it. Catharine recalled that when she visited Mum Bett there daily during her final illness, "I felt as awed as if I had entered the presence of Washington. Even protracted suffering and mortal sickness . . . could not break down her spirit."

On October 18,1829, Elizabeth Freeman signed—with her mark—her last will and testament. It alone reveals that at some point she was married and that she had children, grandchildren, and great-grandchildren.

Elizabeth Freeman died on December 28,1829. Her tombstone stands in the Stockbridge cemetery beside that of her friend Catharine, in the innermost circle of a plot known as the Sedgwick Pie. In the center of the pie are the tall monuments inscribed with the names of Theodore and Pamela Sedgwick; buried in concentric circles around them are generations of Sedgwicks by birth or marriage, all facing in toward the center so that, it is said, on the Day of Judgment, when the dead shall rise, they shall see no one but other

Sedgwicks. The only person who is not a Sedgwick is Elizabeth Freeman—an exception in this as in so many other ways. She is also the only black among all those whites.

The inscription on her tombstone is exceptional too—longer than the others and revealing a personal and profound affection. It was written by Catharine's brother Charles and it reads: "ELIZA-BETH FREEMAN, known by the name of MUMBET died Dec. 28 1829. Her supposed age was 85 years. *She was born a slave and remained a slave for nearly thirty years. She could neither read nor write, yet in her own sphere she had no superior nor equal. She neither wasted time nor property. She never violated a trust, nor failed to perform a duty. In every situation of domestic trial, she was the most efficient helper, and the tenderest friend.* Good mother fare well."

Part III:
Emerging America

A Tax on Whiskey? Never!

Gerald Carson

When one recalls that the President of the United States, the Secretary of War, the Secretary of the Treasury, and the governors of four states once mobilized against the farmers of western Pennsylvania an army almost as large as ever took the field in the Revolutionary War, the event appears at first glance one of the more improbable episodes in the annals of this country. Equipped with mountains of ammunition, forage, baggage, and a bountiful stock of tax-paid whiskey, thirteen thousand grenadiers, dragoons, foot soldiers, pioneers, a train of artillery with six-pounders, mortars, and several "grasshoppers," paraded over the mountains to Pittsburgh against a gaggle of homespun rebels who had already dispersed.

Yet the march had a rationale. President George Washington and his Secretary of the Treasury, Alexander Hamilton, moved to counter civil commotion with overwhelming force because they well understood that the survival of the new U.S. Constitution was involved. Soon after he assumed his post at the Treasury, Hamilton had proposed, to the astonishment of the country, that the United States should meet fully and promptly its financial obligations, including the assumption of the debts contracted by the states in the struggle for independence. Part of the money was to be raised by laying an excise tax upon distilled spirits. The tax became law on March 3, 1791.

In the back country settlements that produced the whiskey and drank the lion's share of it, the news of the passage of the measure was greeted with a roar of indignation. The duty was laid uniformly upon all the states, as the Constitution provided; if the West had to pay more, the Secretary of the Treasury explained, it was only because it used more whiskey. The East could, if it so desired, forego beverage spirits and fall back on cider and beer. The South and the frontier West could not, for they had neither orchards nor breweries. To Virginia and Maryland the excise tax appeared to be as unjust and oppressive as the well-remembered Molasses Act and the tea duties of George III. "The time will come," predicted Georgia's fiery James Jackson in the House of Representatives, "when a shirt shall not be washed without an excise."

Kentucky, then thinly settled, but already producing its characteristic handmade, copper-fired, whole-souled liquor, was of the opinion that the law was unconstitutional. Deputy revenue collectors throughout the Bluegrass region were assaulted, their papers stolen, their horses' ears cropped, and their saddles cut to pieces. On one wild night the people of Lexington dragged a stuffed dummy through the streets and hanged in effigy Colonel Thomas Marshall, the chief collector for the district.

Yet, in no other place did popular fury rise so high, spread so rapidly, involve a whole population so completely, or express so many assorted grievances as in the Pennsylvania frontier counties of Fayette, Allegheny, Westmoreland, and Washington. There, in 1791, a light plume of wood smoke rose from no less than five thousand log stillhouses. The rates went into effect on July 1. The whiskey-maker could choose whether he would pay a yearly levy on his still capacity or a gallonage tax on his actual production.

Before the month was out, "committees of correspondence," in the old Revolutionary phrase, were speeding horsemen over the ridges and through the valleys to arouse the people to arm and assemble. The majority, but not all, of the men who made the whiskey decided to "forbear" from paying the tax. Revenue officers were thoroughly worked over. Robert Johnson, for example, collector for Washington and Allegheny counties, was waylaid near Pigeon Creek by a mob disguised in women's clothing. They cut off his hair, gave him a coat of tar and feathers, and stole his horse.

The Pennsylvania troubles were rooted in the economic importance and impregnable social position of mellow old Monongahela rye whiskey. The frontier people had been reared from childhood on the family jug. They found the taste pleasant, the effect agreeable. Whiskey kept the population cool in summer. In winter, it was the old settlers' equivalent of central heating. Whiskey was usually involved when there was kissing or fighting. It beatified the rituals of birth and death. It provided almost the only diversion, while enjoying at the same time a high reputation as the West's greatest therapeutic agent, effective against fevers, ague, snake bite, or general decline. The doctor kept a bottle in his office for his own use, with the protective label, "Arsenic—Deadly Poison."

Whiskey lubricated the machinery of government. The lawyer produced the bottle when the papers were signed. Whiskey was available at the prothonotary's office when the trial list was made up. Jurors got their dram, and the constable drew his ration for his services on election day. The hospitable barrel and the tin cup were the mark of the successful political candidate. The United States Army issued a gill to a man every day. Ministers of the gospel were paid in rye whiskey, for they were shepherds of a devout flock, Presbyterians mostly, who took their Bible straight, especially where it said:

"Give strong drink unto him that is ready to perish, and wine unto those that be of heavy hearts."

"Let him drink, and forget his poverty, and remember his misery no more."

With grain the most abundant commodity west of the mountains, the farmers could eat it or drink it, but they couldn't sell it in distant markets unless it was reduced in bulk and enhanced in value. Thus a Pennsylvania farmer's "best holt" was whiskey. A pack horse could move only four bushels of grain. But it could carry twenty-four bushels if it was condensed into two large wooden kegs of whiskey slung across its back, while the price of goods would double when they reached the eastern markets. So whiskey became the frontier remittance for salt, sugar, nails, bar iron, pewter plates, powder and shot. Along the western rivers, where men saw few shilling pieces, a gallon of good, sound rye whiskey was a stable measure of value.

The bitter resistance of the western men to the whiskey tax involved both practical considerations and principles. First, the excise payment was due and must be paid in scarce hard money as soon as the water-white distillate flowed from the condensing coil. The principle concerned the whole repulsive idea of an internal revenue levy. The settlers of western Pennsylvania were a bold, hardy, emigrant race from Scotland and northern Ireland, who had set up their mashing tubs, fermenters, and pot stills before the last Indian war whoop ceased to echo among the hills. They brought with them also bitter memories of oppression in the old country under the excise laws, involving invasion of their homes, confiscation of their property, and a system of paid informers. Revenue collectors were social outcasts in a society which might have warmly seconded Doctor Samuel Johnson's definition of excise: "a hateful tax levied upon commodities, and adjudged not by the common judges of property, but wretches hired by those to whom excise is paid."

The whiskey boys of Pennsylvania, then, saw it as simply a matter of sound Whig principles to resist the exciseman as he made his rounds with a Dicas hydrometer to measure the proof of the whiskey and his marking iron to brand the casks with his findings. Earlier, the state had taxed spirits, except that whiskey produced for purely private use was exempt. William Findley of Westmoreland County, a member of Congress at the time and a sympathetic interpreter of the western point of view, looked into this angle. To his astonishment, he learned that all of the whiskey distilled in the west was for purely personal use. So far as the excise tax was concerned, or any other state tax, the sturdy Celtic peoples of the Monongahela region had cheerfully returned to a state of nature: they just didn't pay. About every sixth man made whiskey. But all were involved in the problem, since the other five took their rye and corn to the stillhouse where the master distiller turned it into liquid form.

But now matters had taken a more serious turn. The new federal government in Philadelphia was dividing the whole country up into "districts" for the purpose of collecting the money, and cutting the districts up into smaller inspection "surveys." The transmontane Pennsylvanians found themselves in the grip of something known as the fourth survey, with General John Neville, hitherto a popular citizen and leader, getting ready to enforce the law. Rewards would be paid to informers and a percentage of the taxes given to the collectors, who appeared to be a rapacious set.

The first meeting of public protest against the United States excise of 1791 was held in July at Redstone Old Fort (now Brownsville, Pennsylvania). The proceedings were moderate on that occasion, and scarcely went beyond the right of petition. Another meeting in August, more characteristic of others which were to follow, was radical in tone, disorderly, threatening. It passed resolves that any person taking office under the revenue law was an enemy of society.

When warrants were issued in the affair of the molested revenue agent, Robert Johnson, the process server was robbed, beaten, tarred and feathered, and left tied to a tree in the forest. As the inspectors' offices were established, they were systematically raided. The familiar Liberty poles of the Revolution reappeared as whiskey poles. The stills of operators who paid the tax were riddled with bullets in attacks sardonically described as "mending" the stills. This led to a popular description of the whiskey boys as "Tom the Tinker's Men," an ironical reference to the familiar, itinerant repairer of pots and kettles. Notices proposing measures for thwarting the law, or aimed at coercing the law-abiding distillers, were posted on trees or published in the Pittsburgh *Gazette* signed, "Tom the Tinker," nom de plume of John Holcroft and other anti-tax propagandists. Congressman Findley, one of the prominent men of the region who tried to build a bridge of understanding between the backwoodsmen and the central government, described the outbreak as not the result of any concerted plan, but rather as a flame, "an infatuation almost incredible."

An additional complaint against the tax grew out of the circumstance that offenders were required to appear in the federal court at Philadelphia, three hundred miles away. The whiskey-makers saw this distant government as being no less oppressive than one in London, and often drew the parallel. Some democrats, oriented sympathetically toward the Jacobin Clubs of Paris, whispered that the whole whiskey issue was a scheme of the Federalists to transfer the powers of government from the people to an aristocratic junto.

A mounting clamor of protest led Congress to modify the severity of the excise tax law in 1792 and again in 1794. A further conciliatory step was taken. To ease the hardships of the judicial process, Congress gave to the state courts jurisdiction in excise offenses so that accused persons might be tried in their own vicinity. But some fifty or sixty writs already issued and returnable at Philadelphia resulted in men being carried away from their fields during harvest time. This convinced the western leaders that the aristocrats in the east were seeking a pretext to discipline the democratic west.

One day in July, 1794, while the processes were being served, William Miller, a delinquent farmer-distiller and political supporter of General Neville, saw the General riding up his lane accompanied by a stranger who turned out to be a United States marshal from Philadelphia. The marshal unlimbered a paper and began to read a summons. It ordered the said Miller to "set aside all manner of business and excuses" and appear in his "proper person" before a judge in Philadelphia. Miller had been planning to sell his property and remove to Kentucky, but the cost of the trip to Philadelphia and the fine for which he was liable would eat up the value of his land and betterments.

"I felt my blood boil, at seeing General Neville along, to pilot the sheriff to my very door," Miller said afterward. "I felt myself mad with passion."

As Neville and the marshal rode away, a party from the county militia which was mustered at Mingo Creek fired upon them, but there were no casualties. When the General reached Bower Hill, his country home above the Chartiers Valley, another party, under the command of John Holcroft, awaited him and demanded his commission and official papers. The demand was refused, and both sides began to shoot. As the rebels closed in on the main house, a flanking fire came from the Negro cabins on the plantation. The whiskey boys were driven off with one killed and four wounded.

The next day, Major James McFarlane, a veteran of the Revolutionary War, led an attack in force upon Neville's painted and papered mansion, furnished with such marvels as carpets, mirrors, pictures and prints, and an eight-day clock. The house was now defended by a dozen soldiers from Fort Fayette at Pittsburgh. A fight followed during which a soldier was shot and McFarlane was killed—by treachery, the rebels said, when a white flag was displayed. The soldiers surrendered and were either released or allowed to escape. Neville was not found, but his cabins, barns, outbuildings, and finally the residence were all burned down. Stocks of grain were destroyed, all fences levelled, as the victors broke up the furniture, liberated the mirrors and clock, and distributed the General's supply of liquor to the thirsty.

The funeral of McFarlane caused great excitement. Among those present were Hugh Henry Brackenridge, author, lawyer, and one of the western moderates, and David Bradford, prosecuting attorney for Washington County. The former wished to find ways to reduce the tension; the latter to increase it. Bradford was a rash, impetuous Marylander, ambitious for power and position. Some thought him a second-rate lawyer. Others disagreed. They said he was third-rate. But he had a gift for rough mob eloquence. Bradford had already robbed the United States mails to find out what information was being sent east against the conspirators. He had already called for the people to make a choice of *"submission or opposition . . . with head, heart, hand and voice."*

At the McFarlane funeral service Bradford worked powerfully upon the feelings of the mourners as he described "the murder of McFarlane." Brackenridge also spoke, using wit and drollery to relieve the pressure and to make palatable his warning to the rebels that they were flirting with the possibility of being hanged. But the temper of the throng was for Bradford, as clearly revealed in the epitaph set over McFarlane's grave: "He fell . . . by the hands of an unprincipled villain in the support of what he supposed to be the rights of his country."

The high-water mark of the insurrection was the occupation of Pittsburgh. After the fight and the funeral, Bradford called out the militia regiments of the four disaffected counties. They were commanded to rendezvous at Braddock's Field, near Pittsburgh, with arms, full equipment, and four days' rations. At the field there was a great beating of drums, much marching and counter-marching, almost a holiday spirit. Men in hunting shirts practiced shooting at the mark until a dense pall of smoke hung over the plain, as there had been thirty-nine years before at General Braddock's disaster. There were between five and seven thousand men on the field, many meditating in an ugly mood upon their enemies holed up in Pittsburgh, talking of storming Fort Fayette and burning the town as "a second Sodom."

Bradford's dream was the establishment of an independent state with himself cast as a sort of Washington of the west. Elected major general by acclaim, he dashed about the field on a superb horse, in a fancy uniform, his sword flashing, plumes floating out from his hat as he issued orders, harangued the multitude, and received applications for commissions in the service of—what? No one quite knew.

Marching in good order, strung out over two-and-a-half miles of road, the rebels advanced on August 1, 1794, toward Pittsburgh in what was hopefully termed a "visit," though the temper of the citizen-soldiers was perhaps nearer to that of one man who twirled his hat on the muzzle of his rifle and shouted, "I have a bad hat now, but I expect to have a better one soon." While the panic-stricken burghers buried the silver and locked up the girls, the mob marched in on what is now Fourth Avenue to the vicinity of the present Baltimore & Ohio Railroad station. A reception committee extended nervous hospitality in the form of hams, poultry, dried venison, bear meat, water, and whiskey, and agreed to banish certain citizens obnoxious to the insurrectionists. One building on a nearby farm was burned; another attempt at arson failed to come off. The day cost Brackenridge four barrels of good old Monongahela. It was better, he reflected, "to be employed in extinguishing the fire of their thirst than of my house."

Later in the month of August armed bands continued to patrol the roads as a "scrub Congress"—in the phrase of one scoffer—met at Parkinson's Ferry, now Monongahela, to debate, pass resolutions, and move somewhat uncertainly toward separation from the United States. Wild and unfounded rumors won belief. It was said that Congress was extending the excise levy to plows at a dollar each, that every wagon entering Philadelphia would be forced to pay a dollar, that a tax was soon to be established at Pittsburgh of fifteen shillings for the birth of every boy baby, and ten for each girl.

It was evident that the crisis had arrived. The President requisitioned 15,000 militia (of whom about 13,000 actually marched) from Pennsylvania, New Jersey, Virginia, and Maryland. Would the citizens of one state invade another to compel obedience to federal law? Here one gets a glimpse of the larger importance of the affair. Both the national government and the state of Pennsylvania sent commissioners to the west with offers of pardon upon satisfactory assurances that the people would obey the laws. Albert Gallatin, William Findley, Brackenridge, and others made a desperate effort to win the people to submission, though their motives were often questioned by both the rebels and the federal authorities. The response to the offer of amnesty was judged not to be sufficiently positive. Pressed by the Secretary of the Treasury, Alexander Hamilton, to have federal authority show its teeth, Washington announced that the troops would march.

The Army was aroused. In particular, the New Jersey militia were ready to exercise lynch law because they had been derided in a western newspaper as a "Water-melon Army" and an uncomplimentary estimate made of their military capabilities. The piece was written as a take-off on the kind of negotiations which preceded an Indian treaty. Possibly the idea was suggested by the fact that the whiskey boys were often called "White Indians." At any rate, in the satire the Indians admonished the great council in Philadelphia: ". . . Brothers, we have that powerful monarch, Capt. Whiskey, to command us. By the power of his influence, and a love to *his person* we are compelled to every great and heroic act . . . We, the Six United

Nations of White Indians . . . have all imbibed his principles and passions—that is a love of whiskey . . . Brothers, you must not think to frighten us with . . . infantry, cavalry and artillery, composed of your watermelon armies from the Jersey shores; they would cut a much better figure in warring with the crabs and oysters about the Capes of Delaware."

Captain Whiskey was answered hotly by "A Jersey Blue." He pointed out that "the water-melon army of New Jersey" was going to march westward shortly with "ten-inch howitzers for throwing a species of melon very useful for curing a *gravel occasioned by whiskey!*" The expedition was tagged thereafter as the "Watermelon Army."

The troops moved in two wings under the command of General Henry (Light Horse Harry) Lee, Governor of Virginia. Old Dan Morgan was there and young Meriwether Lewis, five nephews of President Washington, the governors of Pennsylvania and New Jersey, too, and many a veteran blooded in Revolutionary fighting, including Captain John Fries of the Bucks County militia and his dog, which he had named after a drink he occasionally enjoyed—Whiskey.

The left wing marched west during October, 1794, from Virginia and Maryland to Fort Cumberland on the Potomac, then northwest into Pennsylvania, to join forces with the right wing at Bedford. The Pennsylvania and New Jersey corps proceeded via Norristown and Reading to Harrisburg and Carlisle. There, on October 4, President Washington arrived, accompanied by Colonel Alexander Hamilton. The western representatives told the President at Carlisle that the army was not needed, but Hamilton convinced him that it was. Washington rode down to Fort Cumberland on October 16 to review the troops of the left wing, which had assembled there. He then went on to Bedford, the rendezvous, to survey final plans before returning to Philadelphia for the meeting of Congress. Meanwhile Hamilton ordered a roundup of many of the rebels and personally interrogated the most important ones. Brackenridge, incidentally, came off well in his encounter with Hamilton, who declared that he was satisfied with Brackenridge's conduct.

By the time the expedition had crossed the mountains, the rebellion was already coming apart at the seams. David Bradford, who was excluded from the subsequent amnesty, fled to Spanish Louisiana, where he finished out his life as a planter. About 2,000 of the best riflemen in the west left the country, including many a distiller who loaded his pot stills on a pack horse or a Kentucky boat and sought asylum in Kentucky, where, hopefully, a man could distill "the creature" without giving the public debt a lift.

The punitive expedition moved forward in glorious autumn weather, raiding chicken coops, consuming prodigious quantities of the commodity which lay at the heart of the controversy. Richard Howell, governor of New Jersey and commander of the right wing, revived the spirits of the Jersey troops by composing a marching song, "Dash to the Mountains, Jersey Blue":

> *To arms once more, our hero cries,*
> *Sedition lives and order dies;*
> *To peace and ease then bid adieu*
> *And dash to the mountains, Jersey Blue.*

Faded diaries, old letters, and orderly books preserve something of the gala atmosphere of the expedition. At Trenton, New Jersey, a Miss Forman and a Miss Milnor were most amiable. Newtown, Pennsylvania, was noted as a poor place for hay. At Potts Grove a captain of a cavalry troop got kicked in the shin by his horse. Among the Virginians, Meriwether Lewis enjoyed the martial excitement and wrote to his mother in high spirits of the "mountains of beef and oceans of Whiskey," sent regards "to all the girls," and announced that he would bring "an Insergiant Girl to see them next fall bearing the title of Mrs. Lewis." If there was such a girl, he soon forgot her.

Yet where there is an army in being, there are unpleasant occurrences. Men were lashed. Quartermasters stole government property. A soldier was ordered to put an insurgent under guard. In execution of the order, he ran the rebel through with his bayonet, of which wound the prisoner died. At Carlisle, a dragoon's pistol went off and hit a countryman in the groin; he too died. On November 13, long remembered in many a cabin and clearing as "the dismal night," the Jersey Horse rounded up suspects whom they described grimly as "the whiskey pole gentry," dragging them out of bed, tying them back to back.

In late November, finding no one to fight, the army turned east again, leaving a volunteer force under General Morgan to conciliate and consolidate the position during the winter. Twenty "Yahoos" were carried back to Philadelphia and were paraded by the Philadelphia Horse through the streets of the city with "Insurrection" labels on their hats. It was an odd Federalist version of a Roman triumph. The troop was composed, as an admirer said, of "young gentlemen of the first property of the city," with beautiful mounts and uniforms of the finest blue broadcloth. They held their swords elevated in the right hand, while the light flashed from the silver stirrups, martingales, and jingling bridles. Stretched over half a mile they came, first two cavalrymen abreast, then a pair of prisoners, walking; then two more mounted men, and so on.

The army, meditating upon their fatigues and hardships, called for a substantial number of hangings. Samuel Hodgson, the commissary-general, wrote to a Pittsburgh confidant: "We all lament that so few of the insurgents fell—such disorders can only be cured by copious bleedings . . .," while Philip Freneau, friend and literary colleague of Brackenridge, suggested in retrospect—ironically, of course—the benefits which would have accrued to the country "If Washington had drawn and quartered thirty or forty of the whiskey boys. . . ." Most of the captives escaped any punishment other than that of being held in jail without a trial for ten or twelve months. One died. Two were finally tried and sentenced to death. Eventually both were let off.

If the rising was a failure, so was the liquor tax. The military adventure alone, without ordinary costs of collection, ran up a bill of $1,500,000, or about one-third of all the money that was realized during the life of the act. Meanwhile the movement of the army to the Pennsylvania hinterland had brought with it a flood of cash which furnished the distillers with currency for paying their taxes. Gradually the bitterness receded. During Jefferson's administration, the tax was quietly repealed. Yet the watermelon armies and the whiskey boys made a not inconsiderable contribution to our constitutional history. Through them, the year 1794 completed what 1787 had begun; for it established the reality of a federal union whose law was not a suggestion but a command.

Farewell Address (1796)

George Washington

Observe good faith and justice toward all nations. Cultivate peace and harmony with all. Religion and morality enjoin this conduct. And can it be that good policy does not equally enjoin it? It will be worthy of a free, enlightened, and, at no distant period, a great nation to give to mankind the magnanimous and too novel example of a people always guided by an exalted justice and benevolence. . . .

In the execution of such a plan nothing is more essential than that permanent, inveterate antipathies against particular nations and passionate attachments for others should be excluded, and that, in place of them, just and amicable feelings toward all should be cultivated. The nation which indulges toward another an habitual hatred or an habitual fondness is in some degree a slave. It is a slave to its animosity or to its affection, either of which is sufficient to lead it astray from its duty and its interest. Antipathy in one nation against another disposes each more readily to offer insult and injury, to lay hold of slight causes of umbrage, and to be haughty and intractable when accidental or trifling occasions of dispute occur. . . .

So, likewise, a passionate attachment of one nation for another produces a variety of evils. Sympathy for the favorite nation, facilitating the illusion of an imaginary common interest in cases where no real common interest exists, and infusing into one the enmities of the other, betrays the former into a participation in the quarrels and wars of the latter without adequate inducement or justification. It leads also to concessions to the favorite nation of privileges denied to others . . .

Against the insidious wiles of foreign influence (I conjure you
to believe me, fellow citizens) the jealousy of a free people ought
to be constantly awake, since history and experience prove that
foreign influence is one of the most baneful foes of republican
government. . . . But that jealousy, to be useful, must be impartial.
. . . Excessive partiality for one foreign nation and excessive dislike
of another cause those whom they actuate to see danger only on one
side, and serve to veil and even second the arts of influence on the
other. . . .

The great rule of conduct for us in regard to foreign nations is,
in extending our commercial relations, to have with them as little
political connection as possible. So far as we have already formed
engagements, let them be fulfilled with perfect good faith. Here let
us stop.

Europe has a set of primary interests which to us have none or
a very remote relation. Hence she must be engaged in frequent
controversies, the causes of which are essentially foreign to our
concerns. Hence, therefore, it must be unwise in us to implicate
ourselves by artificial ties in the ordinary vicissitudes of her politics, or the ordinary combinations and collisions of her friendships
or enmities.

Our detached and distant situation invites and enables us to
pursue a different course. If we remain one people, under an efficient government, the period is not far off when we may defy
material injury from external annoyance; when we may take such an
attitude as will cause the neutrality we may at any time resolve upon
to be scrupulously respected; when belligerent nations, under the
impossibility of making acquisitions upon us, will not lightly hazard
the giving us provocation; when we may choose peace or war, as our
interest, guided by justice, shall counsel.

Why forgo the advantages of so peculiar a situation? Why quit
our own to stand upon foreign ground? Why, by interweaving our
destiny with that of any part of Europe, entangle our peace and
prosperity in the toils of European ambition, rivalship, interest,
humor, or caprice?

It is our true policy to steer clear of permanent alliances with
any portion of the foreign world, so far, I mean, as we are now at
liberty to do it. For let me not be understood as capable of patron-
izing infidelity to existing engagements. I hold the maxim no less
applicable to public than to private affairs that honesty is always the
best policy. I repeat, therefore, let those engagements be observed

in their genuine sense. But in my opinion it is unnecessary and would be unwise to extend them.

Taking care always to keep ourselves by suitable establishments on a respectable defensive posture, we may safely trust to temporary alliances for extraordinary emergencies.

Harmony, liberal intercourse with all nations, are recommended by policy, humanity, and interest. But even our commercial policy should hold an equal and impartial hand, neither seeking nor granting exclusive favors or preference; constantly keeping in view that it is folly in one nation to look for disinterested favors from another; that it must pay with a portion of its independence for whatever it may accept under that character; that by such acceptance it may place itself in the condition of having given equivalents for nominal favors, and yet of being reproached with ingratitude for not giving more. There can be no greater error than to expect or calculate upon real favors from nation to nation. It is an illusion which experience must cure, which a just pride ought to discard. . . .

The Secret Life of a Developing Country (Ours)

Jack Larkin

Forget your conventional picture of America in 1810. In the first half of the nineteenth century, we were not at all the placid, straitlaced, white-picketfence nation we imagine ourselves to have been. By looking at the patterns of everyday life as recorded by contemporary foreign and native observers of the young republic and by asking the questions that historians often don't think to ask of another time—what were people really like? how did they greet one another in the street? how did they occupy their leisure time? what did they eat?—Jack Larkin brings us a detailed portrait of another America, an America that was so different from both our conception of its past life and its present-day reality as to seem a foreign country.

We Looked Different

Contemporary observers of early-nineteenth-century America left a fragmentary but nonetheless fascinating and revealing picture of the manner in which rich and poor, Southerner and Northerner, farmer and city dweller, freeman and slave presented themselves to the world. To begin with, a wide variety of characteristic facial expressions, gestures, and ways of carrying the body reflected the extraordinary regional and social diversity of the young republic.

When two farmers met in early-nineteenth-century New England, wrote Francis Underwood, of Enfield, Massachusetts, the author of a pioneering 1893 study of small-town life, "their greeting might seem to a stranger gruff or surly, since the facial muscles were so inexpressive, while, in fact, they were on excellent terms." In

courtship and marriage, countrymen and women were equally con-
strained, with couples "wearing all unconsciously the masks which
custom had prescribed; and the onlookers who did not know the
secret would think them cold and indifferent."

Underwood noted a pervasive physical as well as emotional
constraint among the people of Enfield; it was rooted, he thought,
not only in the self-denying ethic of their Calvinist tradition but in
the nature of their work. The great physical demands of unmechan-
ized agriculture gave New England men, like other rural Americans,
a distinctively ponderous gait and posture. Despite their strength
and endurance, farmers were "heavy, awkward and slouching in
movement" and walked with a "slow inclination from side to side."

Yankee visages were captured by itinerant New England por-
traitists during the early nineteenth century, as rural storekeepers,
physicians, and master craftsmen became the first more or less
ordinary Americans to have their portraits done. The portraits
caught their caution and immobility of expression as well as record-
ing their angular, long-jawed features, thus creating good collective
likenesses of whole communities.

The Yankees, however, were not the stiffest Americans. Even
by their own impassive standards, New Englanders found New York
Dutchmen and Pennsylvania German farmers "clumsy and chill" or
"dull and stolid." But the "wild Irish" stood out in America for
precisely the opposite reason. They were not "chill" or "stolid"
enough, but loud and expansive. Their expressiveness made Anglo-
Americans uncomfortable.

The seemingly uncontrolled physical energy of American
blacks left many whites ill at ease. Of the slaves celebrating at a
plantation ball, it was "impossible to describe the things these
people did with their bodies," Frances Kemble Butler, an English-
born actress who married a Georgia slave owner, observed, "and
above all with their faces. . . ." Blacks' expressions and gestures,
their preference for rhythmic rather than rigid bodily motion, their
alternations of energy and rest made no cultural sense to observers
who saw only "antics and frolics," "laziness," or "savagery." Sometimes perceived as obsequious, childlike, and dependent, or sullen
and inexpressive, slaves also wore masks—not "all unconsciously"
as Northern farm folk did, but as part of their self-protective strate-
gies for controlling what masters, mistresses, and other whites could
know about their feelings and motivations.

American city dwellers, whose daily routines were driven by the quicker pace of commerce, were easy to distinguish from "heavy and slouching" farmers attuned to slow seasonal rhythms. New Yorkers, in particular, had already acquired their own characteristic body language. The clerks and commercial men who crowded Broadway, intent on their business, had a universal "contraction of the brow, knitting of the eyebrows, and compression of the lips . . . and a hurried walk." It was a popular American saying in the 1830s, reported Frederick Marryat, an Englishman who traveled extensively in the period, that "a New York merchant always walks as if he had a good dinner before him, and a bailiff behind him."

Northern and Southern farmers and city merchants alike, to say nothing of Irishmen and blacks, fell well short of the standard of genteel "bodily carriage" enshrined in both English and American etiquette books and the instructions of dancing masters: "flexibility in the arms . . . erectness in the spinal column . . . easy carriage of the head." It was the ideal of the British aristocracy, and Southern planters came closest to it, expressing the power of their class in the way they stood and moved. Slave owners accustomed to command, imbued with an ethic of honor and pride, at ease in the saddle, carried themselves more gracefully than men hardened by toil or preoccupied with commerce. Visiting Washington in 1835, the Englishwoman Harriet Martineau contrasted not the politics but the postures of Northern and Southern congressmen. She marked the confident bearing, the "ease and frank courtesy . . . with an occasional touch of arrogance" of the slaveholders alongside the "cautious . . . and too deferential air of the members of the North." She could recognize a New Englander "in the open air," she claimed, "by his deprecatory walk."

Local inhabitants' faces became more open, travelers observed, as one went west. Nathaniel Hawthorne found a dramatic contrast in public appearances only a few days' travel west of Boston. "The people out here," in New York State just west of the Berkshires, he confided to his notebook in 1839, "show out their character much more strongly than they do with us," in his native eastern Massachusetts. He compared the "quiet, silent, dull decency . . . in our public assemblages" with Westerners' wider gamut of expressiveness, "mirth, anger, eccentricity, all showing themselves freely." Westerners in general, the clergyman and publicist Henry Ward Beecher observed, had "far more freedom of manners, and more frankness and spontaneous geniality" than did the city or country people of the New England and Middle Atlantic states, as did the "odd mortals that wander in from the western border," that Martineau observed in Washington's political population.

We Were Dirty and Smelly

Early-nineteenth-century Americans lived in a world of dirt, insects, and pungent smells. Farmyards were strewn with animal wastes, and farmers wore manure-spattered boots and trousers everywhere. Men's and women's working clothes alike were often stiff with dirt and dried sweat, and men's shirts were often stained with "yellow rivulets" of tobacco juice. The locations of privies were all too obvious on warm or windy days. Unemptied chamber pots advertised their presence. Wet baby "napkins," today's diapers, were not immediately washed but simply put by the fire to dry. Vats of "chamber lye"—highly concentrated urine used for cleaning type or degreasing wool—perfumed all printing offices and many households. "The breath of that fiery bar-room," as Underwood described a country tavern, "was overpowering. The odors of the hostlers' boots, redolent of fish-oil and tallow, and of buffalo-robes and horse-blankets, the latter reminiscent of equine ammonia, almost got the better of the all-pervading fumes of spirits and tobacco."

Densely populated, but poorly cleaned and drained, America's cities were often far more noisome than its farmyards. Horse manure thickly covered city streets, and few neighborhoods were free from the spreading stench of tanneries and slaughterhouses. New York City accumulated so much refuse that it was generally believed the actual surfaces of the streets had not been seen for decades. During her stay in Cincinnati, the English writer Frances Trollope followed the practice of the vast majority of American city housewives when she threw her household "slops"—refuse food and dirty dishwater— out into the street. An irate neighbor soon informed her that municipal ordinances forbade "throwing such things at the sides of the streets" as she had done; "they must just all be cast right into the middle and the pigs soon takes them off." In most cities hundreds, sometimes thousands, of free-roaming pigs scavenged the garbage; one exception was Charleston, South Carolina, where buzzards patrolled the streets. By converting garbage into pork, pigs kept city streets cleaner than they would otherwise have been, but the pigs themselves befouled the streets and those who ate their meat—primarily poor families—ran greater than usual risks of infection.

Privy Matters

The most visible symbols of early American sanitation were privies or "necessary houses." But Americans did not always use them; many rural householders simply took to the closest available patch of woods or brush. However, in more densely settled communities and in regions with cold winters, privies were in widespread use. They were not usually put in out-of-the-way locations. The fashion of some Northern farm families, according to Robert B. Thomas's *Farmer's Almanack* in 1826, had long been to have their "necessary planted in a garden or other conspicuous place." Other countryfolk went even further in turning human wastes to agricultural account and built their outhouses "within the territory of a hog yard, that the swine may root and ruminate and devour the nastiness thereof." Thomas was a long-standing critic of primitive manners in the countryside and roundly condemned these traditional sanitary arrangements as demonstrating a "want of taste, decency, and propriety." The better-arranged necessaries of the prosperous emptied into vaults that could be opened and cleaned out. The dripping horse-drawn carts of the "nocturnal goldfinders," who emptied the vaults and took their loads out for burial or water disposal—"night soil" was almost never used as manure—were a familiar part of nighttime traffic on city streets.

The humblest pieces of American household furniture were the chamber pots that allowed people to avoid dark and often cold nighttime journeys outdoors. Kept under beds or in corners of rooms, "chambers" were used primarily upon retiring and arising. Collecting, emptying, and cleaning them remained an unspoken, daily part of every housewife's routine.

Nineteenth-century inventory takers became considerably more reticent about naming chamber pots than their predecessors, usually lumping them with miscellaneous "crockery," but most households probably had a couple of chamber pots; genteel families reached the optimum of one for each bedchamber. English-made ceramic pots had become cheap enough by 1820 that few American families within the reach of commerce needed to go without one. "Without a pot to piss in" was a vulgar tag of long standing for extreme poverty; those poorest households without one, perhaps more common in the warm South, used the outdoors at all times and seasons.

The most decorous way for householders to deal with chamber-pot wastes accumulated during the night was to throw them down the privy hole. But more casual and unsavory methods of disposal were still in wide use. Farm families often dumped their chamber pots out the most convenient door or window. In densely settled communities like York, Pennsylvania, the results could be more serious. In 1801, the York diarist Lewis Miller drew and then described an event in North George Street when "Mr. Day an English man [as the German-American Miller was quick to point out] had a bad practice by pouring out of the upper window his filthiness . . . one day came the discharge . . . on a man and wife going to a wedding, her silk dress was fouled."

Letting the Bedbugs Bite

Sleeping accommodations in American country taverns were often dirty and insect-ridden. The eighteenth-century observer of American life Isaac Weld saw "filthy beds swarming with bugs" in 1794; in 1840 Charles Dickens noted "a sort of game not on the bill of fare." Complaints increased in intensity as travelers went south or west. Tavern beds were uniquely vulnerable to infestation by whatever insect guests travelers brought with them. The bedding of most American households was surely less foul. Yet it was dirty enough. New England farmers were still too often "tormented all night by bed bugs," complained *The Farmer's Almanack* in 1837, and books of domestic advice contained extensive instructions on removing them from feather beds and straw ticks.

Journeying between Washington and New Orleans in 1828, Margaret Hall, a well-to-do and cultivated Scottish woman, became far more familiar with intimate insect life than she had ever been in the genteel houses of London or Edinburgh. Her letters home, never intended for publication, gave a graphic and unsparing account of American sanitary conditions. After sleeping in a succession of beds with the "usual complement of fleas and bugs," she and her party had themselves become infested: "We bring them along with us in our clothes and when I undress I find them crawling on my skin, nasty wretches." New and distasteful to her, such discoveries were commonplace among the ordinary folk with whom she lodged. The American children she saw on her Southern journey were "kept in such a state of filth," with clothes "dirty and slovenly to a degree," but this was "nothing in comparison with their heads . . . [which]

are absolutely crawling!" In New Orleans she observed women picking through children's heads for lice, "catching them according to the method depicted in an engraving of a similar proceeding in the streets of Naples."

Birth of the Bath

Americans were not "clean and decent" by today's standards, and it was virtually impossible that they should be. The furnishings and use of rooms in most American houses made more than the most elementary washing difficult. In a New England farmer's household, wrote Underwood, each household member would "go down to the 'sink' in the lean-to, next to the kitchen, fortunate if he had not to break ice in order to wash his face and hands, or more fortunate if a little warm water was poured into his basin from the kettle swung over the kitchen fire." Even in the comfortable household of the prominent minister Lyman Beecher in Litchfield, Connecticut, around 1815, all family members washed in the kitchen, using a stone sink and "a couple of basins."

Southerners washed in their detached kitchens or, like Westerners in warm weather, washed outside, "at the doors . . . or at the wells" of their houses. Using basins and sinks outdoors or in full view of others, most Americans found anything more than "washing the face and hands once a-day," usually in cold water, difficult, even unthinkable. Most men and women also washed without soap, reserving it for laundering clothes; instead they used a brisk rubbing with a coarse towel to scrub the dirt off their skins.

Gradually the practice of complete bathing spread beyond the topmost levels of American society and into smaller towns and villages. This became possible as families moved washing equipment out of kitchens and into bedchambers, from shared space to space that could be made private. As more prosperous households furnished one or two of their chambers with washing equipment—a washstand, a basin, and a ewer, or large-mouthed pitcher—family members could shut the chamber door, undress, and wash themselves completely. The daughters of the Larcom family, living in Lowell, Massachusetts, in the late 1830s, began to bathe in a bedchamber in this way; Lucy Larcom described how her oldest sister started to take "a full cold bath every morning before she went to her work . . . in a room without a fire," and the other young Larcoms "did the same whenever we could be resolute enough." By the 1830s better city hotels and even some country taverns were providing individual basins and pitchers in their rooms.

At a far remove from "primitive manners" and "bad practices" was the genteel ideal of domestic sanitation embodied in the "chamber sets"—matching basin and ewer for private bathing, a cup for brushing the teeth, and a chamber pot with cover to minimize odor and spillage—that American stores were beginning to stock. By 1840 a significant minority of American households owned chamber sets and washstands to hold them in their bedchambers. For a handful there was the very faint dawning of an entirely new age of sanitary arrangements. In 1829 the new Tremont House hotel in Boston offered its patrons indoor plumbing: eight chambers with bathtubs and eight "water closets." In New York City and Philadelphia, which had developed rudimentary public water systems, a few wealthy households had water taps and, more rarely, water closets by the 1830s. For all others flush toilets and bathtubs remained far in the future.

The American people moved very slowly toward cleanliness. In "the backcountry at the present day," commented the fastidious author of the *Lady's Book* in 1836, custom still "requires that everyone should wash at the pump in the yard, or at the sink in the kitchen." Writing in 1846, the physician and health reformer William Alcott rejoiced that to "wash the surface of the whole body in water daily" had now been accepted as a genteel standard of personal cleanliness. But, he added, there were "multitudes who pass for models of neatness and cleanliness, who do not perform this work for themselves half a dozen times—nay once—a year." As the better-off became cleaner than ever before, the poor stayed dirty.

We Drank and Fought Whenever We Could

In the early part of the century America was a bawdy, hard-edged, and violent land. We drank more than we ever had before or ever would again. We smoked and chewed tobacco like addicts and fought and quarreled on the flimsiest pretexts. The tavern was the most important gateway to the primarily male world of drink and disorder: in sight of the village church in most American communities, observed Daniel Drake, a Cincinnati physician who wrote a reminiscence of his Kentucky boyhood, stood the village tavern, and the two structures "did in fact represent two great opposing principles."

The great majority of American men in every region were taverngoers. The printed street directories of American cities listed tavernkeepers in staggering numbers, and even the best-churched parts of New England could show more "licensed houses" than meetinghouses. In 1827 the fast-growing city of Rochester, New York, with a population of approximately eight thousand, had nearly one hundred establishments licensed to sell liquor, or one for every eighty inhabitants.

America's most important centers of male sociability, taverns were often the scene of excited gaming and vicious fights and always of hard drinking, heavy smoking, and an enormous amount of alcohol-stimulated talk. City men came to their neighborhood taverns daily, and "tavern haunting, tippling, and gaming," as Samuel Goodrich, a New England historian and publisher, remembered, "were the chief resources of men in the dead and dreary winter months" in the countryside.

City taverns catered to clienteles of different classes: sordid sailors' grogshops near the waterfront were rife with brawling and prostitution; neighborhood taverns and liquor-selling groceries were visited by craftsmen and clerks; well-appointed and relatively decorous places were favored by substantial merchants. Taverns on busy highways often specialized in teamsters or stage passengers, while country inns took their patrons as they came.

Taverns accommodated women as travelers, but their barroom clienteles were almost exclusively male. Apart from the dockside dives frequented by prostitutes, or the liquor-selling groceries of poor city neighborhoods, women rarely drank in public.

Gambling was a substantial preoccupation for many male citizens of the early republic. Men played billiards at tavern tables for money stakes. They threw dice in "hazard," slamming the dice boxes down so hard and so often that tavern tables wore the characteristic scars of their play. Even more often Americans sat down to cards, playing brag, similar to modern-day poker, or an elaborate table game called faro. Outdoors they wagered with each other on horse races or bet on cockfights and wrestling matches.

Drink permeated and propelled the social world of early-nineteenth-century America—first as an unquestioned presence and later as a serious and divisive problem. "Liquor at that time," recalled the builder and architect Elbridge Boyden, "was used as commonly as the food we ate." Before 1820 the vast majority of Americans considered alcohol an essential stimulant to exertion as well as a symbol of hospitality and fellowship. Like the Kentuckians with whom Daniel Drake grew up, they "regarded it as a duty to their families and visitors . . . to keep the bottle well replenished." Weddings, funerals, frolics, even a casual "gathering of two or three neighbors for an evening's social chat" required the obligatory "spirituous liquor"—rum, whiskey, or gin—"at all seasons and on all occasions."

Northern householders drank hard cider as their common table beverage, and all ages drank it freely. Dramming—taking a fortifying glass in the forenoon and again in the afternoon—was part of the daily regimen of many men. Clergymen took sustaining libations between services, lawyers before going to court, and physicians at their patients' bedsides. To raise a barn or get through a long day's haying without fortifying drink seemed a virtual impossibility. Slaves enjoyed hard drinking at festival times and at Saturday-night barbecues as much as any of their countrymen. But of all Americans they probably drank the least on a daily basis because their masters could usually control their access to liquor.

In Parma, Ohio, in the mid-1820s, Lyndon Freeman, a farmer, and his brothers were used to seeing men "in their cups" and passed them by without comment. But one dark and rainy night they discovered something far more shocking, "nothing less than a *woman beastly drunk . . .* with a flask of whiskey by her side." American women drank as well as men, but usually much less heavily. They were more likely to make themselves "tipsy" with hard cider and alcohol-containing patent medicines than to become inebriated with rum or whiskey. Temperance advocates in the late 1820s estimated that men consumed fifteen times the volume of distilled spirits that women did; this may have been a considerable exaggeration, but there was a great difference in drinking habits between the sexes. Americans traditionally found drunkenness tolerable and forgivable in men but deeply shameful in women.

By almost any standard, Americans drank not only nearly universally but in large quantities. Their yearly consumption at the time of the Revolution has been estimated at the equivalent of three and one-half gallons of pure two-hundred-proof alcohol for each person. After 1790 American men began to drink even more. By the late 1820S their imbibing had risen to an all-time high of almost four gallons per capita.

Along with drinking went fighting. Americans fought often and with great relish. York, Pennsylvania, for example, was a peaceable place as American communities went, but the Miller and Weaver families had a long-running quarrel. It had begun in 1800 when the Millers found young George Weaver stealing apples in their yard and punished him by "throwing him over the fence," injuring him painfully. Over the years hostilities broke out periodically. Lewis Miller remembered walking down the street as a teenaged boy and meeting Mrs. Weaver, who drenched him with the bucket of water she was carrying. He retaliated by "turning about and giving her a kick, laughing at her, this is for your politeness." Other York households had their quarrels too; in "a general fight on Beaver Street," Mistress Hess and Mistress Forsch tore each other's caps from their heads. Their husbands and then the neighbors interfered, and "all of them had a knock down."

When Peter Lung's wife, Abigail, refused "to get up and dig some potatoes" for supper from the yard of their small house, the Hartford, Connecticut, laborer recalled in his confession, he "kicked her on the side . . . then gave her a violent push" and went out to dig the potatoes himself. He returned and "again kicked her against the shoulder and neck." Both had been drinking, and loud arguments and blows within the Lung household, as in many others, were routine. But this time the outcome was not. Alice Lung was dead the next day, and Peter Lung was arrested, tried, and hanged for murder in 1815.

In the most isolated, least literate and commercialized parts of the United States, it was "by no means uncommon," wrote Isaac Weld, "to meet with those who have lost an eye in a combat, and there are men who pride themselves upon the dexterity with which they can scoop one out. This is called *gouging*."

The Slave's Lot

Slaves wrestled among themselves, sometimes fought one another bitterly over quarrels in the quarters, and even at times stood up to the vastly superior force of masters and overseers. They rarely, if ever, reduced themselves to the ferocity of eye gouging. White Southerners lived with a pervasive fear of the violent potential of their slaves, and the Nat Turner uprising in Virginia in 1831, when a party of slaves rebelled and killed whites before being overcome, gave rise to tighter and harsher controls. But in daily reality slaves had far more to fear from their masters.

Margaret Hall was no proponent of abolition and had little sympathy for black Americans. Yet in her travels south she confronted incidents of what she ironically called the "good treatment of slaves" that were impossible to ignore. At a country tavern in Georgia, she summoned the slave chambermaid, but "she could not come" because "the mistress had been whipping her and she was not fit to be seen. Next morning she made her appearance with her face marked in several places by the cuts of the cowskin and her neck handkerchief covered with spots of blood."

Southern stores were very much like Northern ones, Francis Kemble Butler observed, except that they stocked "negro-whips" and "mantraps" on their shelves. A few slaves were never beaten at all, and for most, whippings were not a daily or weekly occurrence. But they were, of all Americans, by far the most vulnerable to violence. All slaves had, as William Wells Brown, an ex-slave himself, said, often "heard the crack of the whip, and the screams of the slave" and knew that they were never more than a white man's or woman's whim away from a beating. With masters' unchecked power came worse than whipping: the mutilating punishments of the old penal law including branding, ear cropping, and even occasionally castration and burning alive as penalties for severe offenses. In public places or along the road blacks were also subject to casual kicks, shoves, and cuffs, for which they could retaliate only at great peril. "Six or seven feet in length, made of cowhide, with a platted wire on the end of it," as Brown recalled it, the negro-whip, for sale in most stores and brandished by masters and overseers in the fields, stood for a pervasive climate of force and intimidation.

Public Punishment

The penal codes of the American states were far less bloodthirsty than those of England. Capital punishment was not often imposed on whites for crimes other than murder. Yet at the beginning of the nineteenth century many criminal offenses were punished by the public infliction of pain and suffering. "The whipping post and stocks stood on the green near the meetinghouse" in most of the towns of New England and near courthouses everywhere. In Massachusetts before 1805 a counterfeiter was liable to have an ear cut off, and a forger to have one cropped or partially amputated, after spending an hour in the pillory. A criminal convicted of manslaughter was set up on the gallows to have his forehead branded with a letter M. In most jurisdictions town officials flogged petty thieves as punishment for their crime. In New Haven, Connecticut, around 1810, Charles Fowler, a local historian, recalled seeing the "admiring students of [Yale] college" gathered around to watch petty criminals receive "five or ten lashes . . . with a rawhide whip."

Throughout the United States public hangings brought enormous crowds to the seats of justice and sometimes seemed like brutal festivals. Thousands of spectators arrived to pack the streets of courthouse towns. On the day of a hanging near Mount Holly, New Jersey, in the 1820s, the scene was that of a holiday: "around the place in every direction were the assembled multitudes—some in tents, and by-wagons, engaged in gambling and other vices of the sort, in open day." In order to accommodate the throngs, hangings were usually held not in the public square but on the outskirts of town. The gallows erected on a hill or set up at the bottom of a natural amphitheater allowed onlookers an unobstructed view. A reprieve or stay of execution might disappoint a crowd intent on witnessing the deadly drama and provoke a riot, as it did in Pembroke, New Hampshire, in 1834.

Rise of Respectability

At a drunkard's funeral in Enfield, Massachusetts, in the 1830s—the man had strayed out of the road while walking home and fallen over a cliff, "his stiffened fingers still grasping the handle of the jug"—Rev. Sumner G. Clapp, the Congregationalist minister of Enfield, mounted a log by the woodpile and preached the town's first temperance sermon before a crowd full of hardened drinkers. In this way Clapp began a campaign to "civilize" the manners of his parishioners, and "before many years there was a great change in the town; the incorrigible were removed by death, and others took warning." Drinking declined sharply, and along with it went "a general reform in conduct."

Although it remained a powerful force in many parts of the United States, the American way of drunkenness began to lose ground as early as the mid-1820s. The powerful upsurge in liquor consumption had provoked a powerful reaction, an unprecedented attack on all forms of drink that gathered momentum in the Northeast. Some New England clergymen had been campaigning in their own communities as early as 1810, but their concerns took on organized impetus with the founding of the American Temperance

Society in 1826. Energized in part by a concern for social order, in part by evangelical piety, temperance reformers popularized a radically new way of looking at alcohol. The "good creature" became "demon rum"; prominent physicians and writers on physiology, like Benjamin Rush, told Americans that alcohol, traditionally considered healthy and fortifying, was actually a physical and moral poison. National and state societies distributed anti-liquor tracts, at first calling for moderation in drink but increasingly demanding total abstinence from alcohol.

To a surprising degree these aggressive temperance campaigns worked. By 1840 the consumption of alcohol had declined by more than two-thirds, from close to four gallons per person each year to less than one and one-half. Country storekeepers gave up the sale of spirits, local authorities limited the number of tavern licenses, and farmers even abandoned hard cider and cut down their apple orchards. The shift to temperance was a striking transformation in the everyday habits of an enormous number of Americans. "A great, though silent change," in Horace Greeley's words, had been "wrought in public sentiment."

But although the "great change" affected some Americans everywhere, it had a very uneven impact. Organized temperance reform was sharply delimited by geography. Temperance societies were enormously powerful in New England and western New York and numerous in eastern New York, New Jersey, and Pennsylvania. More than three-fourths of all recorded temperance pledges came from these states. In the South and West, and in the laborers' and artisans' neighborhoods of the cities, the campaign against drink was much weaker. In many places drinking ways survived and even flourished, but as individuals and families came under the influence of militant evangelical piety, their "men of business and sobriety" increased gradually in number. As liquor grew "unfashionable in the country," Greeley noted, Americans who wanted to drink and carouse turned increasingly to the cities, "where no one's deeds or ways are observed or much regarded."

Closely linked as they were to drink, such diversions as gambling, racing, and blood sports also fell to the same forces of change. In the central Massachusetts region that George Davis, a lawyer in Sturbridge, knew well, until 1820 or so gaming had "continued to prevail, more and more extensively." After that "a blessed change had succeeded," overturning the scenes of high-stakes dice and card games that he knew in his young manhood. Impelled by a new perception of its "pernicious effects," local leaders gave it up and placed "men of respectable standing" firmly in opposition. Race-courses were abandoned and "planted to corn." Likewise, "bear-baiting, cock-fighting, and other cruel amusements" began to dwindle in the Northern countryside. Elsewhere the rude life of the tavern and "cruel amusements" remained widespread, but some of their excesses of "sin and shame" did diminish gradually.

Over the first four decades of the nineteenth century the American people increasingly made churchgoing an obligatory ritual. The proportion of families affiliated with a local church or Methodist circuit rose dramatically, particularly after 1820, and there were fewer stretches of the wholly pagan, unchurched territory that travelers had noted around 1800. "Since 1830," maintained Emerson Davis in his retrospect of America, *The Half Century*, ". . . the friends of the Sabbath have been gaining ground. . . . In 1800, good men slumbered over the desecration of the Sabbath. They have since awoke. . . ." The number of Sunday mails declined, and the campaign to eliminate the delivery of mail on the Sabbath entirely grew stronger. "In the smaller cities and towns," wrote Mrs. Trollope in 1832, worship and "prayer meetings" had come to "take the place of almost all other amusements." There were still communities near the edge of settlement where a traveler would "rarely find either churches or chapels, prayer or preacher," but it was the working-class neighborhoods of America's larger cities that were increasingly the chief strongholds of "Sunday dissipation" and "Sabbath-breaking."

Whipping and the pillory, with their attentive audiences, began to disappear from the statute book, to be replaced by terms of imprisonment in another new American institution, the state penitentiary. Beginning with Pennsylvania's abolition of flogging in 1790 and Massachusetts's elimination of mutilating punishments in 1805, several American states gradually accepted John Hancock's view of 1796 that "mutilating or lacerating the body" was less an effective punishment than "an indignity to human nature." Connecticut's town constables whipped petty criminals for the last time in 1828.

Slaveholding states were far slower to change their provisions for public punishment. The whipping and mutilation of blacks may have become a little less ferocious over the decades, but the whip remained the essential instrument of punishment and discipline. "The secret of our success," thought a slave owner, looking back after emancipation, had been "the great motive power contained in that little instrument." Delaware achieved notoriety by keeping flogging on the books for whites and blacks alike through most of the twentieth century.

Although there were important stirrings of sentiment against capital punishment, all American states continued to execute convicted murders before the mid-1840s. Public hangings never lost their drawing power. But a number of American public officials began to abandon the long-standing view of executions as instructive communal rituals. They saw the crowd's holiday mood and eager participation as sharing too much in the condemned killer's own brutality. Starting with Pennsylvania, New York, and Massachusetts in the mid-1830s, several state legislatures voted to take executions away from the crowd, out of the public realm. Sheriffs began to carry out death sentences behind the walls of the jailyard, before a small assembly of representative onlookers. Other states clung much longer to tradition and continued public executions into the twentieth century.

Sex Life of the Natives

Early-nineteenth-century Americans were more licentious than we ordinarily imagine them to be.

"On the 20th day of July" in 1830, Harriet Winter, a young woman working as a domestic in Joseph Dunham's household in Brimfield, Massachusetts, "was gathering raspberries" in a field west of the house. "Near the close of day," Charles Phelps, a farm laborer then living in the town, "came to the field where she was," and in the gathering dusk they made love—and, Justice of the Peace Asa Lincoln added in his account, "it was the Sabbath." American communities did not usually document their inhabitants' amorous rendezvous, and Harriet's tryst with Charles was a commonplace event in early-nineteenth-century America. It escaped historical oblivion because she was unlucky, less in becoming pregnant than in Charles's refusal to marry her. Asa Lincoln did not approve of Sabbath evening indiscretions, but he was not pursuing Harriet for immorality. He was concerned instead with economic responsibility for the child. Thus he interrogated Harriet about the baby's father—while she was in labor, as was the long-customary practice—in order to force Charles to contribute to the maintenance of the child, who was going to be "born a bastard and chargeable to the town."

Some foreign travelers found that the Americans they met were reluctant to admit that such things happened in the United States. They were remarkably straitlaced about sexual matters in public and eager to insist upon the "purity" of their manners. But to take such protestations at face value, the unusually candid Englishman Frederick Marryat thought, would be "to suppose that human nature is not the same everywhere."

The well-organized birth and marriage records of a number of American communities reveal that in late-eighteenth-century America pregnancy was frequently the prelude to marriage. The proportion of brides who were pregnant at the time of their weddings had been rising since the late seventeenth century and peaked in the turbulent decades during and after the Revolution. In the 1780s and 1790s nearly one-third of rural New England's brides were already with child. The frequency of sexual intercourse before marriage was surely higher, since some couples would have escaped early pregnancy. For many couples sexual relations were part of serious courtship. Premarital pregnancies in late-eighteenth-century Dedham, Massachusetts, observed the local historian Erastus Worthington in 1828, were occasioned by "the custom then prevalent of females admitting young men to their beds, who sought their company in marriage."

Pregnancies usually simply accelerated a marriage that would have taken place in any case, but community and parental pressure worked strongly to assure it. Most rural communities simply accepted the "early" pregnancies that marked so many marriages, although in Hingham, Massachusetts, tax records suggest that the families of well-to-do brides were considerably less generous to couples who had had "early babies" than to those who had avoided pregnancy.

"Bundling very much abounds," wrote the anonymous author of "A New Bundling Song," still circulating in Boston in 1812, "in many parts in country towns." Noah Webster's first *Dictionary of the American Language* defined it as the custom that allowed couples "to sleep on the same bed without undressing"—with, a later commentator added, "the shared understanding that innocent endearments should not be exceeded." Folklore and local tradition, from Maine south to New York, had American mothers tucking bundling couples into bed with special chastity-protecting garments for the young woman or a "bundling board" to separate them.

In actuality, if bundling had been intended to allow courting couples privacy and emotional intimacy but not sexual contact, it clearly failed. Couples may have begun with bundling, but as courtship advanced, they clearly pushed beyond its restraints, like the "bundling maid" in "A New Bundling Song" who would "sometimes say when she lies down/She can't be cumbered with a gown."

Young black men and women shared American whites' freedom in courtship and sexuality and sometimes exceeded it. Echoing the cultural traditions of West Africa, and reflecting the fact that their marriages were not given legal status and security, slave communities were somewhat more tolerant and accepting of sex before marriage.

Gradations of color and facial features among the slaves were testimony that "thousands," as the abolitionist and former slave Frederick Douglass wrote, were "ushered into the world annually, who, like myself, owe their existence to white fathers, and those fathers most frequently their own masters." Sex crossed the boundaries of race and servitude more often than slavery's defenders wanted to admit, if less frequently than the most outspoken abolitionists claimed. Slave women had little protection from whatever sexual demands masters or overseers might make, so that rapes, short liaisons, and long-term "concubinage" all were part of plantation life.

As Nathaniel Hawthorne stood talking with a group of men on the porch of a tavern in Augusta, Maine, in 1836, a young man "in a laborer's dress" came up and asked if anyone knew the whereabouts of Mary Ann Russell. "Do you want to use her?" asked one of the bystanders. Mary Ann was, in fact, the young laborer's wife, but she had left him and their child in Portland to become "one of a knot of whores." A few years earlier the young men of York, Pennsylvania, made up a party for "overturning and pulling to the ground" Eve Geese's "shameful house" of prostitution in Queen Street. The frightened women fled out the back door as the chimney collapsed around them; the apprentices and young journeymen—many of whom had surely been previous customers—were treated by local officials "to wine, for the good work."

From medium-sized towns like Augusta and York to great cities, poor American women were sometimes pulled into a darker, harsher sexual world, one of vulnerability, exploitation, and commerce. Many prostitutes took up their trade out of poverty and domestic disaster. A young widow or a country girl arrived in the city and, thrown on her own resources, often faced desperate economic choices because most women's work paid too poorly to provide decent food, clothing, and shelter, while other women sought excitement and independence from their families.

As cities grew, and changes in transportation involved more men in long-distance travel, prostitution became more visible. Men of all ages, married and unmarried, from city lawyers to visiting country storekeepers to sailors on the docks, turned to brothels for sexual release, but most of the customers were young men, living away from home and unlikely to marry until their late twenties. Sexual commerce in New York City was elaborately graded by price and the economic status of clients, from the "parlor houses" situated not far from the city's best hotels on Broadway to the more numerous and moderately priced houses that drew artisans and clerks, and finally to the broken and dissipated women who haunted dockside grogshops in the Five Points neighborhood.

From New Orleans to Boston, city theaters were important sexual marketplaces. Men often bought tickets less to see the performance than to make assignations with the prostitutes, who sat by custom in the topmost gallery of seats. The women usually received free admission from theater managers, who claimed that they could not stay in business without the male theatergoers drawn by the "guilty third tier."

Most Americans—and the American common law—still did not regard abortion as a crime until the fetus had "quickened" or began to move perceptibly in the womb. Books of medical advice actually contained prescriptions for bringing on delayed menstrual periods, which would also produce an abortion if the woman happened to be pregnant. They suggested heavy doses of purgatives that created violent cramps, powerful douches, or extreme kinds of physical activity, like the "violent exercise, raising great weights . . . strokes on the belly . . . [and] falls" noted in William Buchan's *Domestic Medicine*, a manual read widely through the 1820s. Women's folklore echoed most of these prescriptions and added others, particularly the use of two American herbal preparations— savin, or the extract of juniper berries, and Seneca snakeroot—as abortion-producing drugs. They were dangerous procedures but sometimes effective.

Reining in the Passions

Starting at the turn of the nineteenth century, the sexual lives of many Americans began to change, shaped by a growing insistence on control: reining in the passions in courtship, limiting family size, and even redefining male and female sexual desire.

Bundling was already on the wane in rural America before 1800; by the 1820s it was written about as a rare and antique custom. It had ceased, thought an elderly man from East Haddam, Connecticut, "as a consequence of education and refinement." Decade by decade the proportion of young women who had conceived a child before marriage declined. In most of the towns of New England the rate had dropped from nearly one pregnant bride in three to one in five or six by 1840; in some places prenuptial pregnancy dropped to 5 percent. For many young Americans this marked the acceptance of new limits on sexual behavior, imposed not by their parents or other authorities in their communities but by themselves.

These young men and women were not more closely supervised by their parents than earlier generations had been; in fact, they had more mobility and greater freedom. The couples that courted in the new style put a far greater emphasis on control of the passions. For some of them—young Northern merchants and professional men and their intended brides—revealing love letters have survived for the years after 1820. Their intimate correspondence reveals that they did not give up sexual expression but gave it new boundaries, reserving sexual intercourse for marriage. Many of them were marrying later than their parents, often living through long engagements while the husband-to-be strove to establish his place in the world. They chose not to risk a pregnancy that would precipitate them into an early marriage.

Many American husbands and wives were also breaking with tradition as they began to limit the size of their families. Clearly, married couples were renegotiating the terms of their sexual lives together, but they remained resolutely silent about how they did it. In the first two decades of the nineteenth century, they almost certainly set about avoiding childbirth through abstinence; coitus interruptus, or male withdrawal; and perhaps sometimes abortion. These contraceptive techniques had long been traditional in preindustrial Europe, although previously little used in America.

As they entered the 1830s, Americans had their first opportunity to learn, at least in print, about more effective or less self-denying forms of birth control. They could read reasonably inexpensive editions of the first works on contraception published in the United States: Robert Dale Owen's *Moral Physiology* of 1831 and Dr. Charles Knowlton's *The Fruits of Philosophy* of 1832. Both authors frankly described the full range of contraceptive techniques, although they solemnly rejected physical intervention in the sexual act and recommended only douching after intercourse and coitus interruptus. Official opinion, legal and religious, was deeply hostile. Knowlton, who had trained as a physician in rural Massachusetts, was prosecuted in three different counties for obscenity, convicted once, and imprisoned for three months.

But both works found substantial numbers of Americans eager to read them. By 1839 each book had gone through nine editions, putting a combined total of twenty to thirty thousand copies in circulation. An American physician could write in 1850 that contraception had "been of late years so much talked of." Greater knowledge about contraception surely played a part in the continuing decline of the American birthrate after 1830.

New ways of thinking about sexuality emerged that stressed control and channeling of the passions. Into the 1820s almost all Americans would have subscribed to the commonplace notion that sex, within proper social confines, was enjoyable and healthy and that prolonged sexual abstinence could be injurious to health. They also would have assumed that women had powerful sexual drives.

Starting with his "Lecture to Young Men on Chastity" in 1832, Sylvester Graham articulated very different counsels about health and sex. Sexual indulgence, he argued, was not only morally suspect but psychologically and physiologically risky. The sexual over-stimulation involved in young men's lives produced anxiety and nervous disorders, "a shocking state of debility and excessive irritability." The remedy was diet, exercise, and a regular routine that pulled the mind away from animal lusts. Medical writings that discussed the evils of masturbation, or "solitary vice," began to appear. Popular books of advice, like William Alcott's *Young Man's Guide*, gave similar warnings. They tried to persuade young men that their health could be ruined, and their prospects for success darkened, by consorting with prostitutes or becoming sexually entangled before marriage.

A new belief about women's sexual nature appeared, one that elevated them above "carnal passion." Many American men and women came to believe during the nineteenth century that in their true and proper nature as mothers and guardians of the home, women were far less interested in sex than men were. Women who defined themselves as passionless were in a strong position to control or deny men's sexual demands either during courtship or in limiting their childbearing within marriage.

Graham went considerably farther than this, advising restraint not only in early life and courtship but in marriage itself. It was far healthier, he maintained, for couples to have sexual relations "very seldom."

Neither contraception nor the new style of courtship had become anything like universal by 1840. Prenuptial pregnancy rates had fallen, but they remained high enough to indicate that many couples simply continued in familiar ways. American husbands and wives in the cities and the Northern countryside were limiting the number of their children, but it was clear that those living on the farms of the West or in the slave quarters had not yet begun to. There is strong evidence that many American women felt far from passionless, although others restrained or renounced their sexuality. For many people in the United States, there had been a profound change. Reining in the passions had become part of everyday life.

Smoking and Spitting

"Everyone smokes and some chew in America," wrote Isaac Weld in 1795. Americans turned tobacco, a new and controversial stimulant at the time of colonial settlement, into a crucially important staple crop and made its heavy use a commonplace—and a never-ending source of surprise and indignation to visitors. Tobacco use spread in the United States because it was comparatively cheap, a homegrown product free from the heavy import duties levied on it by European governments. A number of slave rations described in plantation documents included "one hand of tobacco per month." Through the eighteenth century most American smokers used clay pipes, which are abundant in colonial archeological sites, although some men and women dipped snuff or inhaled powdered tobacco.

Where the smokers of early colonial America "drank" or gulped smoke through the short, thick stems of their seventeenth-century pipes, those of 1800 inhaled it more slowly and gradually; from the early seventeenth to the late eighteenth century, pipe stems became steadily longer and narrower, increasingly distancing smokers from their burning tobacco.

In the 1790s cigars, or "segars," were introduced from the Caribbean. Prosperous men widely took them up; they were the most expensive way to consume tobacco, and it was a sign of financial security to puff away on "long-nines" or "principe cigars at three cents each" while the poor used clay pipes and much cheaper "cut plug" tobacco. After 1800 in American streets, barrooms, stores, public conveyances, and even private homes it became nearly impossible to avoid tobacco chewers. Chewing extended tobacco use, particularly into workplaces; men who smoked pipes at home or in the tavern barroom could chew while working in barns or workshops where smoking carried the danger of fire.

"In all the public places of America," wrote Charles Dickens, multitudes of men engaged in "the odious practice of chewing and expectorating," a recreation practiced by all ranks of American society. Chewing stimulated salivation and gave rise to a public environment of frequent and copious spitting, where men every few minutes were "squirting a mouthful of saliva through the room."

Spittoons were provided in the more meticulous establishments, but men often ignored them. The floors of American public buildings were not pleasant to contemplate. A courtroom in New York City in 1833 was decorated by a "mass of abomination" contributed to by "judges, counsel, jury, witnesses, officers, and audience." The floor of the Virginia House of Burgesses in 1827 was "actually flooded with their horrible spitting," and even the aisle of a Connecticut meetinghouse was black with the "ejection after ejection, incessant from twenty mouths," of the men singing in the choir. In order to drink, an American man might remove his quid, put it in a pocket or hold it in his hand, take his glassful, and then restore it to his mouth. Women's dresses might even be in danger at fashionable balls. "One night as I was walking upstairs to valse," reported Margaret Hall of a dance in Washington in 1828, "my partner began clearing his throat. This I thought ominous. However, I said to myself, 'surely he will turn his head to the other side.' The gentleman, however, had no such thought but deliberately shot across me. I had not courage enough to examine whether the result landed in the flounce of my dress."

The segar and the quid were almost entirely male appurtenances, but as the nineteenth century began, many rural and lower-class urban women were smoking pipes or dipping snuff. During his boyhood in New Hampshire, Horace Greeley remembered, "it was often my filial duty to fill and light my mother's pipe."

After 1820 or so tobacco use among women in the North began to decline. Northern women remembered or depicted with pipe or snuffbox were almost all elderly. More and more Americans adopted a genteel standard that saw tobacco use and womanliness—delicate and nurturing—as antithetical, and young women avoided it as a pollutant. For them, tobacco use marked off male from female territory with increasing sharpness.

In the households of small Southern and Western farmers, however, smoking and snuff taking remained common. When women visited "among the country people" of North Carolina, Frances Kemble Butler reported in 1837, the "proffer of the snuff-box, and its passing from hand to hand, is the usual civility." By the late 1830s visiting New Englanders were profoundly shocked when they saw the women of Methodist congregations in Illinois, including nursing mothers, taking out their pipes for a smoke between worship services.

From Deference to Equality

The Americans of 1820 would have been more recognizable to us in the informal and egalitarian way they treated one another. The traditional signs of deference before social superiors—the deep bow, the "courtesy," the doffed cap, lowered head, and averted eyes—had been a part of social relationships in colonial America. In the 1780s, wrote the American poetess Lydia Huntley Sigourney in 1824, there were still "individuals . . . in every grade of society" who had grown up "when a bow was not an offense to fashion nor . . . a relic of monarchy." But in the early nineteenth century such signals of subordination rapidly fell away. It was a natural consequence of the Revolution, she maintained, which, "in giving us liberty, obliterated almost every vestige of politeness of the 'old school.' " Shaking hands became the accustomed American greeting between men, a gesture whose symmetry and mutuality signified equality. Frederick Marryat found in 1835 that it was "invariably the custom to shake hands" when he was introduced to Americans and that he could not carefully grade the acknowledgment he would give to new acquaintances according to their signs of wealth and breeding. He found instead that he had to "go on shaking hands here, there and everywhere, and with everybody." Americans were not blind to inequalities of economic and social power, but they less and less gave them overt physical expression. Bred in a society where such distinctions were far more clearly spelled out, Marryat was somewhat disoriented in the United States; "it is impossible to know who is who," he claimed, "in this land of equality."

Well-born British travelers encountered not just confusion but conflict when they failed to receive the signs of respect they expected. Margaret Hall's letters home during her Southern travels outlined a true comedy of manners. At every stage stop in the Carolinas, Georgia, and Alabama, she demanded that country tavernkeepers and their households give her deferential service and well-prepared meals; she received instead rancid bacon and "such an absence of all kindness of feeling, such unbending frigid heartlessness." But she and her family had a far greater share than they realized in creating this chilly reception. Squeezed between the pride and poise of the great planters and the social debasement of the slaves, small Southern farmers often displayed a prickly insolence, a considered lack of response, to those who too obviously considered themselves their betters. Greatly to their discomfort and incomprehension, the Halls were experiencing what a British traveler more sympathetic to American ways, Patrick Shirreff, called "the democratic rudeness which assumed or presumptuous superiority seldom fails to experience."

Land of Abundance

In the seventeenth century white American colonials were no taller than their European counterparts, but by the time of the Revolution they were close to their late-twentieth-century average height for men of slightly over five feet eight inches. The citizens of the early republic towered over most Europeans. Americans' early achievement of modern stature—by a full century and more—was a striking consequence of American abundance. Americans were taller because they were better nourished than the great majority of the world's peoples.

Yet not all Americans participated equally in the nation's abundance. Differences in stature between whites and blacks, and between city and country dwellers, echoed those between Europeans and Americans. Enslaved blacks were a full inch shorter than whites. But they remained a full inch taller than European peasants and laborers and were taller still than their fellow slaves eating the scanty diets afforded by the more savagely oppressive plantation system of the West Indies. And by 1820 those who lived in the expanding cities of the United States—even excluding immigrants, whose heights would have reflected European, not American, conditions were noticeably shorter than the people of the countryside, suggesting an increasing concentration of poverty and poorer diets in urban places.

Across the United States almost all country households ate the two great American staples: corn and "the eternal pork"' as one surfeited traveler called it, "which makes its appearance on every American table, high and low, rich and poor." Families in the cattleraising, dairying country of New England, New York, and northern Ohio ate butter, cheese, and salted beef as well as pork and made their bread from wheat flour or rye and Indian corn. In Pennsylvania, as well as Maryland, Delaware, and Virginia, Americans ate the same breadstuffs as their Northern neighbors, but their consumption of cheese and beef declined every mile southward in favor of pork.

Farther to the south, and in the West, corn and corn-fed pork were truly "eternal"; where reliance on them reached its peak in the Southern uplands, they were still the only crops many small farmers raised. Most Southern and Western families built their diets around smoked and salted bacon, rather than the Northerners' salt pork, and, instead of wheat or rye bread, made cornpone or hoecake, a coarse, strong bread, and hominy, pounded Indian corn boiled together with milk.

Before 1800, game—venison, possum, raccoon, and wild fowl—was for many American households "a substantial portion of the supply of food at certain seasons of the year," although only on the frontier was it a regular part of the diet. In the West and South this continued to be true, but in the Northeast game became increasingly rare as forests gave way to open farmland, where wild animals could not live.

Through the first half of the eighteenth century, Americans had been primarily concerned with obtaining a sufficiency of meat and bread for their families; they paid relatively little attention to foodstuffs other than these two "staffs of life," but since that time the daily fare of many households had grown substantially more diverse.

Coming to the Table

Remembering his turn of the-century Kentucky boyhood, Daniel Drake could still see the mealtime scene at the house of a neighbor, "Old Billy," who "with his sons" would "frequently breakfast in common on mush and milk out of a huge buckeye bowl, each one dipping in a spoon." "Old Billy" and his family were less frontier savages than traditionalists; in the same decade Gov. Caleb Strong of Massachusetts stopped for the night with a country family who ate in the same way, where "each had a spoon and dipped from the same dish." These households ate as almost all American families once had, communally partaking of food from the same dish and passing around a single vessel to drink from. Such meals were often surprisingly haphazard affairs, with household members moving in and out, eating quickly and going on to other tasks.

But by 1800 they were already in a small and diminishing minority. Over the eighteenth century dining "in common" had given way to individualized yet social eating; as families acquired chairs and dining utensils, they were able to make mealtimes more important social occasions. Most Americans expected to eat individual portions of food at a table set with personal knives, forks, glasses, bowls, and plates. Anything that smacked of the old communal ways was increasingly likely to be treated as a sin against domestic decency. The clergyman Peter Cartwright was shocked at the table manners of a "backward" family who ate off a "wooden trencher," improvised forks with "sharp pieces of cane," and used a single knife, which they passed around the table.

"One and all, male and female," the observant Margaret Hall took note, even in New York's best society, ate "invariably and indefatigably with their knives." As a legacy of the fork's late arrival in the colonies, Americans were peculiar in using their "great lumbering, long, two-pronged forks," not to convey food to the mouth, as their English and French contemporaries did, but merely to keep their meat from slipping off the plate while cutting it. "Feeding yourself with your right hand, armed with a steel blade," was the prevalent American custom, acknowledged Eliza Farrar's elaborate *Young Lady's Friend* of 1836. She added that it was perfectly proper, despite English visitors' discomfort at the sight of a "prettily dressed, nice-looking young woman ladling rice pudding into her mouth with the point of a great knife" or a domestic helper "feeding an infant of seventeen months in the same way."

Mrs. Farrar acknowledged that there were stirrings of change among the sophisticated in the 1830s, conceding that some of her readers might now want "to imitate the French or English . . . and put every mouthful into your mouth with your fork." Later in the nineteenth century the American habit of eating with the knife completely lost its claims to gentility, and it became another relic of "primitive manners." Americans gradually learned to use forks more dexterously, although to this day they hold them in the wrong hand and "upside down" from an Englishman's point of view.

The old ways, so startlingly unfamiliar to the modern reader, gradually fell away. Americans changed their assumptions about what was proper, decent, and normal in everyday life in directions that would have greatly surprised most of the men and women of the early republic. Some aspects of their "primitive manners" succumbed to campaigns for temperance and gentility, while others evaporated with the later growth of mass merchandising and mass communications.

Important patterns of regional, class, and ethnic distinctiveness remain in American everyday life. But they are far less powerful, and less central to understanding American experience, than they once were. Through the rest of the nineteenth century and into the twentieth, the United States became ever more diverse, with new waves of Eastern and Southern European immigrants joining the older Americans of Northern European stock. Yet the new arrivals—and even more, their descendants—have experienced the attractiveness and reshaping power of a national culture formed by department stores, newspapers, radios, movies, and universal public education. America, the developing nation, developed into us. And perhaps our manners and morals, to some future observer, will seem as idiosyncratic and astonishing as this portrait of our earlier self.

First Inaugural Address (1801)

Thomas Jefferson

F riends and Fellow-Citizens:

Called upon to undertake the duties of the first executive office of our country, I avail myself of the presence of that portion of my fellow citizens which is here assembled to express my grateful thanks for the favor with which they have been pleased to look toward me, to declare a sincere consciousness that the task is above my talents, and that I approach it with those anxious and awful presentiments which the greatness of the charge and the weakness of my powers so justly inspire. . . .

During the contest of opinion through which we have passed the animation of discussions and of exertions has sometimes worn an aspect which might impose on strangers unused to think freely and to speak and to write what they think; but this being now decided by the voice of the nation, announced according to the rules of the Constitution, all will, of course, arrange themselves under the will of the law, and unite in common efforts for the common good. All, too, will bear in mind this sacred principle, that though the will of the majority is in all cases to prevail, that will to be rightful must be reasonable; that the minority possesses their equal rights, which equal law must protect, and to violate would be oppression. Let us, then, fellow-citizens, unite with one heart and one mind. . . . every difference of opinion is not a difference of principle. We have called by different names brethren of the same principle. We are all Republicans, we are all Federalists. If there be any among us who would wish to dissolve this Union or to change its republican form, let them stand undisturbed as monuments of the safety with which error of opinion may be tolerated where reason is left free to combat it. I know, indeed, that some honest men fear that a republican government can not be strong, that this Government is not strong enough; but would the honest patriot, in the full tide of successful experiment, abandon a government which has so far kept us free and firm on the theoretic and visionary fear that this Government, the world's best hope, may by possibility want energy to preserve itself?

I trust not. I believe this, on the contrary, the strongest Government on earth. I believe it the only one where every man, at the call of the law, would fly to the standard of the law, and would meet invasions of the public order as his own personal concern. Sometimes it is said that man can not be trusted with the government of himself. Can he, then, be trusted with the government of others? Or have we found angels in the forms of kings to govern him? Let history answer this question.

Let us, then, with courage and confidence pursue our own Federal and Republican principles, our attachment to union and representative government. Kindly separated by nature and a wide ocean from the exterminating havoc of one quarter of the globe; too high-minded to endure the degradations of the others; possessing a chosen country, with room enough for our descendants to the thousandth and thousandth generation; entertaining a due sense of our equal right to the use of our own faculties, to the acquisitions of our own industry, to honor and confidence from our fellow-citizens, resulting not from birth, but from our actions and their sense of them; enlightened by a benign religion, professed, indeed, and practiced in various forms, yet all of them inculcating honesty, truth, temperance, gratitude, and the love of man; acknowledging and adoring an overruling Providence, which by all its dispensations proves that it delights in the happiness of man here and his greater happiness hereafter—with all these blessings, what more is necessary to make us a happy and a prosperous people? Still one thing more, fellow citizens—a wise and frugal Government, which shall restrain men from injuring one another, shall leave them otherwise free to regulate their own pursuits of industry and improvement, and shall not take from the mouth of labor the bread it has earned. This is the sum of good government, and this is necessary to close the circle of our felicities.

About to enter, fellow-citizens, on the exercise of duties which comprehend everything dear and valuable to you, it is proper you should understand what I deem the essential principles of our Government, and consequently those which ought to shape its Administration. I will compress them within the narrowest compass they will bear, stating the general principle, but not all its limitations. Equal and exact justice to all men, of whatever state or persuasion, religious or political; peace, commerce, and honest friendship with all nations, entangling alliances with none; the support of the State governments in all their rights, as the most competent administrations for our domestic concerns and the surest bulwarks against antirepublican tendencies; the preservation of the General Government in its whole constitutional vigor, as the sheet anchor of our peace at home and safety abroad; a jealous care of the right of election by the people—a mild and safe corrective of abuses which are lopped by the sword of revolution where peaceable remedies are unprovided; absolute acquiescence in the decisions of the majority, the vital principle of republics, from which is no appeal but to force, the vital principle and immediate parent of despotism; a well disciplined militia, our best reliance in peace and for the first moments of war, till regulars may relieve them; the supremacy of the civil over the military authority; economy in the public expense, that labor may be lightly burthened; the honest payment of our debts and sacred preservation of the public faith; encouragement of agriculture, and of commerce as its handmaid; the diffusion of information and arraignment of all abuses at the bar of the public reason; freedom of religion; freedom of the press, and freedom of person under the protection of the habeas corpus, and trial by juries impartially selected. These principles form the bright constellation which has gone before us and guided our steps through an age of revolution and reformation. The wisdom of our sages and blood of our heroes have been devoted to their attainment. They should be the creed of our political faith, the text of civic instruction, the touchstone by which to try the services of those we trust; and should we wander from them in moments of error or of alarm, let us hasten to retrace our steps and to regain the road which alone leads to peace, liberty, and safety. . . .

Relying, then, on the patronage of your good will, I advance with obedience to the work, ready to retire from it whenever you become sensible how much better choice it is in your power to make. And may that Infinite Power which rules the destinies of the universe lead our councils to what is best, and give them a favorable issue for your peace and prosperity.

The Monroe Doctrine
(1823)

Meeting in you a new Congress, I deem it proper to present this view of public affairs in greater detail than might otherwise be necessary. . . . A precise knowledge of our relations with foreign powers as respects our negotiations and transactions with each is thought to be particularly necessary. . . .

At the proposal of the Russian Imperial Government, made through the minister of the Emperor residing here, a full power and instructions have been transmitted to the minister of the United States at St. Petersburg to arrange by amicable negotiation the respective rights and interests of the two nations on the northwest coast of this continent. . . . the occasion has been judged proper for asserting, as a principle in which the rights and interests of the United States are involved, that the American continents, by the free and independent condition which they have assumed and maintain, are henceforth not to he considered as subjects for the future colonization by any European powers. . . .

. . . In the wars of the European powers in matters relating to themselves we have never taken any part, nor does it comport with our policy so to do. It is only when our rights are invaded or seriously menaced that we resent injuries or make preparation for our defense. With the movements in this hemisphere we are of necessity more immediately connected, and by causes which must be obvious to all enlightened and impartial observers. The political system of the Allied Powers is essentially different . . . from that of America. . . . We owe it, therefore, to candor and to the amicable relations existing between the United States and those powers to declare that we should consider any attempt on their part to extend their [political] system to any portion of this hemisphere as dangerous to our peace and safety. With the existing colonies or dependencies of any European power, we have not interfered and shall not interfere. But with the governments [of Latin America] who have declared their independence and maintained it, and whose independence we have, on great consideration and on just principles, acknowledged, we could not view any interposition for the purpose of oppressing them, or controlling in any other manner their destiny, by any European power in any other light than as the manifestation of an unfriendly disposition toward the United States . . .

. . . Our policy in regard to Europe, which was adopted at an early stage of the wars which have so long agitated that quarter of the globe, nevertheless remains the same, which is, not to interfere in the internal concerns of any of its powers; to consider the government de facto as the legitimate government for us; to cultivate friendly relations with it, and to preserve those relations by a frank, firm, and manly policy, meeting in all instances the just claims of every power, submitting to injuries from none. . . .

Part IV: Antebellum Society

Children of Darkness

Stephen B. Oates

Until August 1831, most Americans had never heard of Virginia's Southampton County, an isolated, impoverished neighborhood located along the border in the southeastern part of the state. It was mostly a small farming area, with cotton fields and apple orchards dotting the flat, wooded landscape. The farmers were singularly fond of their apple crops: from them they made a potent apple brandy, one of the major sources of pleasure in this hardscrabble region. The county seat, or "county town," was Jerusalem, a lethargic little community where pigs rooted in the streets and old-timers spat tobacco juice in the shade of the courthouse. Jerusalem lay on the bank of the Nottoway River some seventy miles south of Richmond. There had never been any large plantations in Southampton County, for the soil had always been too poor for extensive tobacco or cotton cultivation. Although one gentleman did own eighty slaves in 1830, the average was around three or four per family. A number of whites had moved on to new cotton lands in Georgia and Alabama, so that Southampton now had a population that was nearly 60 per cent black. While most of the blacks were still enslaved, an unusual number—some seventeen hundred, in fact—were "free persons of color."

By southern white standards, enlightened benevolence did exist in Southampton County—and it existed in the rest of the state, too. Virginia whites allowed a few slave schools to operate—then a crime by state law—and almost without complaint permitted slaves to hold illegal religious meetings. Indeed, Virginians liked to boast that slavery was not so harsh in their "enlightened" state as it was in the brutal cotton plantations in the Deep South. Still, this was a dark time for southern whites—a time of sporadic insurrection panics, especially in South Carolina, and of rising abolitionist militancy in the North—and Virginians were taking no chances. Even though their slaves, they contended, were too happy and too submissive to strike back, Virginia was nevertheless almost a military garrison, with a militia force of some hundred thousand men to guard against insurrection.

Southampton whites, of course, were caught in the same paradox: most of the white males over twenty-one voluntarily belonged to the militia and turned out for the annual drills, yet none of them thought a slave revolt would happen here. *Their* blacks, they told themselves, had never been more content, more docile. True, they did get a bit carried away in their religious meetings these days, with much too much singing and clapping. And true, there were white preachers who punctuated their sermons with what a local observer called "ranting cant about equality" and who might inspire black exhorters to retail that doctrine to their congregations. But generally things were quiet and unchanged in this remote tidewater county, where time seemed to stand as still as a windless summer day.

It happened with shattering suddenness, an explosion of black rage that rocked Southampton County to its foundations. On August 22, 1831, a band of insurgent slaves, led by a black mystic called Nat Turner, rose up with axes and plunged southeastern Virginia—and much of the rest of the South—into convulsions of fear and racial violence. It turned out to be the bloodiest slave insurrection in southern history, one that was to have a profound and irrevocable impact on the destinies of southern whites and blacks alike.

Afterward, white authorities described him as a small man with "distinct African features." Though his shoulders were broad from work in the fields, he was short, slender, and a little knock-kneed, with thin hair, a complexion like black pearl, and large, deep-set eyes. He wore a mustache and cultivated a tuft of whiskers under his lower lip. Before that fateful August day whites who knew Nat Turner thought him harmless, even though he was intelligent and did gabble on about strange religious powers. Among the slaves, though, he enjoyed a powerful influence as an exhorter and self-proclaimed prophet.

He was born in 1800, the property of Benjamin Turner of Southampton County and the son of two strong-minded parents. Tradition has it that his African-born mother threatened to kill him rather than see him grow up in bondage. His father eventually escaped to the North, but not before he had helped inculcate an enormous sense of self-importance in his son. Both parents praised

Nat for his brilliance and extraordinary imagination; his mother even claimed that he could recall episodes that happened before his birth— a power that others insisted only the Almighty could have given him. His mother and father both told him that he was intended for some great purpose, that he would surely become a prophet. Nat was also influenced by his grandmother, who along with his white masters taught him to pray and to take pride in his superior intelligence. He learned to read and write with great ease, prompting those who knew him to remark that he had too much sense to be raised in bondage—he "would never be of any service to any one as a slave," one of them said.

In 1810 Benjamin Turner died, and Nat became the property of Turner's oldest son Samuel. Under Samuel Turner's permissive supervision Nat exploited every opportunity to improve his knowledge: he studied white children's school books and experimented in making paper and gunpowder. But it was religion that interested him the most. He attended Negro religious meetings, where the slaves cried out in ecstasy and sang hymns that expressed their longing for a better life. He listened transfixed as black exhorters preached from the Bible with stabbing gestures, singing out in a rhythmic language that was charged with emotion and vivid imagery. He studied the Bible, too, practically memorizing the books of the Old Testament, and grew to manhood with the words of the prophets roaring in his ears.

Evidently Nat came of age a bit confused if not resentful. Both whites and blacks had said he was too intelligent to be raised a slave; yet here he was, fully grown and still in bondage. Obviously he felt betrayed by false hopes. Obviously he thought he should be liberated like the large number of free blacks who lived in Southampton County and who were not nearly as gifted as he. Still enslaved as a man, he zealously cultivated his image as a prophet, aloof, austere, and mystical. As he said later in an oral autobiographical sketch, "Having soon discovered to be great, I must appear so, and therefore studiously avoided mixing in society, and wrapped myself in mystery, devoting myself to fasting and prayer."

Remote, introspective, Turner had religious fantasies in which the Holy Spirit seemed to speak to him as it had to the prophets of old. "Seek ye the kingdom of Heaven," the Spirit told him, "and all things shall be added unto you." Convinced that he "was ordained for some great purpose in the hands of the Almighty," Turner told his fellow slaves about his communion with the Spirit. "And they believed," Turner recalled, "and said my wisdom came from God." Pleased with their response, he began to prepare them for some unnamed mission. He also started preaching at black religious gatherings and soon rose to prominence as a leading exhorter in the slave church. Although never ordained and never officially a member of any church, he was accepted as a Baptist preacher in the slave community, and once he even baptized a white man in a swampy pond. There can be little doubt that the slave church nourished Turner's self-esteem and his desire for independence, for it was not only a center for underground slave plottings against the master class, but a focal point for an entire alternate culture—a subterranean culture that the slaves sought to construct beyond the white man's control. Moreover, Turner's status as a slave preacher gave him considerable freedom of movement, so that he came to know most of Southampton County intimately.

Sometime around 1821 Turner disappeared. His master had put him under an overseer, who may have whipped him, and he fled for his freedom as his father had done. But thirty days later he voluntarily returned. The other slaves were astonished. No fugitive ever came back on his own. "And the negroes found fault, and murmured against me," Turner recounted later, "saying that if they had my sense they would not serve any master in the world." But in his mind Turner did not serve any earthly master. His master was Jehovah—the angry and vengeful God of ancient Israel—and it was Jehovah, he insisted, who had chastened him and brought him back to bondage.

At about this time Nat married. Evidently his wife was a young slave named Cherry who lived on Samuel Turner's place. But in 1822 Samuel Turner died, and they were sold to different masters—Cherry to Giles Reese and Nat to Thomas Moore. Although they were not far apart and still saw each other from time to time, their separation was nevertheless a painful example of the wretched privations that slavery placed on black people, even here in mellowed Southampton County.

As a perceptive man with a prodigious knowledge of the Bible, Turner was more than aware of the hypocrisies and contradictions loose in this Christian area, where whites gloried in the teachings of Jesus and yet discriminated against the "free coloreds" and kept the other blacks in chains. Here slave owners bragged about their benevolence (in Virginia they took care of their "niggers") and yet broke up families, sold Negroes off to whip-happy slave traders when money was scarce, and denied intelligent and skilled blacks something even the most debauched and useless poor whites enjoyed: freedom. Increasingly embittered about his condition and that of his people, his imagination fired to incandescence by prolonged fasting and Old Testament prayers, Turner began to have apocalyptic visions and bloody fantasies in the fields and woods southwest of Jerusalem. "I saw white spirits and blacks spirits engaged in battle," he declared later, "and the sun was darkened—the thunder rolled in the heavens, and blood flowed in streams—and I heard a voice saying, 'Such is your luck, such you are called to see, and let it come rough or smooth, you must surely bare it.' " He was awestruck, he recalled, but what did the voice mean? What must he bare? He withdrew from his fellow slaves and prayed for a revelation; and one day when he was plowing in the field, he thought the Spirit called out, "Behold me as I stand in the Heavens," and Turner looked up and saw forms of men there in a variety of attitudes, "and there were lights in the sky to which the children of darkness gave other names than what they really were—for they were the lights of the Saviour's hands, stretched forth from east to west, even as they extended on the cross on Calvary for the redemption of sinners."

Certain that Judgment Day was fast approaching, Turner strove to attain "true holiness" and "the true knowledge of faith." And once he had them, once he was "made perfect," then the Spirit showed him other miracles. While working in the field, he said, he discovered drops of blood on the corn. In the woods he found leaves with hieroglyphic characters and numbers etched on them; other leaves contained forms of men—some drawn in blood—like the figures in the sky. He told his fellow slaves about these signs—they were simply astounded—and claimed that the Spirit had endowed him with a special knowledge of the seasons, the rotation of the planets, and the operation of the tides. He acquired an even greater reputation among the county's slaves, many of whom thought he could control the weather and heal disease. He told his followers that clearly something large was about to happen, that he was soon to fulfill "the great promise that had been made to me."

But he still did not know what his mission was. Then on May 12, 1828, "I heard a loud noise in the heavens," Turner remembered, "and the Spirit instantly appeared to me and said the Serpent was loosened, and Christ had laid down the yoke he had borne for the sins of men, and that I should take it on and fight against the Serpent." Now at last it was clear. By signs in the heavens Jehovah would show him when to commence the great work, whereupon "I should arise and prepare myself, and slay my enemies with their own weapons." Until then he should keep his lips sealed.

But his work was too momentous for him to remain entirely silent. He announced to Thomas Moore that the slaves ought to be free and would be "one day or other." Moore, of course, regarded this as dangerous talk from a slave and gave Turner a thrashing.

In 1829 a convention met in Virginia to draft a new state constitution, and there was talk among the slaves—who communicated along a slave grapevine—that they might be liberated. Their hopes were crushed, though, when the convention emphatically rejected emancipation and restricted suffrage to whites only. There was also a strong backlash against antislavery publications thought to be infiltrating from the North, one of which—David Walker's *Appeal*—actually called on the slaves to revolt. In reaction the Virginia legislature enacted a law against teaching slaves to read and write. True, it was not yet rigorously enforced, but from the blacks' viewpoint slavery seemed more entrenched in "enlightened" Virginia than ever.

There is no evidence that Turner ever read antislavery publications, but he was certainly sensitive to the despair of his people. Still, Jehovah gave him no further signs, and he was carried along in the ebb and flow of ordinary life. Moore had died in 1828, and Turner had become the legal property of Moore's nine-year-old son—something that must have humiliated him. In 1829 a local wheelwright, Joseph Travis, married Moore's widow and soon moved into her house near the Cross Keys, a village located southwest of Jerusalem. Still known as Nat Turner even though he had changed owners several times, Nat considered Travis "a kind master" and later said that Travis "placed the greatest confidence in me."

In February, 1831, there was an eclipse of the sun. The sign Turner had been waiting for—could there be any doubt? Removing the seal from his lips, he gathered around him four slaves in whom he had complete trust—Hark, Henry, Nelson, and Sam—and confided what he was called to do. They would commence "the work of death" on July 4, whose connotation Turner clearly understood. But they formed and rejected so many plans that his mind was affected. He was seized with dread. He fell sick, and Independence Day came and passed.

On August 13 there was another sign. Because of some atmospheric disturbance the sun grew so dim that it could be looked at directly. Then it seemed to change colors—now pale green, now blue, now white—and there was much excitement and consternation in many parts of the eastern United States. By afternoon the sun was like an immense ball of polished silver, and the air was moist and hazy. Then a black spot could be seen, apparently on the sun's surface—a phenomenon that greatly aroused the slaves in southeastern Virginia. For Turner the black spot was unmistakable proof that God wanted him to move. With awakened resolution he told his men that "as the black spot passed over the sun, so shall the blacks pass over the earth."

It was Sunday, August 21, deep in the woods near the Travis house at a place called Cabin Pond. Around the crackling fire Turner's confederates feasted on roast pig and apple brandy. With them were two new recruits—Jack, one of Hark's cronies, and Will, a powerful man who intended to gain his freedom or die in the attempt. Around midafternoon Turner himself made a dramatic appearance, and in the glare of pine-knot torches they finally made their plans. They would rise that night and "kill all the white people." It was a propitious time to begin, because many whites of the militia were away at a camp meeting. The revolt would be so swift and so terrible that the whites would be too panic-stricken to fight back. Until they had sufficient recruits and equipment, the insurgents would annihilate everybody in their path—women and children included. When one of the slaves complained about their small number (there were only seven of them, after all), Turner was quick to reassure him. He had deliberately avoided an extensive plot involving a lot of slaves. He knew that blacks had "frequently attempted similar things," but their plans had "leaked out." Turner intended for his revolt to happen completely without warning. The "march of destruction," he explained, "should be the first news of the insurrection," whereupon slaves and free blacks alike would rise up and join him. He did not say what their ultimate objective was, but possibly he wanted to fight his way into the Great Dismal Swamp some twenty miles to the east. This immense, snake-filled quagmire had long been a haven for fugitives, and Turner may have planned to establish a slave stronghold there from which to launch punitive raids against Virginia and North Carolina. On the other hand, he may well have had nothing in mind beyond the extermination of every white on the ten-mile route to Jerusalem. There are indications that he thought God would guide him after the revolt began, just as He had directed Gideon against the Midianites. Certainly Turner's command of unremitting carnage was that of the Almighty, who had said through his prophet Ezekiel:

"Slay utterly old and young, both maids and little children, and women. . . ."

The slaves talked and schemed through the evening. Night came on. Around two in the morning of August 22 they left the woods, by-passed Giles Reese's farm, where Cherry lived, and headed for the Travis homestead, the first target in their crusade.

All was still at the Travis house. In the darkness the insurgents gathered about the cider press, and all drank except Turner, who never touched liquor. Then they moved across the yard with their axes. Hark placed a ladder against the house, and Turner, armed with a hatchet, climbed up and disappeared through a second-story window. In a moment he unbarred the door, and the slaves spread through the house without a sound. The others wanted Turner the prophet, Turner the black messiah, to strike the first blow and kill Joseph Travis. With Will close behind, Turner entered Travis' bedroom and made his way to the white man's bed. Turner swung his hatchet—a wild blow that glanced off Travis' head and brought him out of bed yelling for his wife. But with a sure killer's instinct Will moved in and hacked Travis to death with his axe. In minutes Will and the others had slaughtered the four whites they found in the house, including Mrs. Travis and young Putnam Moore, Turner's legal owner. With Putnam's death Turner felt that at last, after thirty years in bondage, he was free.

The rebels gathered up a handful of old muskets and followed "General Nat" out to the barn. There Turner paraded his men about, leading them through every military maneuver he knew. Not all of them, however, were proud of their work. Jack sank to his knees with his head in his hands and said he was sick. But Hark made him get up and forced him along as they set out across the field to the next farm. Along the way somebody remembered the Travis baby. Will and Henry returned and killed it in its cradle.

And so it went throughout that malignant night, as the rebels took farm after farm by surprise. They used no firearms, in order not to arouse the countryside, instead stabbing and decapitating their victims. Although they confiscated horses, weapons, and brandy, they took only what was necessary to continue the struggle, and they committed no rapes. They even spared a few homesteads, one because Turner believed the poor white inhabitants "thought no better of themselves than they did of negroes." By dawn on Monday there were fifteen insurgents—nine on horses—and they were armed with a motley assortment of guns, clubs, swords, and axes. Turner himself now carried a light dress sword, but for some mysterious reason (a fatal irresolution? the dread again?) he had killed nobody yet.

At Elizabeth Turner's place, which the slaves stormed at sunrise, the prophet tried once again to kill. They broke into the house, and there, in the middle of the room, too frightened to move or cry out, stood Mrs. Turner and a neighbor named Mrs. Newsome. Nat knew Elizabeth Turner very well, for she was the widow of his second master, Samuel Turner. While Will attacked her with his axe the prophet took Mrs. Newsome's hand and hit her over the head with his sword. But evidently he could not bring himself to kill her. Finally Will moved him aside and chopped her to death as methodically as though he were cutting wood.

With the sun low in the east, Turner sent a group on foot to another farm while he and Will led the horsemen at a gallop to Caty Whitehead's place. They surrounded the house in a rush, but not before several people fled into the garden. Turner chased after somebody, but it turned out to be a slave girl, as terrified as the whites, and he let her go. All around him, all over the Whitehead farm, there were scenes of unspeakable violence. He saw Will drag Mrs. Whitehead kicking and screaming out of the house and almost sever her head from her body. Running around the house, Turner came upon young Margaret Whitehead hiding under a cellar cap between two chimneys. She ran crying for her life, and Turner set out after her—a wild chase against the hot August sun. He overtook the girl in a field and hit her again and again with his sword, but she would not die. In desperation he picked up a fence rail and beat her to death. Finally he had killed someone. He was to kill no one else.

After the Whitehead massacre the insurgents united briefly and then divided again, those on foot moving in one direction and Turner and the mounted slaves in another. The riders moved across the fields, kicking their horses and mules faster and faster, until at last they raced down the lane to Richard Porter's house, scattering dogs and chickens as they went. But the Porters had fled—forewarned by their own slaves that a revolt was under way. Turner knew that the alarm was spreading now, knew that the militia would soon be mobilizing, so he set out alone to retrieve the other column. While he was gone Will took the cavalry and raided Nathaniel Francis' homestead. Young Francis was Will's owner, but he could not have been a harsh master: several free blacks voluntarily lived on his farm. Francis was not at home, and his pregnant young wife survived Will's onslaught only because a slave concealed her in the attic. After killing the overseer and Francis' two nephews, Will and his men raced on to another farm, and another, and then overran John Barrow's place on the Barrow Road. Old man Barrow fought back manfully while his wife escaped in the woods, but the insurgents overwhelmed him and slit his throat. As a tribute to his courage they wrapped his body in a quilt and left a plug of tobacco on his chest.

Meanwhile Turner rode chaotically around the countryside, chasing after one column and then the other, almost always reaching the farms after his scattered troops had done the killing and gone. Eventually he found both columns waiting for him at another pillaged homestead, took charge again, and sent them down the Barrow Road, which intersected the main highway to Jerusalem. They were forty strong now and all mounted. Many of the new recruits had joined up eager "to kill all the white people." But others had been forced to come along as though they were hostages. A Negro later testified that several slaves—among them three teen-age boys— "were constantly guarded by negroes with guns who were ordered to shoot them if they attempted to escape."

On the Barrow Road, Turner's strategy was to put his twenty most dependable men in front and send them galloping down on the homesteads before anybody could escape. But the cry of insurrection had preceded them, and many families had already escaped to nearby Jerusalem, throwing the village into pandemonium. By midmorning church bells were tolling the terrible news—*insurrection, insurrection*—and shouting men were riding through the countryside in a desperate effort to get the militia together before the slaves overran Jerusalem itself.

As Turner's column moved relentlessly toward Jerusalem one Levi Waller, having heard that the blacks had risen, summoned his children from a nearby schoolhouse (some of the other children came running too) and tried to load his guns. But before he could do so, Turner's advance horsemen swept into his yard, a whirlwind of axes and swords, and chased Waller into some tall weeds. Waller managed to escape, but not before he saw the blacks cut down his wife and children. One small girl also escaped by crawling up a dirt chimney, scarcely daring to breathe as the insurgents decapitated the other children—ten in all—and threw their bodies in a pile.

Turner had stationed himself at the rear of his little army and did not participate in these or any other killings along the Barrow Road. He never explained why. He had been fasting for several days and may well have been too weak to try any more killing himself. Or maybe as God's prophet he preferred to let Will and the eight or nine other lieutenants do the slaughtering. All he said about it afterward was that he "sometimes got in sight in time to see the work of death completed" and that he paused to view the bodies "in silent satisfaction" before riding on.

Around noon on Monday the insurgents reached the Jerusalem highway, and Turner soon joined them. Behind them lay a zigzag path of unredeemable destruction: some fifteen homesteads sacked and approximately sixty whites slain. By now the rebels amounted to fifty or sixty—including three or four free blacks. But even at its zenith Turner's army showed signs of disintegration. A few reluctant slaves had already escaped or deserted. And many others were roaring drunk, so drunk they could scarcely ride their horses, let alone do any fighting. To make matters worse, many of the confiscated muskets were broken or too rusty to fire.

Turner resolved to march on Jerusalem at once and seize all the guns and powder he could find there. But a half mile up the road he stopped at the Parker farm, because some of his men had relatives and friends there. When the insurgents did not return, Turner went after them—and found his men not in the slave quarters but down in Parker's brandy cellar. He ordered them back to the highway at once.

On the way back they met a party of armed men—whites. There were about eighteen of them, as far as Turner could make out. They had already routed his small guard at the gate and were now advancing toward the Parker house. With renewed zeal Turner rallied his remaining troops and ordered an attack. Yelling at the top of their lungs, wielding axes, clubs, and gun butts, the Negroes drove the whites back into Parker's cornfield. But their advantage was shortlived. White reinforcements arrived, and more were on the way from nearby Jerusalem. Regrouping in the cornfield, the whites counterattacked, throwing the rebels back in confusion. In the fighting some of Turner's best men fell wounded, though none of them died. Several insurgents, too drunk to fight any more, fled pell-mell into the woods.

If Turner had often seemed irresolute earlier in the revolt, he was now undaunted. Even though his force was considerably reduced, he still wanted to storm Jerusalem. He led his men away from the main highway, which was blocked with militia, and took them along a back road, planning to cross the Cypress Bridge and strike the village from the rear. But the bridge was crawling with armed whites. In desperation the blacks set out to find reinforcements: they fell back to the south and then veered north again, picking up new recruits as they moved. They raided a few more farms, too, only to find them deserted, and finally encamped for the night near the slave quarters on Ridley's plantation.

All Monday night news of the revolt spread beyond Southampton County as express riders carried the alarm up to Petersburg and from there to the capitol in Richmond. Governor John Floyd, fearing a statewide uprising, alerted the militia and sent cavalry, infantry, and artillery units to the stricken county. Federal troops from Fortress Monroe were on the way, too, and other volunteers and militia outfits were marching from contiguous counties in Virginia and North Carolina. Soon over three thousand armed whites were in Southampton County, and hundreds more were mobilizing.

With whites swarming the countryside, Turner and his lieutenants did not know what to do. During the night an alarm had stampeded their new recruits, so that by Tuesday morning they had only twenty men left. Frantically they set out for Dr. Simon Blunt's farm to get volunteers—and rode straight into an ambush. Whites barricaded in the house opened fire on them at pointblank range, killing one or more insurgents and capturing several others—among them Hark Travis. Blunt's own slaves, armed with farm tools, helped in the defense and captured a few rebels themselves.

Repulsed at Blunt's farm, Turner led a handful of the faithful back toward the Cross Keys, still hoping to gather reinforcements. But the signs were truly ominous, for armed whites were everywhere. At last the militia overtook Turner's little band and in a final, desperate skirmish killed Will and scattered the rest. Turner himself, alone and in deep anguish, escaped to the vicinity of the Travis farm and hid in a hole under some fence rails.

By Tuesday evening a full-scale manhunt was under way in southeastern Virginia and North Carolina as armed whites prowled the woods and swamps in search of fugitive rebels and alleged collaborators. They chased the blacks down with howling dogs, killing those who resisted—and many of them resisted zealously—and dragging others back to Jerusalem to stand trial in the county court. One free black insurgent committed suicide rather than be taken by white men. Within a week nearly all the bona fide rebels except Turner had either been executed or imprisoned, but not before white vigilantes—and some militiamen—had perpetrated barbarities on more than a score of innocent blacks. Outraged by the atrocities committed on whites, vigilantes rounded up Negroes in the Cross Keys and decapitated them. Another vigilante gang in North Carolina not only beheaded several blacks but placed their skulls on poles, where they remained for days. In all directions whites took Negroes from their shacks and tortured, shot, and burned them to death and then mutilated their corpses in ways that witnesses refused to describe. No one knows how many innocent Negroes died in this reign of terror—at least a hundred twenty, probably more. Finally the militia commander of Southampton County issued a proclamation that any further outrages would be dealt with according to the articles of war. Many whites publicly regretted these atrocities but argued that they were the inevitable results of slave insurrection. Another revolt, they said, would end with the extermination of every black in the region.

Although Turner's uprising ended on Tuesday, August 24, reports of additional insurrections swept over the South long afterward, and dozens of communities from Virginia to Alabama were seized with hysteria. In North Carolina rumors flew that slave armies had been seen on the highways, that one—maybe led by Turner himself—had burned Wilmington, butchered all the inhabitants, and was now marching on the state capital. The hysteria was even worse in Virginia, where reports of concerted slave rebellions and demands for men and guns swamped the governor's office. For a time it seemed that thousands of slaves had risen, that Virginia and perhaps the entire South would soon be ablaze. But Governor Floyd kept his head, examined the reports carefully, and concluded that no such widespread insurrection had taken place. Actually no additional uprisings had happened anywhere. Out of blind panic whites in many parts of the South had mobilized the militia, chased after imaginary insurgents, and jailed or executed still more innocent blacks. Working in cooperation with other political and military authorities in Virginia and North Carolina, Floyd did all he could to quell the excitement, to reassure the public that the slaves were quiet now. Still, the governor did not think the Turner revolt was the work of a solitary fanatic. Behind it, he believed, was a conspiracy of Yankee agitators and black preachers—especially black preachers. "The whole of that massacre in Southampton is the work of these Preachers," he declared, and demanded that they be suppressed.

Meanwhile the "great bandit chieftain," as the newspapers called him, was still at large. For more than two months Turner managed to elude white patrols, hiding out most of the time near Cabin Pond where the revolt had begun. Hunted by a host of aroused whites (there were various rewards totalling eleven hundred dollars on his head), Turner considered giving himself up and once got within two miles of Jerusalem before turning back. Finally on Sunday, October 30, a white named Benjamin Phipps accidentally discovered him in another hideout near Cabin Pond. Since the man had a loaded shotgun, Turner had no choice but to throw down his sword.

The next day, with lynch mobs crying for his head, a white guard hurried Turner up to Jerusalem to stand trial. By now he was resigned to his fate as the will of Almighty God and was entirely fearless and unrepentant. When a couple of court justices examined him that day, he stated emphatically that *he* had conceived and directed the slaughter of all those white people (even though he had killed only Margaret Whitehead) and announced that God had endowed him with extraordinary powers. The justices ordered this "fanatic" locked up in the same small wooden jail where the other captured rebels had been incarcerated.

On November 1 one Thomas Gray, an elderly Jerusalem lawyer and slaveholder, came to interrogate Turner as he lay in his cell "clothed with rags and covered with chains." In Gray's opinion the public was anxious to learn the facts about the insurrection—for whites in Southampton could not fathom why their slaves would revolt. What Gray wanted was to take down and publish a confession from Turner that would tell the public the truth about why the rebellion had happened. It appears that Gray had already gathered a wealth of information about the outbreak from other prisoners, some of whom he had defended as a court-appointed counsel. Evidently he had also written unsigned newspaper accounts of the affair, reporting in one that whites had located Turner's wife and lashed her until she surrendered his papers (remarkable papers, papers with hieroglyphics on them and sketches of the Crucifixion and the sun). According to Gray and to other sources as well, Turner over a period of three days gave him a voluntary and authentic confession about the genesis and execution of the revolt, recounting his religious visions in graphic detail and contending again that he was a prophet of Almighty God. "Do you not find yourself mistaken now?" Gray asked. Turner replied testily, "Was not Christ crucified?" Turner insisted that the uprising was local in origin but warned that other slaves might see signs and act as he had done. By the end of the confession Turner was in high spirits, perfectly "willing to suffer the fate that awaits me." Although Gray considered him "a gloomy fanatic," he thought Turner was one of the most articulate men he had ever met. And Turner could be frightening. When, in a burst of enthusiasm, he spoke of the killings and raised his manacled hands toward heaven, "I looked on him," Gray said, "and my blood curdled in my veins."

On November 5, with William C. Parker acting as his counsel, Turner came to trial in Jerusalem. The court, of course, found him guilty of committing insurrection and sentenced him to hang. Turner, though, insisted that he was not guilty because he did not feel so. On November 11 he went to his death in resolute silence. In addition to Turner, the county court tried some forty-eight other Negroes on various charges of conspiracy, insurrection, and treason. In all, eighteen blacks—including one woman—were convicted and hanged. Ten others were convicted and "transported"—presumably out of the United States.

But the consequences of the Turner revolt did not end with public hangings in Jerusalem. For southern whites the uprising seemed a monstrous climax to a whole decade of ominous events, a decade of abominable tariffs and economic panics, of obstreperous antislavery activities, and of growing slave unrest and insurrection plots, beginning with the Denmark Vesey conspiracy in Charleston in 1822 and culminating now in the worst insurrection Southerners had ever known. Desperately needing to blame somebody besides themselves for Nat Turner, Southerners linked the revolt to some sinister Yankee-abolitionist plot to destroy their cherished way of life. Southern zealots declared that the antislavery movement, gathering momentum in the North throughout the 1820's, had now burst into a full-blown crusade against the South. In January, 1831, William Lloyd Garrison had started publishing *The Liberator* in Boston, demanding in bold, strident language that the slaves be immediately and unconditionally emancipated. If Garrison's rhetoric shocked Southerners, even more disturbing was the fact that about eight months after the appearance of *The Liberator* Nat Turner embarked on his bloody crusade—something southern politicians and newspapers refused to accept as mere coincidence. They charged that Garrison was behind the insurrection, that it was his "bloodthirsty" invective that had incited Turner to violence. Never mind that there was no evidence that Turner had ever heard of *The Liberator*; never mind that Garrison categorically denied any connection with the revolt, saying that he and his abolitionist followers were Christian pacifists who wanted to free the slaves through moral suasion. From 1831 on, northern abolitionism and slave rebellion were inextricably associated in the southern mind.

But if Virginians blamed the insurrection on northern abolitionism, many of them defended emancipation itself as the only way to prevent further violence. In fact, for several months in late 1831 and early 1832 Virginians engaged in a momentous public debate over the feasibility of manumission. Out of the western part of the state, where antislavery and anti-Negro sentiment had long been smoldering, came petitions demanding that Virginia eradicate the "accursed," "evil" slave system and colonize all blacks at state expense. Only by removing the entire black population, the petitions argued, could future revolts be avoided. Newspapers also discussed the idea of emancipation and colonization, prompting one to announce that "Nat Turner and the blood of his innocent victims have conquered the silence of fifty years." The debate moved into the Virginia legislature, too, and early in 1832 proslavery and antislavery orators harangued one another in an unprecedented legislative struggle over emancipation. In the end most delegates concluded that colonization was too costly and too complicated to carry out. And since they were not about to manumit the blacks and leave them as free men in a white man's country, they rejected emancipation. Indeed, they went on to revise and implement the slave codes in order to restrict blacks so stringently that they could never mount another revolt. The modified codes not only strengthened the patrol and militia systems, but sharply curtailed the rights of free blacks and all but eliminated slave schools, slave religious meetings, and slave preachers. For Turner had taught white Virginians a hard lesson about what might happen if they gave slaves enough education and religion to think for themselves.

In the wake of the Turner revolt, the rise of the abolitionists, and the Virginia debates over slavery, the other southern states also expanded their patrol and militia systems and increased the severity of their slave codes. What followed was the Great Reaction of the

1830's and 1840's, during which the South, threatened it seemed by internal and external enemies, became a closed, martial society determined to preserve its slave-based civilization at whatever cost. If Southerners had once apologized for slavery as a necessary evil, they now trumpeted that institution as a positive good—"the greatest of all the great blessings," as James H. Hammond phrased it, "which a kind providence has bestowed." Southern postmasters set about confiscating abolitionist literature, lest these "incendiary" tracts invite the slaves to violence. Some states actually passed sedition laws and other restrictive measures that prohibited Negroes and whites alike from criticizing slavery. And slave owners all across the South tightened up slave discipline, refusing to let blacks visit other plantations and threatening to hang any slave who even looked rebellious. By the 1840's the Old South had devised such an oppressive slave system that organized insurrection was all but impossible.

Even so, southern whites in the ante-bellum period never escaped the haunting fear that somewhere, maybe even in their own slave quarters, another Nat Turner was plotting to rise up and slit their throats. They never forgot him. His name became for them a symbol of terror and violent retribution.

But for ante-bellum blacks—and for their descendants—the name of Nat Turner took on a profoundly different connotation. He became a legendary black hero who broke his chains and murdered white people because slavery had murdered Negroes. Turner, said an elderly black man in Southampton County only a few years ago, was "God's man. He was a man for war, and for legal rights, and for freedom."

The Working Ladies of Lowell

Bernard A. Weisberger

Dusk fell over the city of Lawrence, Massachusetts, a few minutes before five o'clock on January 10, 1860. In the five–story brick textile factory owned by the Pemberton Manufacturing Company, lamps began to flicker in the ritual of "lighting-up time." The big building—nearly three hundred feet long and eighty–five wide—rumbled unceasingly with the noise of its hundreds of machines for turning cotton into cloth: its scutchers and spreaders, carders, drawing frames and spreaders; its warpers and dressers; and its power looms for weaving the finished fabric. Inside, the noise was higher-pitched, a relentless squeak, clatter, and whirr from the belt-and-shift system that transmitted water power to the machinery. Some six or seven hundred "hands," mostly women, were at work that afternoon. Those near the windows could look through the twilight at the factory yard, with its two lower buildings running out at right angles from the ends of the main plant. Next to the yard lay the canal which carried the waters of the Merrimack River to the giant water wheels, and beyond that was a row of frame boardinghouses for the employees. Sometime after seven o'clock, bells would jangle and the workers would stream across footbridges over the canal, home to dinner.

But not that night. Suddenly there was a sharp rattle, and then a prolonged, deafening crash. A section of the building's brick wall seemed to bulge out and explode, and then, literally in seconds, the Pemberton Mill collapsed. Tons of machinery crashed down through crumpling floors, dragging trapped, screaming victims along in their downward path. At a few minutes after five, the factory was a heap of twisted iron, splintered beams, pulverized bricks, and agonized, imprisoned human flesh.

Bonfires, lit to aid rescue workers, made pockets of brightness in the gathering light. But the darkness was merciful, hiding sights of unforgettable horror. Girls and men were carried out on stretchers, with arms and legs torn from their bodies, faces crushed beyond recognition, open wounds in which the bones showed through a paste of dried blood, brick dust, and shredded clothing. The worst was yet to come, however. At about 9:30 P.M., the moans of pain, delirium, and cold coming from those still pinned in the wreckage changed to screams of panic. Someone scrambling through the ruins had upset an oil lantern. Flames raced through the oil-soaked wood and cotton waste, drove back doctors, rescue crews, and spectators (many of them relatives of the mill workers), and snuffed out the final shrieks. Next morning saw only a black and smoking mass of "brick, mortar and human bones . . . promiscuously mingled" at the scene of the tragedy.

There were ninety dead—fourteen of them unidentifiable or never found—and a long list of crippled and hospitalized. The casualty list read like a cross section of New England's labor force. There were Yankee girls like Mary York, of Brighton, Maine, and men life Ira Locke of Derry, New Hampshire. But there were also Nancy Connelly and Bridget Doyle and Kate Harridy, and many others whose names were of Ireland's "ould sod." There were men like the Swiss George Kradolfer, the German Henry Bakeman, and the Scotch-Irish Robert Hayer, who had come a long way to suffer at the edge of a New England canal. And there was not a church in Lawrence—Catholic, Methodist, Baptist, Presbyterian, Congregational, Unitarian, Universalist, Episcopalian—that did not have parishioners to mourn or to console on the Sunday after the accident.

What had gone wrong? A lengthy coroner's inquest did a certain amount of hedging, but certain unpleasant facts emerged. During the factory's construction, in 1835, cast-iron pillars supporting the floor beams had been shown to be cheap and brittle. They went in nevertheless. Extra machinery had been crowded into the upper floors, ignoring already questionable load limits. Brick walls had not been sufficiently reinforced against the outward thrust of those overburdened floors. After the disaster, the ministers of Lawrence spoke sermons on God's inscrutable wrath, but it was clear that human oversight and corner-cutting on expenses bore much of the blame.

This seemed to point the finger at the owners, David Nevins and George Howe, who had bought the factory from its first owners in 1857, during a financial panic. Yet neither man was callous or dishonest. Both undoubtedly shared the shocked dismay of their fellow businessmen in the New England Society for the Promotion of Manufactures and the Mechanic Arts, who, ironically, had scheduled a dinner in Boston for that dreadful January 10. Nevins and Howe had acted in response to pressures which they themselves did not fully understand, and such guilt as they bore was partly the guilt of the generation of men who had brought industry to New England's hills forty years before. Those men had nursed lordly dreams of progress and profit through the machine, and some of their visions of growth and gain and uplift had been realized. But industrialism, as America was to learn, brought pain and perplexity with it as well. The horror at the Pemberton Mills was a symbol of another collapse: that of an experiment in creating a strifeless industrial society showering blessings alike on workers and capitalists. Like most such experiments, it expected too much of human nature and counted too little on the unforeseen. For a time, however, it gave a thrill of promise. Its beginnings went back beyond Lawrence, to the early days of the Republic.

In the years just after 1789, the "establishment of manufactures" was the focus of debate. Men like Alexander Hamilton and Tench Coxe looked upon the few domestic workshops of the infant nation and found them good. They urged that the national government should protect and nurture these producers of "American" clothing, gunpowder, rope, paper, rum, iron, leather, and a miscellany of other articles. From other quarters, however, came warnings that liberty and industry made poor partners. Thomas Jefferson was only one among many to point to England's experience and predict that factory workers would inexorably sink into pauperism. They would be forced by the workings of human nature and economic law to "the maximum of labor which the construction of the human body can endure, & to the minimum of food . . . which will preserve it in life." Malthus, Marx, and Ricardo together could not have put it more grimly. Jefferson's implication needed no spelling out—plainly, an impoverished (and therefore vice-ridden and ignorant) laboring class would be indigestible in a democratic republic.

By and large, the Jeffersonians had the better of the argument for some twenty-five years. Capital, markets, and skilled labor—all necessary to a manufacturing economy—were scare in an undeveloped America, which still found adequate rewards for its work in the soil, the ocean, and the forest. There were a few significant experiments in industry. In Rhode Island, by way of example, two farsighted Quaker merchants, Moses Brown and William Almy, set up in 1790 a "factory" for spinning cotton yarn and thread. They used many of the new machines developed in England during the preceding fifty years to mechanize the spinning process. (The British jealously guarded against the export of those machines or plans for them, but Almy and Brown found a young immigrant from England named Samuel Slater. Slater had stored away the details of the new devices in an incredible memory and come to the United States precisely in the hope of finding sponsors like Almy and Brown. He built their first plant "by heart" and made his fortune and theirs as planned [*See* "Father of Our Factory System," AMERICAN HERITAGE, April, 1958.])

Almy and Brown had their new machinery tended by the children of families whom they induced to settle in the factory neighborhood, and they paid their workers, sometimes, in store orders for Almy and Brown merchandise. Thus high-mindedly did they plant the seeds of the company town and child labor in New England soil. With the coming of the cotton gin in 1793, and with years of wartime high prices, they prospered, and even had a few imitators. Yet for all these, "industry" in any real economic sense remained all but nonexistent in the United States. The real breakthrough came in 1812, and one of the many forces behind it was, as so often, a hunch in a gifted man's mind.

The man was Francis Cabot Lowell, member of a family which was to crowd the American hall of fame with merchants, ministers, legislators, judges, poets, soldiers, and educators. In 1812, this particular Lowell was visiting England for his health, and, like so many Yankees apparently "resting," was deep in meditation. His mind ranged over a number of diverse facts. One was that the impending war would severely shake the Lowell family importing business. Another was that "yarn factories" were not a bad substitute investment. A third was that fresh inventions in the field of power looms had opened up still newer profit opportunities in clothmaking. In Great Britain, weaving factories were at last keeping pace with the healthy output of spinning factories. Francis Lowell, thirty–six years old in 1812, synthesized these facts into a dazzling American vision. Why not put spinning and weaving machines under one roof? Why not have southern cotton delivered at one end of a factory, while from the other end bales of finished yard goods emerged to find a ready market swept clean of British competitors by war. Power would come from New England streamlets; capital from

Boston's countinghouse aristocracy. Machinery? That was a little harder, but not impossible. Lowell, an amateur mathematician and scientist, visited the factories of unsuspecting British business contacts, and gave himself a quick course in the intricate process of machine weaving, which saw cotton fibers fluffed, combed, rolled, twisted, stretched, toughened, and cross-laced, moving from winding to winding and machine to machine in a complex and brilliantly-timed ballet of rollers, spindles, and flyers. Returning home to Boston, he took Paul Moody, a talented Massachusetts mechanic, into his confidence. The two of them perspired over drawings, imported a few devices, copied, redesigned, invented where they had to—and had their factory set up in Waltham, new Boston, by 1815. Meanwhile, Lowell's brother-in-law, Patrick Tracy Jackson, had helped to round up the initial capital, and its donors had been incorporated in 1813 as the Boston Manufacturing Company.

Power, capital, machinery—all were ready. But what of labor? The more complex weaving machinery could not be run by children, and yet the cotton factory did not demand the skill and strength of grown men for most of its jobs. Obviously women workers were the answer. New England indeed had what was then called a "fund" of "female labor" in the daughters of its rural fold. But what of that supposed indissoluble bond of union between "manufactures" on the one hand, and "vice and poverty" on the other? Would Yankee farmers send their daughters into the factories to become part of a permanent force of degraded wage workers? Clearly not! Then how would the Boston Manufacturing Company recruit its labor? The answer was an invention as intriguing as any new mechanical gadget for mass-producing cloth. One of Patrick Jackson's biographers explained it, years later.

> By the erection of boarding houses at the expense and under the control of the factory; putting at the head of them matrons of tried character and allowing no boarders to be received except the female operatives of the mill: by stringent regulations for the government of these houses; by all these precautions, they gained the confidence of the rural population who were now no longer afraid to trust their daughters in a manufacturing town. A supply was thus obtained of respectable girls; and these, from pride of character as well as principle, have taken especial care to exclude all others.

> It was soon found that an apprenticeship in a factory entailed no degradation of character, and was no impediment to a reputable

connection in marriage. A factory-girl was no longer condemned to pursue that vocation for her life: she would retire, in her turn, to assume the higher and more appropriate responsibilities of her sex; and it soon came to be considered that a few years in a mill was an honorable mode of securing a dower. The business could thus be conducted without any permanent manufacturing population. The operatives no longer form a separate caste, pursuing a sedentary employment, from parent to child, in the heated rooms of a factory; but are recruited, in a circulating current, from the healthy and virtuous population of the country.

In a circulating current! There was the trick. The fathers of Waltham had not invented the notion of an employer's personal responsibility for the physical and moral welfare of the worker. That was a legacy from indentured labor, apprenticeship—even slavery. But the new factory owners had built a new structure on that foundation. If they brought young girls to the factory for a brief period between maturing and marrying, and if they boarded them under safeguards approved by church, family, and all the gods of respectability, then a *rotating* labor force would escape the ills of industrial decay. It was simple country logic. Standing water stank; a running stream or a spring-fed pond stayed pure and dear.

So the experiment was tried at Waltham. Not much is known about early working conditions, but from a business viewpoint, success was enormous. The owners played a shrewd game from the start. They concentrated on plain and simple fabrics, marketed through a single firm, and they successfully lobbied, in 1816, for a certain measure of tariff protection. Francis Lowell died prematurely in 1817. He did not live to see another twenty years of dividends rarely falling below ten per cent, even while the price to the consumer dropped from twenty–one to six cents a yard. He did not need to; even by 1817, his kind of textile factory, mass-producing cheap, utilitarian goods, had won a clear decision over the dying system of decentralized craft production. By 1821, the leaders of the Boston Manufacturing Company were looking for new worlds to conquer, hunting for a site for a new factory, to turn out printed calicoes.

They found their spot in December of 1821, in a peaceable little farm community called East Chelmsford, some twenty–five miles from Boston. It was at the junction of the Concord and Merrimack rivers—a quiet place, where men could still fish tranquilly for salmon and alewives in their season. A no-longer-used canal around a fall in the Merrimack was quickly bought by the promoters of the new factory. It gave them water power and an iron grip on any future mill-building in the area. A new corporation, the Merrimack Manufacturing Company, was created—but its owners were predominantly the Waltham founders. For years they remained a well-knit group, holding tightly to patents and controlling blocks of stock, and admitting outsiders only when they could pass inspection—and pay!

But if the ownership elite did not grow swiftly, the enterprise did. The Merrimack factory was up in December of 1823. Within three years more, little East Chelmsford, with its scattered farmhouses, gristmills, store, and tavern, was ready for incorporation as a village. Its leading businessmen, landowners, and citizens—the mill owners, naturally—renamed it Lowell. And Lowell mushroomed, geysered, exploded. Two new mills went up in 1828, another in 1830, three more in 1831, still another in 1835. The population of 200 in 1820 jumped to 6,477 in 1830, and 17,633 in 1836. A bank appeared, then another, then a hotel, a library, two schoolhouses, and Episcopalian, Baptist, Congregational, Universalist, and Unitarian churches. In 1835 the Boston and Lowell Railroad— one of the country's earliest—was opened in a flourish of band music and spread-eagle oratory. By 1845 Lowell, population over 30,000, had become a modern factory town in less time than it took small boys who once had fished undisturbed in the Concord to reach the ripe age of thirty.

Lowell was more than a success. It was a showpiece. Its population consisted mostly of factory girls living in the company boardinghouses. From 1823 to about 1845, it seemed to show that the fond hopes of those who planned a rotating and virtuous labor force might be realized. Foreign tourists—Michel Chevalier of France, Harriet Martineau and Charles Dickens of England—and famous Americans like Andrew Jackson, Henry Clay, and David Crockett visited it to wonder and admire. The focus of attention was the band of New England country girls who had turned themselves into mill hands. They had done so for a number of reasons, among them to show, as one of their number put it, that "it is the laborer's privilege to ennoble his work by the aim with which he undertakes it, and by the enthusiasm and faithfulness he puts into it."

What kind of girls were they? Precisely as planned, they were farm girls, and not only did they come off the farms as expected, they went back to them according to prediction. In 1845 the author of a small book on Lowell inquired of several mill owners to learn whence came their "hands," and how long they stayed. In one factory employing 173 workers, 21 were from Massachusetts, 45 from Maine, 55 from New Hampshire, 52 from Vermont. Only five had worked more than ten years, and 114 of them—nearly two–thirds of the total force—had been there for less than four. Even allowing for some shifting from mill to mill, the turnover in Lowell's population was brisk.

The New England farmer's daughter was anything but a peasant. She might be classed technically as an "unskilled" laborer, but that was only so far as factory production was concerned. She could grow fruits and vegetables, and put them into pies and preserves of breathtaking quality. She could cook for one man or for twenty at harvest time. She could knit, sew, embroider, and sometimes spin and weave. She could keep a two-story frame house spotless, raise small animals and baby brothers and sisters, and nurse sick aunts and grannies as occasion demanded. She could make such varied household products as cheese, brooms, candles, and soap. Independence came as naturally to her as to her brothers, who at seventeen and eighteen were working their own fields or commanding fishing smacks, trading schooners, and whalers. She had the equivalent of a grade-school education, often kept her father's books if he was a small businessman on the side, and took as naturally as she breathed to reading or to attending two-hour lectures and sermons.

One of these girls, Lucy Larcom, who later became a well-known poet and editor of a children's magazine, recalled her childhood in the port town of Newburyport. She remembered leisure hours spent in devouring Aesop, Bunyan, *Gulliver's Travels, The Vicar of Wakefield*, and *Arabian Nights*. The stories in them were no more wonderful than those that she got from retired seamen, who brought home gorgeously colored tropical parrots to squawk from perches in New England parlors, and who spoke to friends (addressed as "shipmate") about voyages to Calcutta and Hong Kong as casually as they might refer to a pony ride to the next village. Lucy knew the local farmers, too, who tramped into her father's store in thick boots and coarse trousers, smelling of hay, dung, and honest sweat. When her widowed mother moved to Lowell to run one of the boardinghouses, Lucy, aged eleven, was prepared for hard work and for leisure rigorously spent in self-improvement.

In the mills there was work in plenty. From April to October, operations began about 5 a.m. and ran until close to 7:30 in the evening, with half-hour interruptions for breakfast at 7 a.m. and dinner at 12:30 in the afternoon. In the shorter months, breakfast was served before daylight, and the working day was finished under lamps. Six days of eleven to thirteen hours' actual work made a long week, but not necessarily a prohibitive one to girls used to being up with the rooster and rarely idle until the sewing basket was set aside for nine o'clock bedtime. (The American factory schedule, in fact, copied farmer's hours—up at dawn to feed stock before breakfast, home for dinner in hottest daytime, late supper after barnyard chores.)

Nor was the factory work unremittingly taxing. Lucy's first job was as a bobbin girl, watching a spinning frame and replacing filled spools with empty ones. It was almost fun to watch a bobbin wax fat, and lift it off at the right moment. Those at spooling, warping, and dressing machines had harder work. The "buzzing and hissing and whizzing of pulleys and rollers and spindles and flyers . . . often grew tiresome." But a lucky girl, near a window, could tend flowers in a window box or read (when such things were permitted, as they were at first) or simply daydream. Daydreaming was discouraged, of course, for one real purpose of having attendants at the machinery was to watch for broken threads, overfilled bobbins, twisted belts, spindles that slipped off their shafts—any one of which could in seconds create an ungodly jam of twisted fibers and stalled machinery.

At the looms, the girls had more to watch—warp threads rising and falling regularly to the tug of the heddles, shuttles jerking back and forth between the warp threads at an even 120 picks to the minute, warp-beam and cloth-beam rolling, and reed beating the cross-threads tight together in even thumps. A wary eye was needed here for breaks and snarls and for shuttle boxes that needed to be changed; but if a girl had only one or two looms to tend, it was not overly burdensome. Then there were other jobs of varying skill and distastefulness—from minding the whippers and pickers which fluffed the newly arrived cotton, to folding, measuring, and packing finished goods in the cloth room. When Lucy Larcom grew up, she chose to work there. It paid less than machine-tending, but left more quiet hours for reading; an overseer once found his intellectual little mill girl deeply absorbed in Cotton Mather's pedantic *Magnalia Christi Americana* while she was folding cloth.

For the girl who grew a little weary of it all, it was always possible to go home for a month or two. With Lowell booming and growing, there would always be a job when she returned to the factory. What was more, farm girls did not need to accept assignments that they regarded as unfair. A young woman who knew that she was only a day's trip from home, where there were chickens in the henyard, milk in the springhouse, and squash in the garden, took no "sass" from an overseer. Early mill records duly chronicled the dismissal of some girls for "insolence," which undoubtedly meant telling overseers what they thought of them. Wherever industry had not completely displaced a rural way of life, workers had an extra bit of protection. The Englishwoman, Harriet Martineau, noted that the boot and shoe makers of Lynn, Massachusetts, as late as 1835, knocked off in summers to earn money by fishing. In Pennsylvania in the 1820's, the overseer at an iron foundry carefully recorded that a batch of molten iron had been ruined because, when it was ready to pour, nobody was on hand. "The men," he sorrowfully noted, "was out hunting with their guns."

And if, somehow, the hours did seem to stretch a bit toward the close of the day, there were the tangible rewards in cash to consider. It is not easy to generalize about Lowell wages from 1830 to 1845, particularly since much of the pay was by the piece. In 1840 a careful Scot, James Montgomery, made a study of the comparative costs of cotton manufacture in Great Britain and the United States. He estimated that American owners had to figure on paying girls at various spinning machines $2.50 to $3.50 a week. Weavers could earn twenty-five cents per "piece," which meant that a girl who was willing to work an extra loom might earn as much as $4.50 or even $5.50. (The gap in pay between the rank and file and the "non-coms" in the industrial army was not very great. Bookkeepers rated $9.50 weekly, overseers $12, and superintendents $25. It seems safe to say that the mill girls, in this period, averaged $3.50 a week in wages. In Lowell in 1840, five cents bought a half-dozen eggs, fifteen cents an entire chicken, and two dollars a carcass of mutton. The companies charged the girls $1.25 for their board and lodging, which left $2.25—nearly $5 every fortnight, or $9 every month, according to how paydays fell—for spending or for saving.

In rural New England a century and a quarter ago, that was no inconsiderable sum of cash. The girls saved what must have been a considerable amount of it. In 1845, according to the Reverend Henry Miles in his *Lowell As It Was And As It Is*, half of the two thousand depositors in the Lowell Savings Bank were factory girls, and their bankbooks showed a total of more than $100,000 laid away. Between 1829 and 1845, the bank had taken in $2,103,500 and paid out $1,423,500, much of it in the girls' earnings. The girls used this money for their own dowries; they lifted mortgages from fathers' farms; they supported fatherless nephews, nieces, and cousins; and, apparently not infrequently, they put brothers through college.

But what counted was not whether the girls spent their pay on ribbons and shawls or saved it for the future. What counted was that as women, they had money of their own. This was an age when a woman's property was still in the absolute control of her husband, and when the single or widowed woman who did not choose to become a seamstress or a housemaid lived on family charity. Another of those literate mill girls, Harriet Hanson Robinson, summed up the advantages of having one's own income:

> The law took no cognizance of woman as a money-spender. She was a ward, an appendage, a relict. Thus it happened, that if a woman did not choose to marry, or, when left a widow, to re-marry, she had no choice but to enter one of the few employments open to her, or to become a burden on the charity of some relative. . . . The cotton-factory was a great opening to these lonely and dependent women. . . . At last they had found a place in the universe; they were no longer obliged to finish out their faded lives mere burdens to male relatives. . . . For the first time in this country woman's labor had a money value. . . . And thus a long upward step in our material civilization was taken; woman had begun to earn and hold her own money, and through its aid had learned to think and to act for herself.

Harriet remembered what a blessing the factory was to those unhappy and lonely older women who sat in New England chimney corners, meekly enduring the teasing of the children, the gruffness of the men, and the sharpness of female in-laws who had kitchens and hearthsides of their own. Some went into the factories, and

> . . . after the first pay-day came, and they felt the jingle of silver in their pockets, and had begun to feel its mercurial influence, their bowed heads were lifted, their necks seemed braced with steel, they looked you in the face, sang blithely among their looms or frames, and walked with elastic step to and from work.

To talk of wage slavery to such women was futile; to them the factory gates had opened the way to independence.

When work was done, the girls returned to the boardinghouses. They were usually two or three story frame buildings, standing in neat rows separated from the factory by squares of greenery. They were run by older women, often widows like Mrs. Larcom, or like the mothers of Nathaniel Banks and Benjamin F. Butler, both of whom were to become Massachusetts political leaders and Civil War generals. The houses had kitchens attached in the back, dining rooms and parlors on the ground floor, and bedrooms in which two or four girls roomed together.

They did not seem to regard that a hardship. Companionship, as a matter of fact, took the sting out of initial homesickness. Harriet Robinson remembered how the wagons which had gone into the back country to recruit would pull up before a boardinghouse and discharge a cluster of farm girls, followed by a pile of neat, small trunks, often bound in home-tanned, spotted calfskin on which the hair still showed. The new arrivals would gaze wide-eyed and white-faced at the huge buildings, the crowds, and the rushing canal. As an old woman, Harriet still recalled one girl with a large tear in each eye, pathetically clutching a bandbox on which the name "Plumy Clay" was carefully lettered.

Yet after a few weeks in which Plumy and Samantha and Keziah and Elgardy and Leafy and Ruhamah had come to be friends, it all seemed rather adventuresome. The girls chatted in their rooms in the evening, or sometimes read to each other from books that might have been found on the shelves of any middle-class home of the period. There were such "holy" works as Baxter's *Saints' Rest*, and *Pilgrim's Progress*, of course, but in addition, such popular (and less uplifting) novels as *Charlotte Temple, The Castle of Otranto*, and *The Mysteries of Udolpho*. On the table in the parlor were the newspapers to which the girls jointly subscribed—religious sheets like the *Christian Register, Christian Herald*, and *Signs of the Times*, abolitionist journals such as *The Liberator* and *Herald of Freedom*, and ordinary dailies like the *Boston Daily Times*. The mill girls read and discussed the contents of these organs of opinion, and debated among themselves the fads and fancies of the yeasty 1830's and 1840's—phrenology, mesmerism, Grahamism, Fourierism. One boardinghouse even contained a Mormon Bible!

Undoubtedly it was only a small number of the girls who were grimly intellectual, but they gave a tone to the entire enterprise. They were the ones who went to lectures at the lyceum in Lowell, and solemnly took note of the pearls of wisdom that fell from the lips of John Quincy Adams, Edward Everett, Ralph Waldo Emerson, John Greenleaf Whittier, and the other gods of New England. They were the girls who took books into the factories, and later, when this was tabooed, pasted pages of newspaper poetry to their looms and frames and memorized as they worked. Some girls felt that the Bible ought to be exempt from the rule, and brought their pocket Testaments to work, creating a nice problem for pious overseers. Under the rules, they had to confiscate all literature discovered, but it went hard for some to wrest the Scriptures from a girl. "I did think," said one of them ruefully to a victim of such a seizure, "you had more conscience than to bring that book in here." One group of these "factory ladies," relentlessly bent upon improving each shining hour, flabbergasted Charles Dickens (who visited Lowell in 1841) by clubbing together to buy a piano for their boardinghouse parlor. The novelist was not merely confounded by such a genteel instrument in what was, after all, a home for "working-class" women, but he shared the amazement which a modern reader must feel that girls who worked a fourteen-hour day could be interested in anything more taxing in the evening than climbing wearily into bed.

Perhaps the most astonishing fact of all was that some of the girls, after a dawn-to-dusk session in the mill, not only found time to read literature, but to make it. Some of the ministers whose congregations included a sprinkling of highly literate mill girls had taken the lead in forming "improvement circles" as early as 1838. At the meetings of these groups—as in the literary clubs of the colleges of that day—members read their own compositions to each other for mutual criticism. The Reverend Abel Thomas, of Lowell's First Universalist Church, gradually accumulated a drawerful of essays, short stories, and poems by the members of his "circle." Enthused by what he read, he raised enough money to issue a collection of the pieces in a pamphlet entitled *The Lowell Offering*. Some of the money came from the company, which sensed the publicity value of the scheme, in the form of a large order for copies.

Having still more material on hand, Thomas undertook to edit the *Offering* as a regular periodical. Four numbers appeared in 1840 and 1841. Meanwhile an "improvement circle" in the First Congregationalist Church had independently launched an *Operatives'*

Magazine. In, 1842, the Reverend Mr. Thomas turned the editorship of the *Offering* over completely to two of the millworkers, Harriot F. Curtis and Harriet Farley. Presumably, he wanted to prove once and for all that the "operatives" could write, edit, and publish a magazine entirely under their own power. The two women merged the *Lowell Offering* and *Operatives' Magazine*, and managed to run it for five volumes. It finally died, as conditions began to change in Lowell, and a few efforts to revive it under other titles failed.

The *Lowell Offering* was by no means the cream of American periodical literature of the mid-nineteenth century. Yet it was an incredible production to emerge from a factory working force. It contained, Harriet Robinson recalled, "allegories, poems, conversations on physiology, astronomy, and other scientific subjects, dissertations on poetry, and on the beauties of nature, didactic pieces on highly moral and religious subjects, translations from French and Latin, stories of factory and other life, sketches of local New England history, and sometimes chapters of a novel." The poetry was in the mold of popular female bards of the period like Lydia Sigourney; the prose had overtones of Addison, Goldsmith, and the briskly selling lady novelist, Lydia Maria Child. The fifty-seven girls who contributed to it chose pen names as far from "Harriet," "Lucy," "Abby," and "Sarah" as they could get—"Ella," "Adelaide," "Aramantha," "Oriana," "Dolly Dindle," and "Grace Gayfeather." Two or three of the contributors continued as writers in later life; others became missionaries, schoolteachers, and suffragettes, and at least one—Margaret Foley—was a successful sculptor.

All of this was a long way from the factory slums of Birmingham and Manchester, which, in those very 1840's, were furnishing ammunition for the assaults on capitalism of Engels and Marx. The girls were aware of their uniqueness, and in the brief moments between sleep and work they undertook their mental cultivation proudly and self-consciously. They were; in their own eyes, pioneers, demonstrating that "woman" could be independent, that "manual labor" could be combined with character and intellect, and that the "impossible" concept of a highly educated working class was realizable in the United States. *They* knew that in their dignity and pride they were the equals of the capitalists who employed them, whatever their incomes. Their writing and poetizing and piano playing were meant to prove, as Lucy Larcom said, that "honest work has no need to assert itself or to humble itself in a nation like ours, but simply to take its place as one of the foundation stones of the republic." At Brook Farm, not too far from Lowell, a number of better-educated men and women were conducting an experiment that was not too different. Pitching hay in the afternoons and reading Greek in the evenings in West Roxbury were ways of vindicating the dignity of labor, too. (*See* "A Season in Utopia," AMERICAN HERITAGE, April, 1959.)

And so, willingly, the girls accepted the discipline of the boardinghouses. They went to church regularly, were in by 10 P.M., avoided improper conduct and language, and shunned idle companions—all of which came to them easily enough. They were trying to make of their factory community "a rather select industrial school for young people," Lucy Larcom wrote in 1889. And then she added, proudly: "The girls were just such girls as are knocking at the doors of young women's colleges today."

So there was Lowell in 1845 at its high noon, and whether the credit belonged to the tariff or American democracy or creative capital or the frontier or Jehovah who smiled upon America was hard to say. It was not really typical of the growing factory system. But all observers agreed that it was a sight to admire. President Jackson visited Lowell in June of 1833, and rode under triumphal arches amid a procession of drums, militiamen, citizens, schoolchildren, and 2,500 of the factory girls, carrying parasols and wearing stockings of silk. Reputedly Jackson swore that "by the Eternal," they were pretty women. Congressman Crockett of Tennessee came the next year, and if we can believe the statement in the largely fraudulent *Autobiography* ghostwritten for him, found the girls "well-dressed, lively, and genteel," looking as if "they were coming from a quilting frolic." Henry Clay came to beam at the success, in 1834, of the domestic manufactures whose protection he had so long and eloquently advocated.

Charles Dickens, as late as 1841, found that the whole city still had a fresh, new appearance (except for the mud). Its shiny buildings looked like those of a cardboard toy town, fresh out of the wrappings. He inspected the factories, he watched the girls at work, and he carried off four hundred pages of the *Offering* to read. Dickens disliked industrialism, and at that time he disliked the United States. He would have been glad, undoubtedly, to pour a little humanitarian spite on an exploitative American industrialism. But after looking long and hard, he declared: "I cannot recall or separate one young face that gave me a painful impression; not one young girl whom, assuming it to be a matter of necessity that she should gain her daily bread by the labour of her hands, I would have removed from those works if I had had the power."

In another twenty years Dickens' thoughts might have been different. For shortly after that first visit of his, Lowell began to decline. The cotton factories moved away from the golden day, toward the era of Lawrence, the Pemberton Mill disasters, and bitterness.

The change came gradually, but even in the heyday a sharp eye might have seen the warning signals going up. There was, to begin with, an iron streak in the companies' paternalism. Their control of the force was as rigid as that of any army. Girls who quit "properly," giving their employer two weeks' notice, received an "honorable discharge" (the very words entered on company records) signed by their superintendent. Not a single mill would hire an experienced worker without such a discharge, which meant that a girl who was fired, or left for any reason not approved by her employers, was barred from factory work for good. It also meant that there was no competitive bidding among bosses, and no way of improving conditions, therefore, except as the bosses chose. And since the companies did not hesitate to discharge girls who received bad conduct reports from the boardinghouse matrons, their "stewardship" sometimes became a kind of punitive spying into the employees' personal lives.

As the bloom wore off the noble experiment, there were murmurs of discontent. Fourteen hours of daily indoor work, broken only for two hastily gulped meals, took some of the spring out of the millworkers. Those whose health broke down could enter a company-built hospital, but had to pay three dollars a week for the privilege, and often emerged with a heavy debt to be worked off. The hardy few who had energy left to enjoy the "advantages" of the boardinghouses began to leave. Labor reformer Seth Luther sardonically compared those who remained to the horse of a hard-fisted farmer, who explained that his animal had "a bushel and a half of oats, *only he ain't got no time to eat 'em.*" Luther, and others like him, resented the corporation owners' growing sense of superiority, however patriarchal it might be. A small but articulate labor press denounced the "mushroom aristocracy of New England, who so arrogantly aspire to lord it over God's heritage."

The real sin of the mushroom aristocrats, however, was nothing so impalpable as an attitude. The truth was that as early as 1836, in the face of growing competition, they began to cut costs at the expense of the workers. In that year the wages of the Lowell mill girls were reduced by a dollar each week. Some 1,500 girls staged a "turn-out" in protest. It was a decorous enough affair: they walked through the streets waving their handkerchiefs and singing a parody of a popular tune:

> *Oh! isn't it a pity, such a pretty girl as I—*
> *Should be sent to the factory to pine away and die?*
> *Oh! I cannot be a slave,*
> *I will not be a slave,*
> *For I'm so fond of liberty*
> *That I cannot be a slave.*

It was charming, intelligent, and utterly futile. The companies did not restore the cuts—then or later. In addition, they began to increase the number of frames and looms each girl had to watch, and then to overcrowd the boardinghouses, assigning as many as eight to a room. The operatives began, after all, to look like the washed-out and exhausted creatures of Jefferson's most dire predictions.

For the girls who had come on the scene early, of course, there was the option of going home. That appealed to them even more than striking, which had an unladylike and un-Christian character about it, hardly becoming to the virtuous daughters of independent yeomen. They would return to the farm until the owners, short of hands, saw reason. In time, the girls believed, they must see it, for in America there was no "irrepressible conflict" between capital and labor.

So the more aggressive and independent girls drifted away from Lowell. But the owners were not concerned with the problem of replacements. For in the 1840's a mighty tide of immigration was setting in, much of it Irish. A few of Erin's sons had been in Lowell in Lucy Larcom's day—some six hundred in 1835—living with their large families in shanties on the town's fringe. Sometimes on their way to work Lucy and her friends would toss a slice of boarding-house bread to an elderly Irishwoman in order to elicit a musical flood of grateful brogue.

There was nothing quaint about the effect of the Irish on the labor market, however. By 1860 they constituted nearly half the population of Lowell. There were no friendly farms to which *they* could retreat when conditions worsened. The roofs that they could call their own were in Lowell only, and they were not the decent roofs of the boardinghouses, but overcrowded, jerry-built, or decaying homes. The companies were spared the expense of boardinghouses in this way, a point not lost upon them. And the millowners did not worry especially about the "moral character" of their Hibernian operatives, being quite willing to leave that to the priests and the police.

While the labor force thus changed, so did the nature of the owning group. The new ownership was well represented by a man like Amos Lawrence, ancestor of many pious churchmen, whose name was bestowed on a new mill town on the Merrimack, built up in the 1840's. Lawrence was a nonsmoker and nondrinker who demanded the same abstinence of his male employees. Plagued with stomach trouble, he dined briefly and frugally on watery gruel, and he was not a man to listen sympathetically to complaints that a worker's salary did not buy an adequate diet. Reproached by some critics with his great wealth, he is said to have snarled: "There is one thing you may as well understand; I know how to make money, and *you* cannot prevent it." There was something hard here that made the older, paternalistic, nationalistic outlook of the founders of Waltham seem archaic. The difference between Lawrence and Lowell, the towns, was something like the difference between Lawrence and Lowell, the men.

In addition, as stockholding in the corporations finally became a little more widespread, the personal link between owner and worker was snapped. The original Boston promoters had been drawn from the same Yankee stock as the mill hands. But the difference between a Boston attorney with a few shares of Suffolk Manufacturing Company in his safe, and Bridget Doyle at her spinning frame, was more than one of money. It was a gap between ways of life and understanding. Moreover, as some stock passed into the hands of guardians and estate administrators, company treasurers were at last able to invoke piously the interests of widows and orphans, as they maintained dividends while slashing wages and stretching out tasks.

Through the 1850's the labor scene darkened as industry spread through the nation. Prices rose in response to gold strikes and industrial booms, but wages remained at ancient levels. Factory workers struck more frequently—and were more frequently replaced by immigrant strikebreakers. Some leaders, despairing of direct action by labor, turned to state legislatures and petitioned for laws restricting the hours of labor and the employment of women and children. Some small gains were made in legislative cutting of the work burden of children under twelve, but most "ten-hour" legislation proposed in New England in the fifties died in the state capitals. The slogans of progress which had justified the beginnings of Waltham and Lowell now rang out to justify a *status quo* maintained at the price of increasing bitterness.

So it was that in 1860 something more than a single defectively built factory lay in ruins in Lawrence. In all New England there was evidence that the United States was going to have to find another way toward justice for labor—was going to have to walk the long road through decades of violence, organization, degradation, cruelty, bitterness, and protest, before the light would dawn again. The short cut to Utopia had run into a dead end, and Lowell was not, as it turned out, the harbinger of a perfect, harmonious, and just industrial society, in which a "circulating current" of laborers gained bread, education, and stature at the machines. It was not the only utopian experiment of the Jacksonian era to fail. Like the others, it remains in American history as a memory, the surviving token of a lost innocence that believed in the impossible, and for a few short hours in a simpler time, seemed to make it work.

A Slave's Description of Life On the Plantation (1845)

Frederick Douglass

My master's family consisted of two sons, Andrew and Richard; one daughter, Lucretia, and her husband, Captain Thomas Auld. They lived in one house, upon the home plantation of Colonel Edward Lloyd. . . . I spent two years of childhood on this plantation in my old master's family. . . . and as I received my first impressions of slavery on this plantation, I will give some description of it, and of slavery as it there existed. . .

Colonel Lloyd kept from three to four hundred slaves on his home plantation, and owned a large number more on the neighboring farms belonging to him . . . . The overseers of these, and all the rest of the farms, numbering over twenty, received advice and direction from the managers of the home plantation. This was the great business place. It was the seat of government for the whole twenty farms. All disputes among the overseers were settled here. If a slave was convicted of any high misdemeanor, became unmanageable, or evinced a determination to run away, he was brought immediately here, severely whipped, put on board the sloop, carried to Baltimore, and sold to Austin Woolfolk, or some other slave-trader, as a warning to the slaves remaining.

Here, too, the slaves of all the other farms received their monthly allowance of food, and their yearly clothing. The men and women slaves received, as their monthly allowance of food, eight pounds of pork, or its equivalent in fish, and one bushel of corn meal. Their yearly clothing consisted of two coarse linen shirts, one pair of linen trousers, like the shirts, one jacket, one pair of trousers for winter, made of coarse negro cloth, one pair of stockings, and one pair of shoes; the whole of which could not have cost more than seven dollars. The allowance of the slave children was given to their mothers, or the old women having the care of them. The children unable to work in the field had neither shoes, stockings, jackets, nor trousers, given to them; their clothing consisted of two coarse linen shirts per year. When these failed them, they went naked until the next allowance-day. Children from seven to ten years old, of both sexes, almost naked, might be seen at all seasons of the year.

There were no beds given the slaves, unless one coarse blanket be considered such, and none but the men and women had these. This, however, is not considered a very great privation. They find less difficulty from the want of beds, than from the want of time to sleep; for when their day's work in the field is done, the most of them having their washing, mending, and cooking to do, and having few or none of the ordinary facilities for doing either of these, very many of their sleeping hours are consumed in preparing for the field the coming day; and when this is done, old and young, male and female, married and single, drop down side by side, on one common bed,—the cold, damp floor,—each covering himself or herself with their miserable blankets; and here they sleep till they are summoned to the field by the driver's horn. At the sound of this, all must rise, and be off to the field. There must be no halting; every one must be at his or her post; and woe betides them who hear not this morning summons to the field; for if they are not awakened by the sense of hearing, they are by the sense of feeling; no age or sex finds any favor. Mr. Severe, the overseer, used to stand by the door of the quarter, armed with a large hickory stick and heavy cowskin, ready to whip any one who was so unfortunate as not to hear, or, from any other cause, was prevented from being ready to start for the field at the sound of the horn.

Mr. Severe was rightly named; he was a cruel man. I have seen him whip a woman, causing the blood to run half an hour at the time; and this, too, in the midst of her crying children, pleading for their mother's release. . . . The field was the place to witness his cruelty and profanity. . . . From the rising till the going down of the sun, he was cursing, raving, cutting, and slashing among the slaves of the field, in the most frightful manner. His career was short. He died very soon after I went to Colonel Lloyd's; . . . His death was regarded by the slaves as the result of a merciful providence.

Mr. Severe's place was filled by a Mr. Hopkins. He was a very different man. He was less cruel, less profane, and made less noise, than Mr. Severe. His course was characterized by no extraordinary demonstrations of cruelty. He whipped, but seemed to take no pleasure in it. He was called by the slaves a good overseer.

The home plantation of Colonel Lloyd wore the appearance of a country village. All the mechanical operations for all the farms were performed here. The shoemaking and mending, the blacksmithing, cartwrighting, coopering, weaving, and grain-grinding, were all performed by the slaves on the home plantation. The whole place wore a business-like aspect very unlike the neighboring farms. It was called by the slaves the Great House Farm. Few privileges were esteemed higher, by the slaves of the out-farms, than that of being selected to do errands at the Great House Farm. . . . They regarded it as evidence of great confidence reposed in them by their overseers; and it was on this account, as well as a constant desire to be out of the field from under the driver's lash, that they esteemed it a high privilege, one worth careful living for. He was called the smartest and most trusty fellow, who had this honor conferred upon him the most frequently. . . .

The slaves selected to go to the Great House Farm, for the monthly allowance for themselves and their fellow-slaves, were peculiarly enthusiastic. While on their way, they would make the dense old woods, for miles around, reverberate with their wild songs, revealing at once the highest joy and the deepest sadness. They would compose and sing as they went along, consulting neither time nor tune. . . .

. . . They told a tale of woe which was then altogether beyond my feeble comprehension; they were tones loud, long, and deep; they breathed the prayer and complaint of souls boiling over with the bitterest anguish. Every tone was a testimony against slavery, and a prayer to God for deliverance from chains. The hearing of those wild notes always depressed my spirit, and filled me with ineffable sadness. . . . To those songs I trace my first glimmering conception of the dehumanizing character of slavery. . . . If any one wishes to be impressed with the soul-killing effects of slavery, let him go to Colonel Lloyd's plantation, and, on allowance-day, place himself in the deep pine woods, and there let him, in silence, analyze the sounds that shall pass through the chambers of his soul,—and if he is not thus impressed, it will only be because "there is no flesh in his obdurate heart."

A Defense of Slavery (1837)

John C. Calhoun

We of the South will not, cannot surrender our institutions. To maintain the existing relations between the two races, inhabiting that section of the Union, is indispensable to the peace and happiness of both. . . . Be it good or bad, it has grown up with our society and institutions, and is so interwoven with them that to destroy it would be to destroy us as a people. But let me not be understood as admitting, even by implication, that the existing relations between the two races in the slaveholding States is an evil—far otherwise; I hold it to be a good, as it has thus far proved itself to be to both, and will continue to prove so if not disturbed by the fell spirit of abolition. I appeal to facts. Never before has the black race of Central Africa attained a condition so civilised and so improved, not only physically, but morally and intellectually. It came among us in a low, degraded, and savage condition, and in the course of a few generations it has grown up under the fostering care of our institutions, reviled as they have been, to its present comparatively civilised condition. . . .

. . . I hold that in the present state of civilisation, where two races of different origin, and distinguished by colour, and other physical differences, as well as intellectual, are brought together, the relation now existing in the slaveholding States between the two, is, instead of an evil, a good—a positive good. I feel myself called upon to speak freely upon the subject where the honor and interest of those I represent are involved. I hold then, that there never has yet existed a wealthy and civilized society in which one portion of the community did not, in point of fact, live on the labor of the other. Broad and general as is this assertion, it is fully borne out by history.

. . . I fearlessly assert that the existing relation between the two races in the South, against which blind fanatics are waging war, forms the most solid and durable foundation on which to rear free and stable political institutions. It is useless to disguise the fact. There is and always has been in an advanced stage of wealth and civilisation, a conflict between labour and capital. The condition of society in the South exempts us from the disorders and dangers resulting from this conflict . . . which explains why it is that the political condition of the slaveholding States has been so much more stable and quiet than that of the North. . . .

The Prairie Schooner Got Them There

George R. Stewart

One of life's ironies is that no generation knows what history will make of its doings, or upon what symbols the future will seize to sum up the past's greatest strivings. The bold, pioneering emigrants who led the way across the Great Plains would never have suspected that their symbol would be the humble and utilitarian vehicle in which they made their journey. As the long rifle and the log cabin stand for the settling of the first frontier across the Alleghenies, the sturdy covered wagon will forever call to mind the winning of the West.

To be sure, subsequent generations have somewhat distorted the reality. Most modern illustrations of covered wagons, for example, depict the huge and lumbering Conestoga, with its boat-shaped bed and sloping sides, its cover overhanging front and rear to give the whole a "swayback" appearance. Originating about 1750 in Pennsylvania, it flourished for a century. But it was almost never used beyond the Missouri except by freighters along the Santa Fe Trail. The Conestoga was uselessly heavy for the long pull to Oregon or California, and most of the few that were ill-advisedly taken on that journey had to be abandoned somewhere along the road. Physically, the emigrants' vehicles were about the same as the so-called "movers' wagons" that had taken earlier travelers on shorter, less heroic journeys. To go from one point to another farther west—from Connecticut to Ohio, say, or from Georgia to Alabama—the mover merely packed his wagon, hitched up, and went off over an already established road. He passed through a familiar type of country. He bought needed supplies at village stores. If a wagon broke down, or an ox died, or a child took sick, he could find whatever assistance was needed. The journey was seldom of more than a few hundred miles, and was not likely to require more than a month or six weeks.

Then, about 1840, the situation changed. Partly the change was geographical; partly political; partly, perhaps, psychological. Geographically, the central frontier now lay in Iowa and Missouri. Beyond it, in what is now eastern Nebraska and Kansas, there was some land that by the standards of the time was potentially good for farming. But this was a rather narrow belt, and in the eyes of a farmer of 1840 there was nothing much to be expected of it. Moreover, there was the political barrier, since Congress had established this nearer region as Indian territory. There was also room for settlers in Minnesota, but this was a cold and inhospitable region from the point of view of a southerner—and the cutting edge of the frontier was largely southern. Finally, by 1840 there had been a good deal of favorable publicity about both Oregon and California. The latter, to be sure, was still a part of Mexico. "But," anyone could say, "look at what happened in Texas!"

Thus the problem in 1840 was vastly different from that faced by earlier movers. The distance to be traversed totaled about two thousand miles, and it must be made in one jump, between winter and winter. The intervening country was unsettled, so that any emergency must be met with the materials at hand. There was nothing that could be called an established road for wagons. The country was not the well-watered and generally benign eastern terrain, but was largely mountainous and arid. The Indians had not already retreated before the advancing white man, but were wholly untamed; many were powerful and warlike.

Thus presented, the odds seem impossible. A saying later current in California begins, "The cowards never started." One would be inclined to go a little further and say, "Only the madmen started!" Yet start they did, and after some failures they were successful. Thus, rightly, an epic achievement placed the covered wagon in its present niche of glory.

Behind that achievement lay a psychic drive, a desire, almost a passion, to keep moving—and there was only one direction: westward! Many of the emigrants have left records of their motives. Negatively, they specify the wish to escape the agricultural depression that followed the panic of 1837, or the desire to get away from the malaria that raged throughout the Mississippi Valley. Positively, they mention the attractions of Oregon and California—the climate, the rich farmland, the chance to get ahead. Many went out of the sheer love of adventure—and an occasional one, like the absconding banker in the emigration of 1841, because he was fleeing the police.

The other motives seem to have been obscure to the emigrants themselves, but hindsight enables us to see them clearly. With many of these people moving had become a habit, even an ancestral habit. Their journey to the Pacific Coast was not their first one. Joseph Chiles was only thirty-one years old when he headed west in '41, but he had already moved from Kentucky to Missouri. George Donner, captain of the ill-fated party in '46, had been born in North Carolina, but had lived in Kentucky, Indiana, Texas, and Illinois. Many, indeed, were Englishmen, Scotsmen, Irishmen, or Germans, to whom the Mississippi Valley was only a way stop. To all of these people, "going west" was as natural as swimming upstream is to a salmon.

Mere monotony and ennui must have been a second unconscious but important reason. After a man, or a woman, had vegetated on a frontier farm for ten years, sheer boredom would be likely to make the risks of the journey seem rather attractive. One man put it simply. He had always liked to fish, he said, and he had heard that there was good fishing in Oregon.

These, then, were the forces that drove men west. How would they get there?

First among those factors that made desire practical were the trappers and missionaries who had already gained some knowledge of the country. This knowledge, indeed, was far from complete. The idea that the mountain men "knew every foot of the West" is sheer nonsense, as the history of the migration makes startlingly clear. Still, what they did know was invaluable. They had even taken wheeled vehicles—carts, generally—a long way along the road.

The ignorance of the first emigrants and the comparative knowledge of these others is strikingly demonstrated by the situation in '41. The emigrants had assembled their wagons on the Missouri frontier, ready to start, when they discovered that not one of them had the slightest idea of what the route was. Luckily, they were able to attach themselves to a company of missionaries led by the famous Belgian Jesuit Pierre Jean De Smet and guided by "Broken Hand" Fitzpatrick, one of the famous mountain men. This guidance served the emigrants excellently for about half the distance, and then they were forced to press on into a country about which even the mountain men could tell them little—and with disastrous results. Still, however limited, the information and leadership supplied by the mountain men—Fitzpatrick, Joseph Walker, Caleb Greenwood, Isaac Hitchcock—were essential aids to the migration.

Granted the desire and some information, the frontier people next had to make the choice among three traditional modes of transportation: the cart, the pack train, or the wagon.

The two-wheeled cart seems scarcely to have been considered. At first glance, this seems curious. Carts were in use on many farms. They were strong and highly maneuverable. To the south, in Mexico, the *carreta* had served excellently during the magnificent push of the frontier northward. To the north, the so-called Red River cart, pulled by two or three mules in tandem, had become the standard means of transport on the Canadian prairies; American fur traders had adopted them, too, and had taken long trains of them as far as the Rocky Mountains.

But the cart was primarily adapted to the transportation of goods, not of families. And the emigration was primarily a family matter. A house on wheels was what was needed and this the cart simply did not provide. Occasionally, when his team was reduced by death or exhaustion, some emigrant cut his wagon down to cartsize and thus was able to continue, but this is about all we hear of carts in the migration proper.

On the other hand, the pack train had its definite place. The mule, and less commonly the horse, already served as a pack animal for the mountain men, and during the migration, notably in 1849, was often employed. The advantages were obvious. The greater speed of movement meant carrying a smaller weight of supplies; the over-all time could be cut by at least a month, and the dangerous stretches of desert could be traversed more quickly. Pack trains could ford streams and cross mountains and rough country much more easily than could wagons.

But for migrating families the disadvantages of the pack train were extreme. Most farm women could ride, but few could withstand the day-after-day jouncing that would add up to two thousand miles. If the wife was pregnant (and many set out in that condition), it was obviously foolish to attempt such a ride. Small children were equally unsuited to the pack train. And there were other handicaps. As an ox driver noted: "The pack-mule companies are a pitiful set of slaves. They have to sit on their mules roasting in the sun all day. If they get down to walk or rest themselves, they must be bothered leading the animals. When they stop at night, they must unpack everything. In the mornings they have to repack everything."

Finally, in the event of accident or severe illness to one of its members, the pack train faced disaster. In a wagon train a man with a broken leg or a case of dysentery could be trundled along. If such a situation arose in a pack train (and difficulties were only to be expected), there was no humane solution. The barbarous abandonment of comrades on the road, such as was recorded in '49 especially, must have resulted from this dilemma.

Pack-train companies, therefore, generally consisted of young men, willing to risk their chances of getting through quickly against their chances of not getting through at all.

There remained, then, the wagon. Its disadvantages were obvious—it was slow, heavy, cumbersome, subject to breakage, difficult to take across rivers, ravines, and mountains or through rocky country. But it served as a moving home, involved less daily unpacking and repacking, allowed more pounds to be transported per animal, supplied an ambulance for the sick, and—when properly placed in formation—offered a fortress against attack. Thus it became a standard vehicle of the westward migration.

The wagon consisted of three parts—body, top, and running gear. The body, or bed, was a wooden box—often, indeed, so-called—nine or ten feet long and about four feet wide. Generally the sides and ends, about two feet high, went up perpendicularly, but on wagons of the so-called Murphy type they flared outward, as if imitating the Conestoga in miniature. Many emigrants built a false floor twelve or fifteen inches from the bottom of the bed. The lower space was divided into compartments and used for storing reserve supplies. With this clutter out of the way, the false floor was used for ordinary living.

The wagon boxes served their purpose, were subjected to no particular strain, and gave no trouble. They are seldom mentioned at all in the diaries. The top or cover was the most conspicuous part of the whole outfit, and has supplied the distinguishing adjective in the phrase "covered wagon."

This top was of canvas (then usually called twill) or else of some cloth which had been waterproofed with paint or linseed oil. It was supported by bows of bent hickory, usually five or six in number. On the ordinary straight-sided bed these went straight up. There was thus no overhang at front or rear and no swayback. Flaps at the front and a "puckering string" at the back allowed ventilation or complete closing. Inside, the wagon was thus a tiny room, about ten by four, with sides partly of wood and partly of canvas rising almost perpendicularly to a height of four or five feet and then arching over. A man could stand upright along the center line. On wagons with flaring sides the bows followed the lines of the sides before arching over, producing a more cylindrical effect, with perhaps a front and rear overhang. The top effectively protected goods and people against the weather. In an upset, it might be torn and some of the bows broken, and in thick forest country overhanging branches sometimes ripped the cloth, but there was not much country of that kind. When going head-on into the strong westerly winds of the plains, some companies put the tops down to reduce wind resistance. But on the whole the tops, like the boxes, produced few problems.

Not so the running gear. In the numerous booklets of advice surviving from the period, there is always the admonition that the wagons should be light and strong. Obviously, the two qualities are somewhat incompatible, and even the best materials and workmanship could not always produce a vehicle that would get through without breakage.

By the mid-nineteenth century the construction of running gear had reached a high degree of sophistication. Readers of Oliver Wendell Holmes' poem about the one-hoss shay will remember the care and the many different woods that went into construction of the deacon's masterpiece. Though the emigrant's wagon might not have been that carefully constructed, it would well have had hubs of elm or Osage orange, spokes of oak, felloes of ash, and tongue and hounds of hickory. Moreover, the tires were of iron, and iron was used for reinforcement at critical points.

Yet lightness was essential too, or the teams would be worn out by the mere dead weight of the wagon. The result, as in the airplane decades later, was a compromise. In the end, breakages were frequent, precipitating many a crisis and many a tragedy.

Tongues snapped on sharp turns. Front axles gave way on sudden down-drops. These were the commonest accidents, and were taken almost as routine. "Occasionally we break a tongue or an axletree," wrote an emigrant of '49, as if thinking it all in the day's work. Some emigrants carried extra parts, but this added to the total weight, and so was doubtful practice. Usually the nearest suitable tree supplied timber, though "nearest" was sometimes not very near.

In '46, when one of J. F. Reed's wagons suffered a broken axle near Great Salt Lake, his teamsters had to go fifteen miles to find a tree large enough to furnish a replacement. Not many were as unlucky as Ira Butterfield, who in 1861 snapped both axles at once while crossing Skull Creek. Fortunately he was with a large, well-equipped company, so that the accident meant only a twenty-four hour delay, and not disaster.

Wheels, however, were irreplaceable; if one broke, the wagon might have to be abandoned. But usually, wheels were extremely tough and rarely gave way except in the roughest mountain passages. True, many a wheel gave trouble because of shrinkage in the dry air of the desert, but then wedges could be driven under the tire. Eventually the tire might have to be taken off, heated red-hot, and reset on the wheel.

Although we are not well informed as to the exact dimensions of most parts of the wagon, for one wheel at least there is a meticulous measurement, made by William Clayton, a Mormon of the 1847 migration. Having decided to make an odometer, he carefully measured a hind wheel, and found it to be fourteen feet, eight inches in circumference, or four feet, eight inches in height. This was undoubtedly a large wheel; the average one probably stood almost a foot lower.

Front wheels were always smaller than hind wheels, to make the vehicle more maneuverable. On many wagons they were not more than six inches lower, preventing turns exceeding about thirty degrees. An occasional one had wheels so low that they would pass under the bed, and thus permit turns of ninety degrees or more, but small wheels made for harder pulling.

The ordinary wagon had neither springs nor brakes, but an essential part of the equipment was the "tar bucket." Traditionally it hung from the rear axle but was carried elsewhere when fording streams or traversing rock passages. The term "tar" must be taken as highly flexible. Often the bucket contained tar or resin mixed half-and-half with tallow. Since these contents were used steadily to grease the heels and kingbolt, the supply decreased, and before the end of the journey the emigrants might be using anything that came in handy and would serve. A Mormon in '47 shot a wolf, apparently for mere rifle practice. He found the animal to be exceptionally fat, so he tried the fat out and added wolf grease to the mixture in the bucket. Later these same Mormons found an oil seep, and filled their buckets at it—thus being among the first Americans to use a petroleum lubricant.[1]

Such was the wagon in which the average pioneer rode to Oregon or California. And since his comfort—and sometimes his very life—depended on it, a man had an appreciation for a good one. The youthful Isaac Jones Wistar, late a Union general, started for California early in '49. On the street in Cincinnati a wagon caught his eye, and he sized it up as he might a horse or a woman—"light, strong, shot-coupled." Then and there though the wagon was in use, he made an offer. Later, he was able to write proudly:

> I made no mistake, for that wagon proved to be one of the only two of our entire outfit which survived the searching trials of the rocks and mountains, of alkali plains and desicating deserts, and actually reached the Pacific Coast.

Granted, then, that the four-wheeled wagon was to be the vehicle of empire, how was it to be hauled? There were three possibilities—horses, mules, oxen.

Many modern representations to the contrary, the horse was really ruled out from the beginning. Though that noble animal could move faster than the ox and could pull more than the mule, he could not match the ability of either to endure the long haul, the constant work, and the insufficient food. To do his best work, a horse needed grain, and grain could not be transported. Every train, indeed, had its riding horses and these often got through. They were not, however, worked as hard as the team animals, and being more valuable, were given special care.

Only in the later years of the trail, from 1850 onward, did horse teams begin to be fairly common. By this time the road was better established, and swifter-moving transport had its advantages: grain was sometimes carried along so that the animals could have proper feed, at least during the first few weeks. To give them their due, the

---

1   The Mexican *carreta*, by contrast, was never greased—a lack which Americans considered shiftless—and its screeching was notorious. An interesting etymological question is thus raised. Why, except by the ancient principle of *lucus a non lucendo*, should not the Americans, who were so fond of lubricant, (instead of the Mexicans, who never touched the stuff) be called *greasers*?

horses seem to have stood up well enough then, when the journey was not so arduous.

As between the mule and the ox, however, there doubtless were endless arguments around the campfires, punctuated by tobacco juice spat into the embers.

"Mules move faster."
"Yes, but oxen can pull more."
"Oxen don't stampede so easy."
"Yes, but when they do, they run worse."

It could go on forever. Mules bogged down in mud, but could live on cottonwood bark. The Plains Indians would steal mules, but not oxen. Oxen, however, were more likely to get sore feet.

As a "mule man" we may cite William Johnston, who crossed in '49 under the pilotage of James Stewart, an old Santa Fe trader who loved mules and handled them expertly. As Johnston wrote, "Stewart's concern is always for the mules—he wastes no thought on the men." Thus coddled, the animals responded vigorously: "It was a noble sight to see those small, tough, earnest, honest Spanish mules, every nerve strained to the utmost, examples of obedience, and of duty performed under trying circumstances." As the result of Stewart's efficiency, the men could claim that theirs was the first wagon train to get to California that year—and the mules were still in good condition.

As an "ox man" we have Peter H. Burnett, of '43, later to be the first governor of the state of California. In his train were both oxen and mules, and he found the oxen "greatly superior." He narrated their virtues thus: "The ox is a most noble animal, patient, thrifty, durable, gentle, and easily driven, and does not run off. Those who come to this country will be in love with their oxen by the time they reach here."

The expression "dumb ox" is not found in diaries of the migration. Oxen seem to have been at least as intelligent as mules and much more so than most horses. They were individually named, and had personality. J. Q. Thornton, of '46, may be called to testify. He has left us the names and characters of the eight in his four yoke. There was Brady, who died at South Pass. Thornton called Star and Golden "unreliable," though perhaps they were just intelligent and strong-willed: they used to hide in the thickets at yoking-up time, and then look innocent when found. Thornton mentioned four others as being good enough and "tolerably honest"—Sam, John, Tom, and Nig. But his love was Dick, who was all that an ox ought to be and was labeled in one word: "faultless."

The long-continued case of *Mule v. Ox*, as J. S. Holliday points out in his doctoral dissertation, could never really be decided.

Numerically, however, the verdict was in favor of the ox. In 1850 a count at Fort Laramie showed 36,116 oxen passing through and only 7,548 mules—and the latter figure apparently included pack-train animals. Quite possibly the deciding factor was the expense. One price list of the period gives the cost of a mule as $75 and of an ox as $25. Though the prices varied from year to year, the ratio probably remained about the same. In the long run the use of oxen became so prevalent that "ox-team emigrant" became a generic term.

The number of oxen to the wagon varied considerably. Four—that is, two yoke—was the minimum. Three yoke was perhaps the average, but four was not uncommon; six yoke was probably the maximum that could be handled on the twisting mountain roads. The bigger teams could haul heavier loads, and the strain on the individual animal was less. On the other hand, the more animals, the more work to guard and care for them, and pasturage had to be found.

Generally some of the cattle—especially in trains that included children—were milch cows. These were usually just driven along, but sometimes were put under the yoke. Extra cattle were usually taken along as spares and for a supply of fresh meat, though some people thought that such a herd was more nuisance than it was worth. The total number of cattle was thus regularly about twice that of the men and women.

The fate of most of these faithful beasts was a sad one. Rare was the ox or cow that lived to a quiet and respected old age on the deep-grassed pastures of Oregon or California. Many of them were slaughtered on the trail for beef, and we can scarcely even imagine that the best-loved ones were spared the longest. There was little place for sentiment on the desert, and the ox that began to fail was undoubtedly the one to be butchered. Remembering, however, that the ancient Greeks sacrificed an ox only after ritual weeping for the death of "man's companion," we can believe that on Goose Creek or along the Humboldt there were sad thoughts in him who did the deed, and tears in women's eyes, and the wailing of children—and perhaps the beef did not sit well, even on a very empty stomach. Yet this was another virtue of the ox, that he could thus yield food. Of course, the mule also could be, and was, eaten—but always with prejudice.

To every ox slaughtered, however, a dozen or a score died of disease, of drinking alkali water, of Digger arrows, of thirst, or of slow starvation and overwork. Notations on dead oxen are a monotonous feature of the diaries. J. Goldsborough Bruff of '49, a great counter, kept busy during five days on the Rabbit Hole and Black Rock stretch in northwestern Nevada, where someone had left a posted notice on a bit of broken axle: *This is the place of destruction to team.* Bruff's total was 603 dead oxen.

Such mass catastrophe may not move us as much as the death of one known individual animal. We may quote James Mason's elegy of August 2, 1850, on Cassia Creek: "Here we lost old Sock. He died rather sudden. He was much lamented by the boys as he was our main Sanby [stand-by] at the start."

We should remember a little the faithful beasts that died. Sometimes they dropped under the yokes and were left lying. Often they were merely abandoned, standing, too weak to follow, left a prey to the wolves. Sometimes a kindly bullet finished the matter. Except for a little meat cut off for food, no one bothered with the carcasses; on some stretches they lay so thick that a blind man could have followed the trail by the stench. Then for a few years the skeletons lay dazzling white in the desert sun, pale white under the moon.

In reckoning the price of the land we might well be no less thoughtful of the animals than that kindhearted Lord, the God of heaven, when he spoke to Jonah of saving the men—and beasts—of Nineveh. Yes, in that reckoning of the price we might remember his final words: ". . . and also much cattle."

Thus, in the end, the covered wagon is to be considered a kind of double symbol—the wagon itself and the oxen that pulled it. With this equipment the epic movement was accomplished.

In 1841 came the first attempts—unsuccessful, in that the emigrants were forced to leave their wagons and proceed on horseback or muleback or afoot. In '42, the wagons got through to Oregon. In '43 came the great migration to Oregon, and Joe Walker made a gallant try for California, though in the end he had to leave the three wagons. At last in '44 Elisha Stevens broke the Sierra

barrier and took wagons across what would one day be called
Donner Pass.

Thus, the emigration first pointed toward Oregon, and the term
Oregon Trail has stuck. But from '46 onward, California tended to
steal the show. In '49 came the cataclysm of the Gold Rush, and for
a few years anyone going to Oregon was a curiosity. Indeed, '50 was
probably bigger than '49, and, according to some, '52 was the
biggest of all. The migration died down somewhat in the later fifties,
and Oregon began to get a better share again.

The "trail" it was called—seldom the "road." The distinction is
significant. "Trail," an Americanism in this sense, meant a route
of travel that had been established merely by use. "Road" was reserved
for something that had been definitely laid out and constructed, as was
Lander's Road from the Sweetwater River to Fort Hall.

In many places you can still see the trail, sometimes even
follow it for miles. Across the prairies and through the sagebrush
there was easy going. Even there, however, the trail never runs
straight, but always slightly sinuously—where the oxen of the lead
team adjusted their course to inequalities of ground or growth, and
where the following thousands, over two decades and more, kept to
the same trace.

The trail never follows the contours of a hill, because the
wagons had a high center of gravity and tipped easily, and because
the making of a "dugway" was too much work for the emigrants. But
almost no steepness of ascent deflects the trail, because the teams
could be doubled. Nor does a sharp downgrade: one, two, or all four
wheels could be locked, or the wagons could even be let down by
ropes snubbed around trees. Lakes and swampy places could be
skirted. Smaller streams were forded as a matter of course, the
difficulty of getting down the bank into the stream often being
greater than crossing it. Larger streams, up to about four feet in
depth, could also be forded. Across the deeper ones the wagon beds
were raised upon blocks set upon the axle and bolster, an uplift of
about a foot being considered safe. The few streams that were still
deeper had to be ferried, either by improvising rafts of logs or by
calking and floating the wagon beds.

To generalize about the conditions of the long trek is difficult.
The teams plodded monotonously westward. Heat, dust, and mosquitoes! Quarrels, resulting from too-long association in the same

company! But the emigrants (they were always "emigrants" and never "immigrants") remembered good times also—dancing on the prairie, singing around the campfire, exciting chases after buffalo, breathtaking first sights of the wonders of this new land: snow-covered peaks in July, boiling springs, mirages, ancient volcanic craters.

Some of the wagon people were both strong in body and exuberant in personality, and these traits shine through in their diaries like lamps burning steadily. Such a one was Thomas Turnbull of '52. Nothing downed his optimism and enthusiasm. It was always: "the best feed I mostly ever saw . . . plenty of wood here . . . the handsomest roads I ever saw . . . the best grass of every kind I ever saw in the United States . . . the best road I ever saw, as level as a plank." (But, to be sure, he could also go to superlatives in the opposite direction: "Mosquitoes the worst I ever saw.")

Another one was Lydia Waters of '55. Everything had equal zest for her—driving oxen, or herding the loose cattle, or presiding at a childbirth. She seems quite in character when comparing a wattled hut to a champagne basket. Again, when she crossed the Forty-Mile Desert, she did not write of hell. But on arriving at the Truckee River, she could put it thus: "If I ever saw Heaven, I saw it there." Naturally she was the one who could write in retrospect: "There were many things to laugh about."

Danger and death, like battles in a war, were always a nerve-gnawing possibility, but they occurred on very few days. From year to year, according to the conditions, the face of peril changed. The first trains had the hardest time because of sheer geographical ignorance and the necessity of breaking trail. Partly by skill and stamina, partly by good luck, they got through with remarkably few casualties. The greatest disaster, that of the Donner party, did not come until '46, and then as the result of human duplicity and fallibility, and an early winter. The Forty-niners followed a crowded trail; their cattle died from lack of pasturage.

In '49 and several subsequent years, cholera rode the wagons out onto the plains, and there came to be a string of graves along the trail. In the later fifties there were difficulties with white desperadoes; one group captured an entire train, and sent the people off westward on foot.

And, of course, there were the Indian troubles, which gave rise to the greatest myth of the trail. The wagon train of fiction—in Hough's *Covered Wagon*, for instance—moves from one desperate

Indian attack to another. The record, however, shows little of this sort. The trains actually moved only by favor and friendship of the powerful Plains tribes.

A moment's reflection should show that this must be true. When the Sioux, Cheyenne, and Arapaho really went to war in the sixties, they fought and sometimes defeated whole armies. What would they have done with a few emigrants?

The wagon trains seem to have interested and amused the Indians. (Doubtless, life in the tepee became monotonous at times.) Besides, the emigrants could be cajoled or scared into giving gifts, which the Indians probably considered a kind of tribute. The emigrants had much more trouble with the despised Diggers in the desert country than they ever had with the lordly Sioux. For one reason, the emigrants themselves were on their good behavior among the powerful tribes. No one in his right mind went about insulting or mistreating a Sioux in the land of his own strength. But in '45 a half-breed emigrant wantonly shot a Paiute. Probably there were also unrecorded atrocities, and from that time on there was trouble along the Humboldt. In '46 something of a pitched battle occurred, and one white man was killed. Emigrants learned not to camp within bowshot of the willows that fringed any stream. Otherwise they might wake up to find several oxen crippled by arrows, and perhaps the cattle guard himself laid out, agape at the morning sun. The emigrants were likely to retaliate by shooting on sight.

But all this is very different from the epic legend of the beleaguered wagon train. We all know the picture: the wagons are drawn up in a circle; from them the men fire their rifles; around the outside the mounted Indians circle on their horses, shooting with their bows.

How often did it happen? I have been reading covered-wagon records for a long time now. All I can say is that I have never found one such example.

We can see why, if we consider the realities. The Plains Indian was a good fighter, but he had no more liking than any other man for getting himself killed. Once a wagon train was in position, garrisoned by some determined riflemen, all the odds were against the Indian. The bullets far outranged his arrows, and he and his pony would have had little chance of even getting within bowshot of the enemy before being brought down. Why should any professional warrior thus gallop around and let himself be shot at? Why especially when he could just as well wait until the wagon train was strung out helplessly on the trail? The beleaguered wagon train is one part of the story which I think we shall have to give over to the writers of fiction.

Otherwise, I can see no reason to start debunking the covered-wagon story. It might even be built up a little. Its very audacity—an attempt to cross two thousand miles of wilderness—is breathtaking. Those who love to sing the praises of free enterprise should make more of it. Here was free enterprise at its rawest. Until the later fifties, the travelers got no appreciable government aid, not even for exploration. Except for the Mormons, there is nothing that can be called large-scale corporate action. The unit was the family.

In this last connection we come to another source of continuing interest in the story. The frontier, in most of its dramatic history, is a man's world. Exploration, trapping, Indian fighting—here the women and children had no place except by accident. Even in the mining camp and on the cattle ranch, women were so scarce that the novelist usually had to go to great trouble to import a schoolmarm or someone's far-strayed daughter. But the families were right there in the covered wagons—the women and children often outnumbering the men. And family life kept right on. If there was a preacher along, like the Reverend Mr. Dunleavy in '46, he was likely to be called upon not only for funerals but also for marriages. From the number of children born less than nine months after the arrival of the trains in Oregon or California, we should judge that the amenities of family life were not neglected during the journey. On the other hand, pregnancy was no bar against setting out. The Stevens party of '44 arrived stronger by two than when it left. Even that first migration, of '41, had a woman along. This was Mrs. Nancy Kelsey, a ripe eighteen years of age, who stated roundly, "Where my husband goes, I can go," and went—taking a baby with her. So did others—the women following their men, the children with them.

The graves of all three lined the trail. In the early years the herd was milled over a new-made grave or the wagons run across it, so that the Indians could not find it and dig the body up. In later years, when there were more emigrants and few Indians, little headboards or crosses of wood stood along the trail. But certainly we should not accept that slogan, "The weak died by the way." Since when did Death refuse to take the strong? They may go to him first by their very strength. So, sometimes, we think, reading the words that the keepers of the diaries copied down.

M. De Morst, of Col: Ohio,
died Sep. 16th. 1849
Aged 50 years, Of Camp Fever.

Jno A. Dawson, St. Louis, Mo.
Died Oct. 1st, 1849
from eating a poisonous root at the spring.

Mr. Eastman;—
The deceased was killed by
an Indian arrow; Octr. 4th, 1849

Saml. A. Fitzzimmons, died from
effects of a wound received from
a bowie-knife in the hands of Geo. Symington
Aug. 25th 1849

Died: "Of cholera . . . Of cholera . . . Of cholera." (That most often!) *Died*: "Of accidental discharge of his gun." *Died*: (there was a doctor in this company) "Disease, Gastro Enterites Typhoid." *Died*: "Of drowning." Often, simply: "Died."

Died: "From Southport, Wisconsin . . . Late of Galena, Ill. . . . Of Selma, Alabama . . . From Yorkshire, England . . . Of Buffalo, N.Y." *Died*: sometimes with only the name for identification.

Died: "Mrs. Mildred Moss, wife of D. H. T. Moss." *Died* (as if registering in some last hotel): "Robert Gilmore and wife." *Died*: "Frederic William, son of James M. and Mary Fulkerson." *Died* (two weeks farther westward): "Mary, consort of J. M. Fulkerson."

Died: "Mrs. Emmaline Barnes, Amanda and Mahela Robbins, three sisters in one grave, Indiana."

There were graves without names: "The remains of a dead man dug up by wolves, and reburied."

Some were laid in their graves succinctly, perhaps as time pressed; some were granted a few more words:

Samuel McFarlin, of Wright Co Mo. died
27th Sep. 1849, of fever, Aged, 44 years.—
*May he rest peaceably in this
savage unknown country*

Jno. Hoover, died, June 18. 49
Aged 12 yrs. Rest in peace,
sweet boy, for thy travels are over.

As Virgil wrote: *Tantae molis erat Romanam condere gentem.*
Yes, it was a great labor to establish the Roman people. So also it
was to pass the barrier of mountains and deserts and thus round out
the shape of a republic. The covered wagon stands as the symbol,
and we should not forget its dead. "All this too was part of the price
of the taking-over of the land."

Part V: Politicians and Reformers

The Rise of the Little Magician

Louis W. Koenig

Early one spring evening in 1829, a brougham, handsomely carved and immaculately kept, jogged at a dignified pace down Pennsylvania Avenue toward the White House. Within was a solitary figure sitting with the pompous grace of a Hindu rajah. He was the new Secretary of State, Martin Van Buren of New York, just arrived after a hard journey from Albany through the wilderness and cities of the seaboard. Recollections of that journey made his solitude welcome. He had much to think about. For the step he was to take this evening, in committing his services to the new President, defied the urgent warnings of many friends whose judgment he had leaned upon from the day he had become a figure in national politics. They considered him foolhardy to join this administration, and the force of their reasons still haunted his mind. The Cabinet, they unanimously contended, was packed with the minions of Vice President John C. Calhoun, who proposed to dominate the administration and advance ruthlessly to his long-cherished goal, the Presidency itself. In such company, Martin Van Buren and his political future would be hopelessly submerged.

The alarms of his friends were still ringing in Van Buren's ears even as his carriage entered the White House grounds and approached the front portico. A lackey was on hand to open the door and help him alight. The figure that emerged was in dress and form most outstanding—scarcely more than five and a half feet and free of the corpulence that afflicts middle age. It was a pleasantry of Washington society that he wore a corset. Everything about his features seemed exaggerated; his hair was emphatically yellow and curly, parted over the right temple and combed back in wavy masses, hiding his ears. His forehead was of great proportions. Red sideburns came to the point of his jaw. His long and aggressive Roman nose suggested the fox, and his guileless, deep-set blue eyes seemed to promise, as the mood required, easy laughter and prodigious determination. His clothes were a cartoonist's delight. For years his dandylike dress had been the butt of political broadsides, and on this evening he sustained his reputation: he wore a snuff-colored coat, white trousers, lace-tipped cravat, yellow gloves, and morocco shoes.

Into the White House this impeccable little creature walked, with light tiny steps. The doorman ushered him through the vestibule to the President's office and opened the door. In the dim light of the single candle that lit that enormous room, he saw a haggard face from which bereavement had drained all spirit. For Andrew Jackson had just buried his beloved wife, and that event—coupled with the torment of ceaseless physical illness—had left him with the countenance of Job: cadaverous eyes with anguished lines beneath them, and withered white hair. But when Jackson rose, there occurred a miraculous transformation from despair and exhaustion, and his affectionate and eager greeting melted every anxiety in Van Buren's mind. Leaving his own misfortunes unmentioned, Jackson inquired anxiously about Van Buren's recent illness and, noticing his weariness, insisted that all business be postponed until the next day. Paternally, he ordered Van Buren to bed. In that short interlude, from those few gestures, Van Buren considered his decision vindicated.

The new Secretary of State had been born December 5, 1782, in a long, low, one-and-a-half-story clapboard farmhouse in Kinderhook, New York. His parents were second-generation Dutch-Americans, who regularly spoke the ancestral language at the dinner table. The father, Abraham, a farmer and tavern operator, was one of the few local residents well-to-do enough to meet the stiff suffrage requirement—ownership of land valued at a hundred pounds over and above encumbrances. At school age, Martin was enrolled in the Kinderhook Academy, where he compiled a good record. His heart was set on entering Columbia College, when his father's finances went into an unexpected tailspin and the boy was forced to go to work. The change of plan left its scar. Forever after, Van Buren venerated the learning that had been denied him—so much so that he developed a conspicuous sense of intellectual inferiority.

His dandyish dress had origins in his youth, too. His schooling ended, family friends secured a clerkship for him in the offices of

Francis Sylvester, first lawyer of Kinderhook. Van Buren showed up for his job in coarse homespun linens and woolens made by his economy-minded mother. His employer, appalled by this ungainly apparition, finally took his clerk aside and ardently lectured him on the importance of proper dress. Next day Van Buren had undergone a sartorial transformation that left Sylvester gasping: he was decked out in a complete gentleman's outfit consisting of a black broad-brimmed cocked hat, a waistcoat with layers of frilly lace, velvet breeches, silken hose, and huge flashing silver buckles.

Although Van Buren rose rapidly in the legal profession, politics was his consuming passion. He so excelled at composing differences in the local Democratic caucus that he was rewarded with a major plum—election at twenty-six as surrogate of Columbia County. A year later, in 1809, he cut short his honeymoon with Hannah Hoes to go off into the deep snows for the hustings. In 1812, Van Buren was elected state senator.

Simultaneously, Van Buren was ascending to a leading place in party councils, owing not so much to his devotion to policy as to his gifts at political management. He presided over an enormously successful Democratic organization, the "Albany Regency," a handful of state leaders who traded jobs in the executive branch for votes in the legislature and made their bargains stick.

In 1821, after a term as New York's attorney general, Van Buren stepped onto the national political stage when the Regency boosted him into the United States Senate. By every appearance, his coming made no great splash. Though Van Buren toiled with exemplary diligence on the finance and judiciary committees, he became identified with no significant legislation. He spoke infrequently on the floor and seldom with much impact, his pianissimo style of oratory being hopelessly drowned out by the organ tones of titans like Daniel Webster, Robert Hayne, and John C. Calhoun.

As head of the prevailing party in New York, however, he became a leading influence in the congressional caucus and in the wide-open presidential race of 1824. In choosing among the many candidates entreating his support, Van Buren, in the manner of his hero, Thomas Jefferson, aimed to link the power of New York with that of the South. Accordingly he came out for the leading southern candidate, William H. Crawford, a Georgian who had been Secretary of the Treasury in the Monroe Cabinet.

Van Buren's first venture in the "art and business of President-making," as he called it, was totally disastrous. Hardly had Crawford announced his candidacy when he was felled by a general paralytic stroke. His nervous system was shattered; he permanently lost the use of his lower limbs and temporarily, his sight and speech. Still, pressed by Van Buren, Crawford stayed in the race. The candidate's distraught promoters labored overtime at hiding his distress from public view. He made no speeches; a tightly covered coach carried him about when travel was unavoidable. Whenever a meeting with impressionable visitors was necessary, they were ushered into a room so darkened by heavy curtains and dimmed lights that the pitiful Crawford, propped between several devoted associates, was scarcely visible. Hardly had a visitor settled into his chair when he was, on some pretext or other, whisked out. Notwithstanding these precautions, rumors got around that Crawford was a very sick man. In desperation, Van Buren attempted a bold eleventh-hour deal: he offered Henry Clay of Kentucky the Vice Presidency if he would support Crawford. Clay turned him down cold.

The sly maneuver and the ruthless machination provide the basis for much of Martin Van Buren's lasting political reputation. All his nicknames—and no other public figure in his time or perhaps since has had so many—betoken the unprincipled political trickster. "The Little Magician" and "the Red Fox of Kinderhook" he was first called in New York politics, and later "the American Talleyrand." DeWitt Clinton spoke of Van Buren as "the prince of villains" and "a confirmed knave." Calhoun, a later foe, said of him: "He is not . . . of the race of the lion or of the tiger; he belonged to a lower order—the fox."

In his private ruminations following the calamitous elections of 1824, Van Buren decided to hitch his wagon to the rising star of Andrew Jackson. In the three-way race among Jackson, Crawford, and John Quincy Adams, the hero of New Orleans had, after all, garnered the largest popular vote, and had lost to Adams only when the election was thrown into the House of Representatives. For the next several years, Van Buren worked quietly and successfully to bring the Crawford men into Jackson's fold. In 1828, Old Hickory triumphed at the polls and fittingly offered "the Magician," who in the same year became Governor of New York, the choicest spot in the new administration, the post of Secretary of State.

By every indication, Van Buren proposed to be far more than a mere presidential counselor: he intended to do nothing less than succeed General Jackson in the Presidency itself, and, everything considered, this steadily burning ambition was altogether reasonable. It was widely believed that Jackson did not have long to live. The creeping dropsy, the racking cough, the wizened frame signified a man whose days were numbered. There was, further, an enthralling statistic in Van Buren's favor: in the twenty-eight years subsequent to 1800, four secretaries of state had become President.

Van Buren was not the only party of interest hungering for the succession. His most redoubtable competitor was John C. Calhoun, a man of consuming drive, maturer national political experience, and wider public fame. The Van Buren-Calhoun competition was hardly a matter of conjecture; it was starkly manifested even before the inauguration when both camps launched a series of maneuvers designed to control the selection of the Cabinet. Van Buren trained his guns on the two departments richest in patronage, the Treasury and the Post Office. To his great chagrin, both posts went to loyal Calhounites. As Secretary of War, Jackson chose his longtime friend from Tennessee, John H. Eaton, whose preference between Van Buren and Calhoun was not at all clear. The two other members of the Cabinet, the Attorney General and the Secretary of the Navy, were mediocrities who, when the cards were down, were expected to throw in with Calhoun. However, Van Buren's companionship was much welcomed, both during business hours and after, by a President just emerging from the pit of tragedy. Van Buren was also a widower (Hannah had died in 1819), and Jackson found in him the solace of shared experience. The New Yorker was a constant visitor at the Executive Mansion. Unconstrained by the demands of family, he could respond to every beck and call.

Van Buren moved easily in the considerable circle of personalities residing in the White House. In its size and essential informality, the circle was unprecedented. Besides the President, it included his nephew and confidential secretary, the astute and discreet Andrew Jackson Donelson, and his wife Emily, a spare, aristocratic beauty who presided expertly as official White House hostess. Also in residence were the President's old friend and political bodyguard, William B. Lewis; Mrs. Donelson's attractive cousin, Mary Eastin (Van Buren's eldest son, Abraham, was courting her); and the President's adopted son, Andrew, and his family. Together, the several families contributed four children to the White House population. These were considerably augmented by other juveniles of the far-flung Jackson clan, who constantly visited the President.

Evening callers like Van Buren ordinarily found Jackson well attended in the family sitting room. Reposing in his easy chair, puffing gently on a great Powhatan pipe whose bowl rested upon his knees, Jackson was an island of composure in a sea of chaos. Children would be romping around the room, rolling, climbing, falling, and brawling while the adults were bravely trying to read, sew, or converse. Entering unannounced, Van Buren would retire to a corner with Jackson for conversation that was continually interrupted. After finishing with the President, Van Buren paid heed to the ladies, with whom he got on famously.

Jackson and his friend transacted most of their business not in their evening encounters, however, but in a reserved hour during the day. Every afternoon at about three thirty, Van Buren would meet Jackson at the White House, and the two would slip out the back door for a canter on horseback. Although he preferred a coach, Van Buren threw desire and comfort to the winds and acquired a trusty charger.

It was during such outings that the seed of Jackson's earlier invitation for Van Buren to function as general adviser and confidant was coming to real fruition. Anything and everything was discussed. Legislation, appointments to office, correspondence, messages to Congress—on such instruments of policy Van Buren constantly impressed his influence. Together with Lewis and Donelson, he was also functioning as a drafter of the President's speeches and messages. Jackson, from all indications, required considerable help along these lines. His prose tended to be abrupt and disconnected, his intelligence expressing itself in judgment rather than in analysis. But Van Buren's particular forte, on which Jackson relied most, whether in speech drafting or on other occasions of decision, was his skill in political tactics and in discerning the motives of men.

To the casual observer of the political scene, Washington, in the crisp autumn of 1829, glowed with serenity. This was a condition sedulously cultivated by the two contenders for the succession. Duff Green, editor of the administration organ, the *United States Telegraph*, appears to have been instructed by his *de facto* chief, Calhoun, to scotch all rumors of discord and to chant in his columns a steady song of bliss. Van Buren reciprocated by endorsing Green's appointment to the lush post of Public Printer. Toward Calhoun personally, Van Buren was sweetness itself. He wined and dined the Vice President and his family regularly, and in all other respects their dealings persisted, in Van Buren's phrase, on "a friendly and familiar footing."

Behind the façade of official beatific calm, Van Buren was advancing his fortunes with ruthless vigor. In private sessions with Jackson he was quietly but effectively taking over a principal source of power in the new administration: patronage. With his sure touch, he pursued the policy of holding dismissals of Adams' appointees to moderate numbers, on the assumption that the incumbent clerks were generally sympathetic to his cause, while the clamoring job-seekers were decidedly disposed toward Calhoun and the western faction of Jackson supporters.

Van Buren was also launching his moves against the Calhoun camp in another locale. Being an intensely social animal, the Secretary of State had become a major figure in Washington society, a tireless party-giver and partygoer, and it was in these enterprises that he found his finest opportunities to advance his long-range purposes. The situation that worked to his greatest profit was the marriage of Secretary of War Eaton to Mrs. Margaret "Peggy" O'Neale Timberlake on January 1, 1829.

The uncommonly beautiful Peggy was the daughter of a Washington tavernkeeper and the widow of a Navy purser who had allegedly committed suicide because of her extramarital flirtations. Her wedding to Eaton, which should have been an all-out social event, was boycotted en masse by proper and indignant capital ladies. At the inaugural dinner in March they would not speak to her, and Mrs. Calhoun established the precedent, which others quickly followed, of refusing to call on her. The President, gallant and sensitive to suffering femininity, became concerned. The lady herself, meanwhile, was facing up to the situation not like a frail violet but with the ferocity of a tigress. Given Mrs. Eaton's gameness, the President's interest, and the unyielding opposition of the Calhouns, Van Buren had all the ingredients of a highly profitable situation. He lost no time in exploiting it.

He proceeded to pay, as Jackson was to term it, "the most devoted and assiduous attention to Mrs. Eaton." While other Cabinet members were bulldozed by incensed wives and squeamish daughters into slighting the wife of the Secretary of War against the President's well-known wishes, the unattached Van Buren could maneuver as he pleased. He called on Mrs. Eaton. He gave parties in her honor. He prodded his friends, the British and the Russian ministers, both of whom were bachelors, to give dances at which the Secretary's lady was treated with pointed distinction.

L'affaire Eaton, strenuously fanned by the enterprising Van Buren, quickly became a roaring holocaust. It gutted the Cabinet. The President, who was choleric on the subject, called his Secretaries together and admonished them to order their wives to be hospitable to Mrs. Eaton. At another point, he proposed to fire a Secretary whose wife was one of the shriller buglers of the crusade against her. But Van Buren managed to pull the President off; there was bigger game to bag.

In the White House the ranks were bitterly divided. Although Jackson was pure loyalty to Mrs. Eaton, the Donelsons with equal conviction deemed her a terrible blot on the social register. Not only that, Mrs. Donelson was blaming Van Buren and Van Buren alone for keeping her there, and the intensity of her feelings was becoming increasingly apparent to him. Until these recent rending events, Emily Donelson had been his favorite companion at dances and dinners. Of late, however, she had become noticeably distant.

One evening Van Buren dropped in at the White House, as was his habit, for a chat with anyone who happened to be about the sitting room. Jackson, he was disappointed to find, was not there. But Emily Donelson and several of her friends were. After some small talk, she drew Van Buren aside and with deadly candor told him that she was puzzled about his disposition toward Mrs. Eaton and would appreciate having the point cleared up. Awkwardly and ingloriously, the trapped Van Buren squirmed out of the situation by declaring that he had an engagement for which he had to leave at once. Under Emily's exacting gaze, he felt compelled to add that he would be glad to discuss the subject further at their earliest mutual convenience. Emily insisted on a definite date.

At the appointed time, Van Buren and the piquant Mrs. Donelson commenced a long, lively discussion in the sitting room. Also on hand and quite alert was Emily's cousin, Mary Eastin, who shared her opinion of Mrs. Eaton. The discussion quickly became heated. Greatly affected, Miss Eastin withdrew to the embrasure of a nearby window, sobbing heavily. Alarmed by the deterioration of the situation, and even more concerned that Jackson might enter at any moment, Van Buren worked desperately to set things aright. He launched into a long, consoling monologue; the upshot was that Miss Eastin's tears were checked. Perhaps more important, Emily Donelson agreed that they should never discuss the subject again.

In the weeks that followed, Van Buren zealously plied the ruffled lady with attentions; the Donelsons, after all, were much too close to Jackson to be alienated. It worked. When Emily Donelson's first-born daughter was christened in an elaborate ceremony at the White House, the mother had the pick of Washington's manpower in selecting godfathers for her child; the two she unhesitatingly chose were the President and her recent antagonist, Mr. Van Buren.

A new and momentous issue now rose to restore Martin Van Buren's still uncertain fortunes. While the Eaton affair was running its merry pace, the country's attention was turning to the infinitely more complex and menacing issue of nullification. Nothing less than the safety and future of the Union turned on the outcome. The igniting spark had been provided by the Tariff Act of 1828—"the tariff of abominations" it was called in the South—the last of a series of acts discriminating strongly against that region. In Calhoun's own state of South Carolina, men spoke openly of declaring the act to be null and void and making Charleston a free port; Calhoun himself was nullification's most articulate advocate.

Andrew Jackson was slow to speak out publicly on the great issue until it squarely confronted him. The occasion was Thomas Jefferson's birthday anniversary—April 13, 1830. In the four years since his death it had not been the object of any special celebration, however much Jefferson was venerated by his countrymen and the party he had founded. Now, however, Senators Thomas Hart Benton of Missouri and Robert Hayne of South Carolina proposed a grand subscription dinner, ostensibly to remedy this oversight. To Van Buren, the plot was clear. The celebration, he told Jackson, would be used as "a stalking horse" for linking Jefferson's prestige to the current doctrines expounded by Calhoun and Hayne.

When Van Buren, with Jackson and Donelson, joined the nearly one hundred celebrants in the dining hall of Brown's Indian Queen Hotel on April 13, they found the atmosphere already decidedly chilly. Van Buren quickly discovered the cause when he picked up from one of the tables a card on which had been printed the formal toasts to be offered in the course of the evening. It was clear at a glance that the banquet hall would resound with sentiments dear to the nullifiers. Only a few minutes before the arrival of the presidential party, the Pennsylvania delegation, taking one look at the toast cards, had walked out in a pique. Several other delegations were feverishly conferring on the same decision. The Marine band, meanwhile, was blaring away with extra vigor to drown out the rising tension.

Somehow the meal began and passed without incident. Then, after what seemed interminable preliminaries, the toast of the President of the United States was called for. The room crackled with expectation. The short-statured Van Buren, his view hopelessly blocked by the crowd, climbed up on a chair to observe the President. Jackson at last rose. In a voice rough with defiance, he declared, "Our Union: It must and shall be preserved." Without a word more, he lifted his glass as a sign that the toast was to be drunk standing. Chairs scraped and there was a hum of excited whispering as the company rose. Calhoun stood with them. "His glass," noticed a nearby participant, "trembled in his hand and a little of the amber fluid trickled down the side."

The fight was now in the open. A visitor to the Senate gallery observed, not long after, that the Vice President seemed "more wrinkled and careworn that I had expected from his reputed age. . . . His voice is shrill. . . . His manners have in them an uneasiness, a hurried, incoherent air." With the stealth and evil grace of the fox, Van Buren came in for the kill. His route was typically circuitous, and the weapon he counted upon to destroy Calhoun was a letter. It was a very special letter, solicited by Van Buren's trusted aide, James A. Hamilton, and written long ago by William H. Crawford while serving as Secretary of the Treasury in the Cabinet of James Monroe.

Secretary Crawford's letter centered upon a climactic episode of the Seminole Indian War in 1818, when Jackson as commanding general in the field invaded Florida without consulting President Monroe and seized the Spanish forts of St. Marks and Pensacola. To the nation, Jackson was instantaneously a hero; to the President he was arrant and insubordinate. Monroe took up the problem with his Cabinet. There, according to the Crawford letter, John C. Calhoun, then Secretary of War, forthrightly recommended that General Jackson be arrested and punished.

The letter, which had been retrieved from an old trunk in Crawford's Georgia home, reached Jackson via a number of trusted hands, including those of Van Buren's faithful White House ally, W. B. Lewis. Through Lewis, the letter finally came to Donelson and thence to the President. Jackson, to whom the disclosures were not altogether a surprise—only recently he had discussed the entire incident with ex-President Monroe himself—was still seething from the Jefferson Day dinner. The evidence is impressive that he desired to strike further at Calhoun, and Van Buren's conveniently timed skulduggery gave him a pretext for doing so. The President, accordingly, lost no time in dispatching a peremptory request to Calhoun to explain his conduct in the Monroe Cabinet. In a painstaking answer of some fifty-two pages, the Vice President freely admitted the charges, defended his own conduct, and condemned Crawford for betraying the secrets of the Cabinet. Evidently eager to keep the fight going, Jackson tartly informed Calhoun that his reply was unsatisfactory. Their break was now complete.

Although Calhoun was now in full eclipse, Van Buren's own situation was not without peril. The Cabinet was still strongly pro-Calhoun; the Eaton affair was still roaring along. Calling upon all his skill at co-ordinating seemingly disparate forces, Van Buren hit upon a bit of vivid dramaturgy designed to solve the Eaton affair, reconstitute the Cabinet, and project himself before the public as a selfless magistrate dedicated to the commonweal.

The crux of the plan entailed nothing less than his resigning as Secretary of State, ostensibly for so noble a purpose as the peace and welfare of the administration. His real object was to compel not only the resignation of Eaton but that of Calhoun's supporters in the Cabinet.

With Calhoun out of the way, he need no longer be on hand at the White House to protect his interests and could afford at least a brief absence from that arena of destiny. As a place of temporary refuge once he had resigned, Van Buren fixed his enterprising gaze upon a post outside the country, the ministership to Great Britain, rich in prestige and far from the tumult of Washington. He packed his bag of tricks and waited for an opportune moment to break the news to Jackson. He struggled unavailingly for weeks to muster his courage, so fearful was he of the General's reaction. Finally, Van Buren came to grips with fate while horseback riding with the President one afternoon through Georgetown and down the Tenallytown road. The subject under discussion was the Eatons and the disintegration of the Cabinet. Van Buren somehow managed to seize the gaping opening and blurted out nervously: "No, General, there is but one thing can give you peace!"

"What is that, sir?"

"My resignation."

The President, in Van Buren's word, "blanched." "Never, sir," replied Jackson with peremptory vigor. "Even you know little of Andrew Jackson if you suppose him capable of consenting to such humiliation of his friends by his enemies."

For hours that day and next, Van Buren sought to justify his course to the President. As the discussion wore on inconclusively into the late afternoon of the second day, the western circle—Lewis, Eaton, and Postmaster General Barry—was called in. There was more discussion, equally futile, whereupon Van Buren invited the three westerners to his home for dinner. Along the way, Eaton suddenly stopped as though transfixed. It was wrong for Van Buren, "the most valuable member of the Cabinet," to resign, he exclaimed. Then, after a breath, tumbled out the statement for which the Magician had so expertly and painstakingly built the foundations in the discussions through the long afternoon. It was he, Eaton, who should resign. He, not Van Buren, had brought the administration its woe.

For a long moment no one spoke, a hiatus that must have seemed like ages to Eaton, if he was waiting for someone to say that he was mistaken, that he too was indispensable. No one did, and Van Buren, after a decent interval, swooped in with the clinching blow. "What about Mrs. Eaton?" he asked with quiet finality. The Secretary of War managed to mumble that he was sure she would not object. Within a matter of days Eaton sent in his resignation, and Van Buren's quickly followed. When the President and Van Buren, now the minister-designate to England, went around to the departing Eatons one day to pay their respects, Peggy was decidedly chilly.

The remainder of the Cabinet, as Van Buren had hoped, likewise resigned. As he had also calculated, the reconstituted Cabinet was predominantly loyal to himself. Thereupon he took off for England, bearing a presidential recess appointment, and fell avidly to work in London, having exceptionally long and cordial audiences with King William IV and the royal ministers. With Washington Irving, first secretary of the United States legation, he became fast friends, but best of all, he was sustained by the obvious fact that Jackson missed his counsel. "Any suggestions which your leisure will permit," wrote the President, "you may choose to make on any subject will be kindly received." And in another dispatch, "I am . . . anxious to have you near me."

Jackson's prayer for Van Buren's homecoming was suddenly, and not altogether unexpectedly, answered by no less an agency than the United States Senate. Van Buren's being a recess appointment, Jackson passed along his name to the Senate when the regular legislative session commenced in December. The titans of Capitol Hill, Calhoun, Clay, and Webster, smarting under Van Buren's unchecked rise, were sharpening their claws for vengeance. Burying momentarily their own past differences, these doughty individualists united to consign the nomination to slow death.

Three months dragged by before Van Buren's name was even referred to the Foreign Relations Committee, a step which under normal circumstances was instantaneous. In the committee and on the Senate floor, a long, mudslinging discussion ensued, linking Van Buren with every known evil of the day. A special strategy was concocted to subject the minister-designate to the most excruciating humiliation. The remaining cards were played: his nomination was reported out favorably by the Foreign Relations Committee, and when the floor vote was taken, it resulted, by careful prearrangement, in a tie.

The situation called for John Calhoun, as Vice President of the United States and President of the Senate, to cast the deciding vote. Preening himself under the clamorous encouragement of the onlooking senators, Calhoun committed his long-awaited act of revenge, and voted against Van Buren. The Senate rang with cheers, as the crowd does when the matador makes his death thrust at the fallen bull. In the exhilaration of accomplishment, the Vice President was heard to declare, "It will kill him, sir, kill him dead. He will never kick, sir, never kick."

But Calhoun's victory was short-lived. The stab in the back only succeeded in incensing the local party organizations, which viewed the Senate's action as a gross personal injustice and a travesty on party integrity, and all but clinched the vice presidential nomination for Van Buren. The first national convention of the Democratic party, which assembled in Baltimore on May 21, 1832, unanimously nominated Van Buren on the second ballot. The Magician, spurned in Washington, was now redeemed in Baltimore.

With characteristic foresight, Van Buren had long had in readiness a central issue for the ensuing electoral campaign. His circling eye had alighted on the mighty financial fortress of the Bank of the United States. Chartered in 1816 for a period of twenty years, the Bank was predominantly private in character, with but one-fifth of its capital subscribed by the federal government. But it was the depository of government funds; by demanding or threatening to demand specie for the state bank notes it took in, or by refusing to take them altogether, the great Bank exercised a powerful check upon state banking activity.

In terms of the political necessities of Martin Van Buren, a fight with the Bank of the United States had great allure. His popularity would surely rise. Operating free of the safety-fund requirements imposed by state law upon New York banks, and having its headquarters in Philadelphia, the Bank of the United States made that city the financial capital of the country. New York—its manufacture, trade, and population soaring—was chafing to wrest supremacy from Philadelphia. In the South, Van Buren's supporters could be counted on to jump at the opportunity to avenge their states' rights principles by exterminating a major national institution like the Bank. But to Van Buren the most valuable feature of the Bank was its unpopularity in the West, where it was hated and feared.

As early as December 8, 1829, in his annual message to Congress, Jackson had openly expressed his hostility to the Bank. Meanwhile Van Buren was assaulting it by less direct means. Although he never discussed the Bank publicly or even in his most confidential letters, his trusted lieutenant, James A. Hamilton, busied himself for weeks at Jackson's side arranging the details of a new banking structure. Van Buren himself was quietly working with Amos Kendall, a leading westerner whose influence in the administration was rocketing. A journalist with a gift for piercing invective, he occupied the nominal post of Fourth Auditor of the Treasury, but devoted most of his energies to major drafting chores around the White House.

Not all the maneuvering concerning the Bank was going on at the White House. Henry Clay, his presidential ambitions charged with a new intensity, also regarded it as a useful issue. He prodded the Bank into directing its lieutenants in the House of Representatives to introduce legislation on January 6, 1832, providing for recharter. The great Bank dispatched its shrewdest lobbyists to Washington, and Daniel Webster and John Calhoun added their might and prestige to Clay's cause. Recharter passed both houses of Congress by comfortable margins in the summer of 1832.

By this time Martin Van Buren, having lost his job in London, had returned to the United States. Indeed, he managed to reach Washington by stage on Sunday, July 8, just as the presidential veto, which Jackson had ordered prepared, was being put into final shape. The little band of draftsmen still were hard at it when Van Buren rolled up to the White House portico in his brougham. The President, who was ailing, welcomed him in his bedroom. "Holding my hand in one of his own," the anxious Van Buren later reported, "and passing the other thro' his long white locks, he said, with the clearest indications of a mind composed, and in a tone entirely devoid of passion or bluster—'the bank, Mr. Van Buren, is trying to kill me, *but I will kill it!*' " After fittingly acknowledging his agreement, Van Buren was installed as a guest in the bedroom recently vacated by Sarah Yorke Jackson, the President's favorite daughter-in-law.

The Bank's supporters contended that Van Buren—"before he could unpack his bags"—was put to work polishing up the veto for transmittal to Congress early the next morning. Plainly bearing the touch of a practiced political hand, the veto ultimately prevailed in Congress. In the subsequent presidential campaign, the Jackson-Van Buren ticket triumphed mightily.

The onrushing events in South Carolina, meanwhile, had reached a point of alarming deterioration. The nullifiers had called a special convention and swiftly passed an ordinance holding the existing tariff laws unconstitutional and not binding upon the state. Outright secession was boldly threatened. Jackson responded by dispatching a naval force to Charleston. When the more rabid nullifiers cried out for troops to be raised to "defend" the state, Jackson countered by ordering the federal garrison at Charleston alerted and dispatched General Winfield Scott to take command.

Martin Van Buren, for his part, found himself caught in a vise. At opposite and seemingly irreconcilable extremes of the nullification controversy were the two principal claimants to his loyalty, his party following in the South and Andrew Jackson. If he pleased Jackson, he would displease the southern element of his party, and vice versa.

The line Van Buren proceeded to follow was heralded by the substance of the toast he had offered at the famous Jefferson Day dinner. "Mutual forbearance and reciprocal concessions," he had said, "thro' their agency the Union was established—the patriotic spirit from which they emanated will forever sustain it." Now, late in 1832, Van Buren toiled busily applying his formula for peace. In private letters to his southern friends, he forthrightly disapproved the nullification doctrine. In counsel to Jackson, he tirelessly sought to reduce the intensity of the conflict, or at least head off measures threatening to aggravate it.

While flagging down the President, Van Buren was eyeing the tariff laws for possible reforms as the most promising solution to the nullification crisis. To avoid antagonizing the Calhounites, whose natural interests favored tariff reduction but whose zest for vengeance might tempt them to reject anything identified with himself, Van Buren worked secretly through Congressman Gulian Crommelin Verplanck, Chairman of the House Ways and Means Committee, an independent not previously identified with Van Buren's enterprises.

After weeks of intensive work, Verplanck emerged with a bill to which southerners of all camps so warmed that Van Buren began openly and confidently identifying himself as its real instigator. He stood at the brink of new fame. If the bill passed—and according to every indication it would—the Magician would surely be hailed as "the Great Compromiser." For the first time in his career he would gain a genuine national popularity among a people who desperately did not want a civil war.

The serene progress of Van Buren's plans was suddenly and unexpectedly throttled. His mighty rivals—Clay and Calhoun—met and decided that at any cost the indomitable palace politician must not become a popular hero. So anxious was Clay to block Van Buren that he put aside his long-standing high-tariff convictions and introduced his own reform bill. His object, plainly, was to snatch away the accolade of "Compromiser" from the grasping hands of Van Buren. Although Clay's tariff bill called for only a portion of the cuts that Verplanck had proposed, militant southerners, led in both houses of Congress by John Calhoun, rallied around Clay. The Clay-Calhoun juggernaut swept the Kentuckian's measure into enactment.

While events were reaching their climax behind the scenes in Washington, state legislatures in both North and South were passing resolutions disavowing the nullifiers and assuring the President of their support. In conspicuous contrast, Van Buren's own state organization in Albany was discreetly tight-lipped, fearful of offending their hero's southern followers. Meanwhile, the New York Whigs, led by two wily rising politicos, William H. Seward and Thurlow

Weed, put Van Buren squarely on the spot by introducing their own resolutions into the state legislature, approving Jackson's proclamation in lavish terms.

The Red Fox was trapped; the kill seemed near. Van Buren could not avoid taking a stand, and whatever he did would be ruinous. If he supported the resolution, he would break up his party and lose his status as Jackson's most likely successor. If he opposed it, he risked breaking with Jackson. As always, Van Buren chose his party. He prepared a resolution forthrightly taking issue with the "history given by the President on the formation of our Government." Accompanying it was a labored report expounding a states' rights position which would hardly fail to please his most fastidious southern supporters.

To Jackson he forwarded the resolution, the report, and a letter of explanation. Upon receiving the documents, an eyewitness reported, Jackson perused them thoroughly, drawing hard all the while on his Powhatan pipe. Then, without comment, he handed them over to his secretary for filing.

It was Van Buren's expectation and hope that the veto would bring down the curtain on the drama of the United States Bank until 1836, when its charter was due to expire. Further warfare upon the Bank would clearly invite serious dislocation of the economy and gravely endanger his own prospects for the Presidency. But his policy of passivity quickly ran into an unyielding wall: Amos Kendall. Kendall argued that the Bank, with its huge assets and far-flung branches, was capable of enormous self-interested maneuver. He proposed that the government remove its very large deposits of funds. Kendall was so convincing that Jackson in March of 1833 instructed his aide to draft a withdrawal request to the Secretary of the Treasury, Louis McLane. Encouraged by Van Buren, McLane forthrightly opposed the request.

Van Buren himself met Kendall head-on at a White House "family dinner." During the meal, the New Yorker protested with hearty candor that the removal plan would start a needless fight entailing grave risks for the administration and the party. The ordinarily mild Kendall rose from the table in great excitement. In a voice taut with anger, he said that under Van Buren's policy the Bank would surely win and that faced with the certainty of that dismal prospect, he and other administration journalists might as well lay down their pens. "I can live under a corrupt despotism as well as any other man by keeping out of its way," exclaimed Kendall, resuming his seat. As the evening wore on, Van Buren concluded that Jackson was unmistakably veering toward Kendall's plan. The Vice President of the United States found it politic to apologize fully to the Fourth Auditor of the Treasury and assume blame for the unfortunate incident.

In June of 1833, the Cabinet was reorganized. McLane stepped up as Secretary of State and handpicked the new Secretary of the Treasury, the little-known William J. Duane, primarily for his proven loyalty to Van Buren's interests. These, to be sure, had been undergoing redefinition. Convinced that Jackson was unalterably in favor of withdrawing the government's funds, Van Buren was now arguing that he should not do so until after Congress reconvened, for the statute governing removal seemed to require congressional approval. Kendall, however, in a counterthrust, proposed that removal be accomplished by executive fiat *before* Congress met, rather than risk the embarrassment of legislative defeat. The President again sided with Kendall and on June 26 ordered Duane to arrange the removal. For weeks, the Secretary ingeniously dillydallied, shielded by Van Buren. The latter's friends, Washington Irving and James Gordon Bennett, editor of the New York *Enquirer*, were convinced that Kendall was craftily employing the Bank issue to throttle Van Buren's presidential hopes.

By late summer, Jackson had come around fully to the position of Kendall and his allies, Attorney General Roger Taney and Frank Blair, a leading administration penman. The government's deposits, the President decreed, were to be removed from the great Bank well before Congress reconvened. With this policy settled and ready for launching, the support of Van Buren and his party following was imperative. It was high time to crack down, which Jackson proceeded to do by directing a strong letter to the Vice President, then sojourning in Albany. "It is already hinted," the President wrote bluntly on August 16, 1833, "that you are opposed to the removal of the Deposits, and of course privately a friend to the Bank. *This must be removed* or it will do us both much *harm*."

Van Buren's response was mellifluously noncommittal; Jackson requested that he return to Washington at once. Van Buren, at this moment with Washington Irving on a month's tour of the old Dutch settlements on the North River and Long Island, begged off. While Van Buren pored over Long Island antiquities, the bank crisis rushed towards its climax. Duane was fired, and Attorney General Taney, who took over the Treasury via a recess appointment, promptly announced that the government would cease placing deposits in the Bank of the United States after September 30. When Congress finally reconvened, the pro-Bank majority in the Senate retaliated by refusing to approve Taney's appointment to the Treasury.

Van Buren quickly readjusted his own line to the changing situation by writing to the President, lavishing praise upon his course of action. "I now invite you here," Jackson magnanimously responded. "I have my dear Sarah's room prepared for you, until your own House can be put in order."

For all of his tempestuous interludes and narrow squeaks, the Magician emerged with the hard core of his fortunes intact. No unmendable schisms rent his following. The President still counted him as the heir apparent. Van Buren duly captured the Democratic presidential nomination in May of 1835 and swept on to victory at the polls.

On March 4, 1837, the scepter passed. The day was bright, glistening with the exhilaration of spring and the sense of renewal implicit in an inauguration. Seated side by side in the carriage Constitution, drawn by the famous grays, were the outgoing President and his confidential adviser and chosen successor. After a dignified passage down Pennsylvania Avenue, the two men on whom all interest centered appeared on the east portico of the Capitol. Below was a vast crowd wedged breathlessly together, faces upturned—"a field," said one observer, "paved with human faces." They were silent, still and reverent. The inaugural proceeded. The Chief Justice of the United States stepped forward to administer the oath to the President-elect. The new President began delivering his message, but its urbane substance was lost in the droning monotone of his speaking style. No cheers interrupted it; the applause at the end was polite but unenthusiastic.

The old General, now divested of power, rose to descend the broad steps of the portico to take his seat in the carriage. The feelings of the crowd, so long restrained, rolled forth like a giant thunderclap. The cheers burst and burst again from three thousand hearts. The new President descended too, but he was all but unnoticed and forgotten. All eyes were on General Jackson as he uncovered and bowed, the wind stirring his silver locks. A part, indeed a substantial part, of the tribute being paid the General and his outgoing administration belonged to the unnoticed men behind him, and

Jackson, more than anyone, knew it. But the crowd did not know, and never would know. Martin Van Buren, on his most glorious day, the day for which he had plotted and gambled and maneuvered and flattered for eight anxious years, was paying the price for the secrecy of his success in the palace shadows. "For once," as Thomas Hart Benton remarked, "the rising was eclipsed by the setting sun."

Memorial of the Cherokee Nation (1830)

We are aware that some persons suppose it will be for our advantage to remove beyond the Mississippi. We think otherwise. Our people universally think otherwise. Thinking that it would be fatal to their interests, they have almost to a man sent their memorial to Congress, deprecating the necessity of a removal. . . . We are not willing to remove; and if we could be brought to this extremity, it would be not by argument, not because our judgment was satisfied, not because our condition will be improved; but only because we cannot endure to be deprived of our national and individual rights and subjected to a process of intolerable oppression.

We wish to remain on the land of our fathers. We have a perfect and original right to remain without interruption or molestation. The treaties with us, and laws of the United States made in pursuance of treaties, guaranty our residence and our privileges, and secure us against intruders. Our only request is, that these treaties may be fulfilled, and these laws executed.

But if we are compelled to leave our country, we see nothing but ruin before us. The country west of the Arkansas territory is unknown to us. From what we can learn of it, we have no prepossessions in its favor. All the inviting parts of it, as we believe, are preoccupied by various Indian nations, to which it has been assigned. They would regard us as intruders, and look upon us with an evil eye. The far greater part of that region is, beyond all controversy, badly supplied with wood and water; and no Indian tribe can live as agriculturists without these articles. All our neighbors, in case of our removal, though crowded into our near vicinity, would speak a language totally different from ours, and practice different customs. The original possessors of that region are now wandering savages lurking for prey in the neighborhood. They have always been at war, and would be easily tempted to turn their arms against peaceful emigrants. Were the country to which we are urged much better than it is represented to be, and were it free from the objections which we have made to it, still it is not the land of our birth, nor of our affections. It contains neither the scenes of our childhood, nor the graves of our fathers. . . .

Such we deem, and are absolutely certain, will be the feelings of the whole Cherokee people, if they are forcibly compelled, by the laws of Georgia, to remove; . . . We have been called a poor, ignorant, and degraded people. We certainly are not rich; nor have we ever boasted of our knowledge, or our moral or intellectual elevation. But there is not a man within our limits so ignorant as not to know that he has a right to live on the land of his fathers, in the possession of his immemorial privileges, and that this right has been acknowledged and guaranteed by the United States; nor is there a man so degraded as not to feel a keen sense of injury, on being deprived of this right and driven into exile. . . .

Indian Removal Defended (1830)

Andrew Jackson

It gives me pleasure to announce to Congress that the benevolent policy of the Government, steadily pursued for nearly thirty years, in relation to the removal of the Indians beyond the white settlements is approaching to a happy consummation. Two important tribes have accepted the provision made for their removal at the last session of Congress, and it is believed that their example will induce the remaining tribes also to seek the same obvious advantages.

The consequences of a speedy removal will be important to the United States, to individual States, and to the Indians themselves. The pecuniary advantages which it promises to the Government are the least of its recommendations. . . . It will separate the Indians from immediate contact with settlements of whites; free them from the power of the States; enable them to pursue happiness in their own way and under their own rude institutions; will retard the progress of decay, which is lessening their numbers, and perhaps cause them gradually, under the protection of the Government and through the influence of good counsels, to cast off their savage habits and become an interesting, civilized, and Christian community. These consequences, some of them so certain and the rest so probable, make the complete execution of the plan sanctioned by Congress at their last session an object of much solicitude. . . .

The present policy of the Government is but a continuation of the same progressive change by a milder process. The tribes which occupied the countries now constituting the Eastern States were annihilated or have melted away to make room for the whites. The waves of population and civilization are rolling to the westward, and we now propose to acquire the countries occupied by the red men of the South and West by a fair exchange, and, at the expense of the United States, to send them to a land where their existence may be prolonged and perhaps made perpetual. Doubtless it will be painful to leave the graves of their fathers; but what do they more than our ancestors did or than our children are now doing? . . . Can it be cruel in this Government when, by events which it can not control, the Indian is made discontented in his ancient home, to purchase his lands, to give him a new and extensive territory, to pay the expense of his removal, and support him a year in his new abode? How many thousands of our own people would gladly embrace the opportunity of removing to the West on such conditions! . . .

   . . . Rightly considered, the policy of the General Government toward the red man is not only liberal, but generous. . . . In the consummation of a policy originating at an early period, and steadily pursued by every Administration within the present century—so just to the States and so generous to the Indians—the Executive feels it has a right to expect the cooperation of Congress and of all good and disinterested men.

Veto of the Bank Recharter Bill (1832)

Andrew Jackson

The bill "to modify and continue" the act entitled "An act to incorporate the subscribers to the Bank of the United States" was presented to me on the 4th July instant. Having . . . come to the conclusion that it ought not to become a law, I herewith return it to the Senate, in which it originated, with my objections.

The present corporate body enjoys an exclusive privilege of banking under the authority of the General Government, a monopoly of its favor and support, and, as a necessary consequence, almost a monopoly of the foreign and domestic exchange. The powers, privileges, and favors bestowed upon it in the original charter, by increasing the value of the stock far above its par value, operated as a gratuity of many millions to the stockholder. . . .

. . . It is not our own citizens only who are to receive the bounty of our Government. More than eight millions of the stock of this bank are held by foreigners. By this act the American Republic proposes virtually to make them a present of some millions of dollars . . . .

If we must have a bank with private stockholders, every consideration of sound policy and every impulse of American feeling admonishes that it should be purely American. Its stockholders should be composed exclusively of our own citizens, who at least ought to be friendly to our Government and willing to support it in times of difficulty and danger. . . .

The Bank is professedly established as an agent of the Executive Branch of the government, and its constitutionality is maintained on that ground. Neither upon the propriety of present action nor upon the provisions of this act was the Executive consulted. It has had no opportunity to say that it neither needs nor wants an agent clothed with such powers and favored by such exemptions. There is nothing in its legitimate functions which makes it necessary or proper. Whatever interest or influence, whether public or private, has given birth to this act, it cannot be found either in the wishes or necessities of the Executive Department, by which present action is deemed premature, and the powers conferred upon its agent not only unnecessary but dangerous to the government and country. . . .

It is to be regretted that the rich and powerful too often bend the acts of government to their selfish purposes. Distinctions in society will always exist under every just government. Equality of talents, of education, or of wealth cannot be produced by human institutions. In the full enjoyment of the gifts of heaven and the fruits of superior industry, economy, and virtue, every man is equally entitled to protection by law.

But when the laws undertake to add to these natural and just advantages artificial distinctions, to grant titles, gratuities, and exclusive privileges, to make the rich richer and the potent more powerful, the humble members of society—the farmers, mechanics, and laborers—who have neither the time nor the means of securing like favors to themselves, have a right to complain of the injustice of their government.

There are no necessary evils in government. Its evils exist only in its abuses. If it would confine itself to equal protection, and, as heaven does its rains, shower its favors alike on the rich and the poor, it would be an unqualified blessing. In the act before me there seems to be a wide and unnecessary departure from these just principles. . . .

Experience should teach us wisdom. Most of the difficulties our government now encounters, and most of the dangers which impend over our Union, have sprung from an abandonment of the legitimate objects of government by our national legislation, and the adoption of such principles as are embodied in this act. Many of our rich men have not been content with equal protection and equal benefits, but have besought us to make them richer by act of Congress. By attempting to gratify their desires we have in the results of our legislation arrayed section against section, interest against interest, and man against man, in a fearful commotion which threatens to shake the foundations of our Union.

The Know-Nothing Uproar

Ray Allen Billington

The congressional and state elections of 1854 and 1855 witnessed one of the most remarkable political upheavals in the nation's history. Candidates whose names were not even on ballots were thrust into office; others who had been given no chance to win triumphed over long-established favorites; and a political party that had operated in such secrecy that few knew its name and still fewer its true purposes was catapulted into control in a half dozen states, won a strong minority place in several others, and seemed destined to capture the White House in 1856. More remarkable still, the political infant that accomplished these miracles was dedicated to principles that were basically un-American, for its sole claim to popular favor rested on its pledge to check the growth of the Catholic Church and foreign immigration. As befitted such a party, its history was mercifully brief. Yet the racial and religious hatreds that found expression in its short-lived triumphs reached deep into the American past and were rooted in a surprisingly large number of people. The two incidents that started their spread a generation before they found political manifestation during the 1850's were surprisingly trivial, yet they were of the sort that often alters the lives of men or nations. One concerned a hat, the other a slate pencil.

The hat belonged to Samuel F. B. Morse, and was clapped firmly on his head on a bright June day in 1830 as he watched a papal procession wend its way through the streets of Rome. As a New England Puritan Morse had little love for Catholicism, but as an artist he admired its pomp and pageantry—until that day, that is. For, as he watched, his hat was suddenly struck from his head by a soldier, or rather (as he recorded in his diary that night) "by a poltroon in a soldier's costume, and this courteous manoeuvre was accompanied with curses and taunts and the expression of a demon in his countenance." That this ill-mannered gesture should be blamed on the soldier never occurred to Morse. "The blame," he wrote, "lies after all not so much with the pitiful wretch who perpetrates this outrage, as it does with those who gave him such base and indiscriminate orders." From that day the artist inventor was a sworn enemy of Romanism, and he carried that enmity back to America.

Returning to New York at the end of his grand tour, Morse hurried into print to warn his countrymen of the insidious papal designs on the United States. His essays were later published in two volumes: *Foreign Conspiracy Against the Liberties of the United States* and *Imminent Dangers to the Free Institutions of the United States through Foreign Immigration*. European despots, he told his thousands of readers, were trembling lest the democratic institutions of America inspire revolts on the part of their own peoples. These institutions could not be overthrown by arms, for the United States was too powerful; hence monarchs had allied with the Catholic Church, which Morse considered a giant religious despotism, to dispatch its servile minions across the Atlantic, disguised as immigrants, until they were numerous enough to seize control. "You," he thundered to his fellow Americans, "are marked for their prey, not by foreign bayonets, but by *weapons surer of effecting the conquest of liberty* than all the munitions of physical combat in the military or naval storehouses of Europe." Only by closing the gates to those immigrants, Morse believed, could America be saved.

The slate pencil that reshaped the course of history was accidentally rammed into the head of a young girl named Maria Monk as she played near her childhood home on the outskirts of Montreal. From that day on, her mother later testified, Maria was unable to distinguish right from wrong; she became a wayward Jezebel whose sexual precocity finally led to her confinement in a Catholic asylum for magdalens in Montreal. From there she escaped with the aid of her current lover and, large with his child, made her way to New York, where she fell into the hands of a group of fanatical anti-Catholics who saw in her an opportunity to turn prejudice into profit. The result was the publication in 1836 of Maria's so-called autobiography, *Awful Disclosures of Maria Monk . . . in the Hotel Dieu Nunnery at Montreal*, from that day to this a best-selling tribute to the gullibility of book-buying nativists. The enduring popularity of the *Awful Disclosures* is easy to understand; its frankly pornographic "revelations" of the "criminal intercourse" between priests and nuns were enough to titillate a generation accustomed to the more restricted standards of Victorian morality. And hundreds of thousands, who read its lurid pages—and those of her *Further Disclosures*, published the following year—were convinced that Catholicism was a monstrous evil that must no longer be endured.

That books of such unsavory origins and unpalatable contents could command nationwide attention was due less to their own merits than to the spirit of the times. Since the beginning of the 1830's nativistic prejudices had been slowly, almost imperceptibly, but steadily mounting as immigrants from the Catholic nations of Europe flooded into the seaboard states in ever-increasing numbers to create the first sizable non-Protestant group in the nation's history. Resentment against these newcomers whose religious practices seemed so alien to traditionally American ways might have remained vague and undefined had not their coming coincided with the importation of a considerable body of anti-Catholic literature from England. There, anti-Catholics were making attacks on Parliament for adopting the tolerant Catholic Emancipation Act of 1829; and as Americans eagerly purchased English books, pamphlets, and magazines that heaped calumny on the Roman Church, native writers awakened to the realization that here was an unexploited market for their talents. In New York a band of zealots launched a weekly newspaper, *The Protestant*, in 1830 and a year later organized the New York Protestant Association. Books with such flaming titles as *A Master Key to Popery* and *Female Convents: Secrets of Nunneries Disclosed* began to appear. In 1834 a mob burned down a convent in Charlestown, near Boston. Clearly, by the mid-1830's the time was ripe for a concentrated assault on Romanism, which nativists saw as a growing menace to American liberty and Protestantism.

So they reasoned as they stirred themselves into action—and thus inadvertently set in motion the forces that within two decades would be setting their sights on the White House. Some used the press to preach the No-Popery message; *The Downfall of Babylon*, a weekly published in Philadelphia, and the *American Protestant Vindicator*, a biweekly printed in New York, both appeared as if by magic to carry word of the "Jesuitical abomination" of popery across the land in every edition. Individual nativists, capitalizing on the newly discovered American passion for joining, reorganized the New York Protestant Association along national lines as the Protestant Reformation Society and began flooding the country with propagandist literature and lecturing agents. Still others seized their pens to unleash a torrent of books and pamphlets, all preaching the evils of Romanism, that swept a surprisingly large number of men and women into the nativist fold.

One group of propagandists, expanding on the theme first developed by Morse, capitalized on the nationalist impulses of a generation that was soon to espouse the cause of Manifest Destiny. The Pope, they insisted, was anxious to move the Vatican out of decadent Italy, and what was more natural than his selection of the Mississippi Valley, the veritable garden of the world, for its new site? To this end he was cooperating with despotic European monarchs who were anxious to protect their own thrones by stemming the flow of liberal ideas from the democratic United States; together they would flood the land with papal minions disguised as immigrants, then seize control and establish those twins of oppression, despotism and Romanism, as the nation's new order. This was the warning voiced by such sober religious leaders as the Reverend Lyman Beecher in his *Plea for the West* (1835) and re-echoed in every Protestant religious journal as well as in the numerous publications of the influential American Home Missionary Society. To many ethnocentric Americans of that self-assured generation this was an argument that made sense.

Other persons were won by the plea that Catholics were seeking to undermine the American school system. Nativists began developing this theme shortly after 1839, when the American Bible Society, a Protestant group, announced a plan to place a copy of the Scriptures in every classroom of the nation. Catholics, both the hierarchy and the laity, protested when teachers began daily readings of this Protestant version of the Scriptures, and many Protestants interpreted the opposition to mean that Catholics disapproved of both the Bible and education. The issue was most violently joined in New York City, where the schools were under the control of the Protestant-dominated Public School Society, a private agency that distributed public funds. Led by the vigorous Bishop John Hughes, Catholics carried their fight to the state legislature, where, in 1842, they helped push through a bill abolishing the Public School Society and placing the city's schools under state administration. Protestants retaliated by electing a solidly No-Popery school board that continued Bible reading in the schools. But the harm was done. Protestant America was convinced that this attempt to inflict the minority will on the majority had shown that Catholicism was truly despotic and that Catholics were sworn enemies of the Holy Word.

While the propaganda inspired by the Bible-reading controversy appealed especially to middle-class churchgoers, another brand of calumny was aimed at the semiliterate masses who wanted sensationalism in unadulterated doses. Brazenly paraded before the public in such books as *Open Convents, Priests' Prisons for Women* and *Auricular Confession and Popish Nunneries*, this type of literature capitalized upon the demand for pornography proven by the popularity of Maria Monk's *Awful Disclosures*. Some authors of this school specialized in tales of convent immorality; others fastened upon the confessional to prove that popery stripped the last vestiges of morality from the victims. How, these writers asked, can Catholics be expected to obey the laws of God or man when all sin can be forgiven by a few muttered words from a confessor? How can a maiden remain pure when locked for hours in a confessional booth with a lecherous priest who is more interested in making advances that in saving souls?

In that day, when action spoke louder than words, such lurid sensationalism could not be peddled without inflaming men to violence. Trouble began in Philadelphia during the spring of 1844 when a group of nativists, wrought up by a Bible-reading controversy similar to that in New York, attempted to hold a mass meeting in one of the city's Irish-Catholic sections. In the inevitable clash that followed, a few shots were fired and one of the nativists was fatally wounded. With this, the editor of the leading anti-Catholic newspaper, the *Native American*, completely lost his head. "Another St. Bartholomew's Day is begun on the streets of Philadelphia," he proclaimed. "The bloody hand of the Pope has stretched itself forth to our destruction. We now call on our fellow-citizens, who regard free institutions whether they be native or adopted, to arm." That afternoon rioting began as bands of Protestant workmen marched through Catholic sections, burning and pillaging as they went. Hundreds of homes and two Catholic churches were put to the torch before troops arrived to quell the rioters. A few weeks later the July Fourth celebration touched off another period of carnage in the City of Brotherly Love; it lasted for three days, during which thirteen were killed and fifty wounded.

The Philadelphia riots sent organized nativism into a period of temporary decline. The fruits of anti-Catholicism were church-burning and bloodshed, and the majority of sensible Americans felt a natural revulsion that they took no pains to hide. Amidst their torrents of censure, the Protestant Reformation Society died unmourned, to be replaced at once by the American Protestant Society.

This new national organization pledged itself to illuminate the "spiritual darkness" of popery with "Light and Love" rather than violence, and to "awaken Christian feeling and Christian action for the salvation of Romanists," but the time was not ripe for even such a mild form of prejudice. The people, heatedly debating the slavery issue during and after the Mexican War, clearly felt little fear of a mythical papal invasion while the Union stood in real peril. Not until the Compromise of 1850 settled the sectional crisis, apparently for all time to come, could they rekindle their enthusiasm for the No-Popery crusade.

Times were auspicious for a revival of the assault, for by the end of the 1840's a number of tolerant, middle-class people were coming to the belief that the nativists' charges were not without some basis of truth. The Catholic Church, they were well aware, was no temporal-minded despotism bent on the political subjugation of the United States, but they nevertheless felt that the arrogantly uncompromising attitude of some of its clergy, if unchallenged, threatened the traditional values and institutions of their homeland. Immigrants, they knew, were not Jesuit minions in disguise, but they did believe that the newcomers were threatening to corrupt the political parties, disrupt the time-honored tradition of isolation from Europe's storms, lower the living standard of native workers, and cost the nation heavily in pauperism and crime. As they soberly contemplated the results of a generation of Catholic growth and unrestrained immigration, thousands upon thousands of previously unworried Americans began to reconsider the arguments of the nativists.

Certainly there was little to reassure them in the attitude of many overzealous Catholic clergymen who, misled by the rapid increase of their flocks into believing that Catholicism would soon become dominant in the United States, seemed in Protestant eyes to be behaving as though that day were already at hand. When Archbishop Hughes of New York could declare, as he did in his widely circulated address on "The Decline of Protestantism and Its Cause," that Catholics did intend to convert the entire population of the Mississippi Valley, and that the avowed mission of Catholicism was "to convert the world—including the inhabitants of the United States—the people of the cities, and the people of the country . . . the Senate, the Cabinet, the President, and all!" the time had apparently come to pay attention to the warnings of anti-papists. When Catholics could demand, as they did in a dozen states after 1852, that a share of the tax-raised school funds be diverted for the use of their parochial schools, even tolerant citizens felt they must rally to the defense of their most venerated institutions.

Even more fear was engendered among non-nativists by the rising tide of immigration. They might agree that newcomers bolstered the economic and military strength of the United States, but they were brought up short by the results of a generation of uncontrolled migration. Sober facts told the story: In 1850 only 6.5 per cent of the foreign born attended schools, as compared to 20 percent of the native born. Among aliens, one person in every 32 was a pauper receiving public support, while among natives the ratio was only one in every 260. Nearly half of the 27,000 persons convicted of crimes were aliens, although foreigners constituted only 11 percent of the population. As sobering as these figures was the less tangible evidence that was there for all to see: quiet city streets transformed into unsightly slums, corrupt political machines truckling to foreign-born voters, American workers displaced by new arrivals accustomed to lower living standards, the decline of national isolation from Europe's stormy politics as Irish and Germans loudly demanded support for the revolutionary movements of their homelands. To men and women who witnessed these changes, there seemed more truth than wit in the tale of the schoolboy called upon to parse "America"; " 'America,' ", said he, "is a very common noun, singular number, masculine gender, critical case, and governed by the Irish." Nor did there seem any end to these alterations in the pattern of American life. Boston's foreign-born voting population increased by 195 per cent in the first five years of the 1850's, while the number of its native-born voters mounted by only 15 per cent, indicating a not-too-distant future when the whole United States would be dominated by Catholic aliens.

Doubts such as these haunted Protestant Americans who had scorned organized nativism in the past; to them the time was clearly at hand for an all-out assault on Catholic and immigrant alike. To command their support, a society must be formed that would be free of the taints that had marred earlier nativistic organizations. This emerged when the American Protestant Society joined with two tiny groups dedicated to the herculean task of winning Europe to Protestantism—the Foreign Evangelical Society and the Christian Alliance—to form the American and Foreign Christian Union. Governed by a constitution that did not even mention "popery" or "Romanism," the new society was pledged to "diffuse and promote the principles of Religious Liberty, and a pure and Evangelical Christianity, both at home and abroad, wherever a corrupted Christianity exists." Organized nativism had moved far from the days when Maria Monk and the Protestant Reformation Society spread their crude invective throughout the land.

The new society's relative moderation attracted an unprecedented number of followers from among middle-class, churchgoing Protestants. By 1854 the contributions it received were large enough to support 120 traveling agents, all of them roaming constantly, speaking against Catholicism wherever they could find an audience, and laboring zealously to "save" Catholic souls. More important was the support now attracted from the nation's churches. Almost without exception, the 125 Protestant religious magazines and newspapers published in the United States converted themselves into champions of the crusade, while virtually every Protestant church body opened its doors to agents of the American and Foreign Christian Union, collected funds in the Union's behalf, and encouraged ministers to speak out for the salvation of misguided Romanists. In the same way the powerful interdenominational societies—the American Bible Society, the American Tract Society, and the American Home Missionary Society—all swung into line and became effective organs for disseminating anti-Catholic propaganda. By 1854 American Protestants were caught up in a No-Popery campaign of unprecedented proportions: thousands upon thousands were ready to translate their prejudices into votes whenever the opportunity offered.

Nor did the American and Foreign Christian Union completely ignore the more turbulent working classes in its campaign to save the country from Rome—although its appeal to this group was inadvertent rather than planned. This was inspired by the American visit of a papal nuncio, Archbishop Gaetano Bedini, who had already alarmed Italian nationalists by his alliance with monarchists in the brutal suppression of northern Italy's abortive struggle for independence from Austria in 1848. The American and Foreign Christian Union, eager to parade the Nuncio's unenviable record before the American people, imported an Italian ex-priest, Alessandro Gavazzi, to denounce Bedini in each city the Nuncio was scheduled to visit.

Gavazzi lived up to his assignment too well when he began his tour in 1853. Garbed in somber monk's robes emblazoned with a fiery cross, he shouted to his audiences: "Popery cannot be reformed. *Destruction to Popery!* No Protestantism; no protestations. Nothing but annihilation!" Here was a message that appealed to sensation-loving Americans in a day when tensions bred of the slavery conflict made violence synonymous with adherence to any cause. Wherever Bedini went Gavazzi had been there before him to whip the people into a frenzy against what he called this "Bloody Butcher of Bologna;" mobs in several cities burned the Nuncio in effigy, shouted insults, or threatened bodily harm.

The Bedini rioting touched off a new era of inflammatory attacks on Catholics and Catholicism. In a dozen cities self-appointed rabble rousers mounted their soapboxes, summoned their street-corner audiences, and unleashed their unrestrained invective; aroused by such tactics, the nativists burned churches and convents, molested immigrants, insulted Catholics, and on one occasion tarred and feathered a priest. These disorders bred a near-hysteria in areas where immigrants were most numerous, notably in the Northeast. There housekeepers refused to employ Irish servant girls lest the family food be poisoned on papal orders; placards everywhere warned the people to be on guard against the Pope's legions; and even the paper used by merchants to wrap parcels admonished buyers against the evils of Rome. In Maine mysterious symbols found on the homes in one community caused a near-panic among those who feared they had been marked for destruction by the Inquisition—until an itinerant hairdresser explained that he had thus chalked the houses he had already canvassed. In the nation's capital a block of marble contributed by the Pope to the Washington Monument was dumped into the Potomac by a raging mob. Clearly a surprisingly large portion of the American people had been swept so far along the No-Popery road that a political party reflecting their views would command support. The stage was set for that remarkable exhibit of political nativism that reached a climax in the elections of 1854 and 1855.

Of the dozens of semipolitical nativist groups organized about the beginning of the decade, the one destined to emerge on a national scale was the Order of the Star Spangled Banner. Secretly formed in New York in 1849—probably by Charles B. Allen, a politically ambitious anti-Catholic—it remained so small at first that its influence was scarcely felt beyond the city's borders. But in the spring of 1854 its members, having put their own house in order by healing local schisms, worked out a plan for national expansion on a federal pattern and devised a secret ritual with handshakes, passwords, oaths of membership, and all the other hocus-pocus so dear to Americans to this day. The result was phenomenal. So eager were nativists to express themselves politically that within months the Order, known now as the American party or the Know-Nothing party (from its members' practice of parrying all questions with "I know nothing about it"), had spread over most of the nation and was a political force to be reckoned with.

Its growth was demonstrated in the fall elections of 1854. In the northern and border states the Know-Nothings showed surprising strength, carrying Massachusetts and Delaware solidly and winning a balance of power in Pennsylvania. A year later three more New England states, New Hampshire, Rhode Island, and Connecticut, succumbed; along the middle border Maryland and Kentucky swung into line, with Tennessee almost following; and in the South the party's total vote was only 16,000 less than that of its opponents. Even in the Old Northwest, where the heavy percentage of foreign born doomed any nativist party, the Know-Nothings scored some near-misses, especially in Wisconsin. Little wonder that the party leaders confidently anticipated electing a President in 1856, or that such hostile newspapers as the New York *Herald* were willing to concede them victory.

What was responsible for this amazing political phenomenon? Three factors played an essential role. One was the nativistic propaganda that reached a crescendo just as the party was entering the national scene; hundreds of thousands of Americans voted for the party's candidates because they were sincerely convinced that Catholicism and foreign immigration seriously threatened their institutions. Another was the breakdown of traditional political patterns following the Compromise of 1850; voters during the next years had to decide among Democratic, Whig, Anti-Nebraska, Free Soil, Hard Democratic, Soft Democratic, Conscience Whig, Union Maine Law, and a variety of other candidates. Any well-knit party with a well-defined purpose stood to profit by this disarray. Thirdly, the dramatic reopening of the slavery controversy with the passage of the Kansas-Nebraska Act of 1854 temporarily played into Know-Nothing hands. In the furious debate that followed, thousands deserted the older parties. Many of them joined the Know-Nothings, attracted by the party's neutrality on the slavery issue and its loud promises to preserve the Union.

That these forces were operating in 1854 and 1855 was shown by the Know-Nothings' victory pattern. In the South, where they were only partially successful, their strength was centered in the rich-soil areas, suggesting that they attracted ex-Whig planters who were seeking compromise on the slavery issue rather than expressing dislike of Rome. Yet thousands of poorer southerners also supported the party, probably because their evangelical religions stimulated their hatred of Catholicism just as sectional loyalties sharpened their hostility toward immigrants, who were increasing the population strength of the North. In the border states the party's sweeping victories were traceable more to a desire to compromise the troublesome slavery question than to entrenched nativistic beliefs; men whose homes occupied the probable battlegrounds of a civil war naturally hesitated to support either of the sectional parties that emerged after the Kansas-Nebraska Act. Only in the Northeast did the Know-Nothings match their victories in the border states, and only there was hatred of the Catholic and the immigrant primarily responsible for the party's growth. Yankees and New Yorkers, with no desire to avoid a showdown on slavery, could have rushed into the newly formed Republican party had not their nativistic prejudices taken precedence. Instead they cast their lot with the Know-Nothings because three decades of propaganda had convinced them that Romanism and aliens threatened the institutions of their forefathers.

Whatever their causes, the thumping victories of 1854 and 1855 placed nativists in a position to translate prejudice into action. Yet they failed utterly to do so, and this failure not only revealed the party's weakness but contributed to its decline. Know-Nothings never commanded a majority in Congress, but they did hold a balance of power on several occasions. Despite this favorable position, their crusade against Catholicism could produce nothing more than a few bombastic speeches directed against the alleged temporal designs of the Pope, while their anti-alien program degenerated into a single bill that would have extended the period before naturalization to 21 years.

Even this measure failed to reach a vote. Within the states Know-Nothings proved just as impotent. In Massachusetts a bumbling governor and an inept legislature allowed several bills limiting aliens' voting to die in committee, although they did adopt a law requiring Bible reading in the schools and created a "Nunnery Committee" to report on Catholic schools, seminaries, and convents within the state. After frightening a few nuns and lay teachers by poking about parochial schools in search of firearms and other evidence of conspiracy, the committee disbanded amidst the derisive hoots of most of the sensible people of the nation. Nor was the record of the Know-Nothings more impressive in Maryland or other states under their control. Having no tangible program acceptable in a democratic land, the party, as Horace Greeley remarked, was "as devoid of the elements of persistence as an anti-Cholera or anti-Potato-Rot party would be."

These manifestations of Know-Nothing weakness encouraged spokesmen for human decency who had been cowed into silence by the hysteria of the past few years to raise their voices, feebly at first, and then with growing assurance. Some leveled their verbal lances against the party's secrecy; "one might as well study optics in the pyramids of Egypt or the subterranean tombs of Rome," warned Henry Ward Beecher, "as liberty in secret conclaves controlled by hoary knaves versed in political intrigue."

Others poked fun at the Know-Nothings' fantastic fears of a papal invasion or the transfer of the Vatican to the Mississippi Valley. Still more condemned the party for the rioting and bloodshed it inspired, a charge that gained meaning as each new election brought further clashes between nativists and immigrants. This combination of censure and ridicule proved effective; by the end of 1855 Know-Nothingism was on the wane.

The party's end was hurried by the very force that had stimulated its early growth: the reopened slavery controversy. As battle lines formed following the Kansas-Nebraska Act, and as each dispatch from "bleeding Kansas" inflamed the public mind, nativists found themselves catapulted into the conflict, no matter how loudly they protested their neutrality. Northerners, rallying beneath the antislavery banner, began to view the whole Know-Nothing movement as a southern conspiracy to distract attention from the vital issue of the day. Southerners, forming ranks behind their "peculiar institution," began to look upon nativists as enemies of the solidarity needed to protect slavery from Black Republicans. Thus discredited in North and South, the Know-Nothing party lost its followers in droves, but worse was yet to come. Its 1855 national convention was unable to avoid a debate on slavery and broke up in disorder, with northern and southern Know-Nothings arrayed against each other on this all-prevailing issue.

Thus divided, the party approached the presidential election of 1856 with no chance of victory. Yet its leaders clung to a last hope:

if the major sectional parties fought to a standstill, they believed, the final decision might be made in the House of Representatives, where they had a strategic position. Thus inspired, they sought unsuccessfully to patch up their internal differences, then nominated former President Millard Fillmore of New York as their candidate.

A more unfortunate choice would have been hard to find. Already hated by northerners for having signed the unpopular Fugitive Slave Act of 1850, Fillmore had not only proven himself inept in the Presidency but had exhibited none of the fiery zeal needed to attract nativists to his standard. Actually he scarcely mentioned Catholicism during his campaign, devoting himself instead to vague plans for saving the Union. When the ballots were counted he had received over 800,000 popular votes—almost a fourth of the total—but received the electoral vote of Maryland alone. The Know-Nothing party was as dead as the dodo.

The defeat of Know-Nothingism was also a setback for intolerance. When put to the test, the bigots who had fomented against Romanists and aliens for a generation had nothing to offer save the timeworn cliches of bigotry and a political ineptitude that revealed their own inferiority. Prophets of hatred were to thrust themselves onto the national scene in the future, as the careers of the American Protective Association of the 1890's and the Ku Klux Klan of the 1920's amply demonstrated, yet never was their threat to basic American values so serious as in the 1850's. By discrediting the cause for which they stood, the Know-Nothings, ironically, made a contribution to the principles of human decency that they opposed so violently.

The Seneca Falls Declaration of Sentiments (1848)

When in the course of human events, it becomes necessary for one portion of the family of man to assume among the people of the earth a position different from that which they have hitherto occupied, but one to which the laws of nature and of nature's God entitle them, a decent respect to the opinions of mankind requires that they should declare the causes that impel them to such a course.

We hold these truths to be self-evident: that all men and women are created equal; that they are endowed by their Creator with certain inalienable rights; that among these are life, liberty, and the pursuit of happiness; that to secure these rights governments are instituted, deriving their just powers from the consent of the governed. Whenever any form of government becomes destructive of these ends, it is the right of those who suffer from it to refuse allegiance to it, and to insist upon the institution of a new government, laying its foundation on such principles, and organizing its powers in such form, as to them shall seem most likely to effect their safety and happiness. Prudence, indeed, will dictate that governments long established should not be changed for light and transient causes; and accordingly all experience hath shown that mankind are more disposed to suffer, while evils are sufferable, than to right themselves by abolishing the forms to which they were accustomed. But when a long train of abuses and usurpations, pursuing invariably the same object, evinces a design to reduce them under absolute despotism, it is their duty to throw off such government, and to provide new guards for their future security. Such has been the patient sufferance of the women under this government, and such is now the necessity which constrains them to demand the equal station to which they are entitled.

The history of mankind is a history of repeated injuries and usurpations on the part of man toward woman, having in direct object the establishment of an absolute tyranny over her. To prove this, let facts be submitted to a candid world.

He has never permitted her to exercise her inalienable right to the elective franchise.

He has compelled her to submit to laws, in the formation of which she had no voice.

He has withheld from her rights which are given to the most ignorant and degraded men—both natives and foreigners.

Having deprived her of this first right of a citizen, the elective franchise, thereby leaving her without representation in the halls of legislation, he has oppressed her on all sides.

He has made her, if married, in the eye of the law, civilly dead.

He has taken from her all right in property, even to the wages she earns. . . .

He has so framed the laws of divorce, as to what shall be the proper causes, and in case of separation, to whom the guardianship of the children shall be given, as to be wholly regardless of the happiness of women—the law, in all cases, going upon the false supposition of the supremacy of man, and giving all power into his hands. . . .

He has monopolized nearly all the profitable employments, and from those she is permitted to follow, she receives but a scanty remuneration. He closes against her all the avenues to wealth and distinction which he considers most honorable to himself. . . .

He has created a false public sentiment by giving to the world a different code of morals for men and women, by which moral delinquencies which exclude women from society, are not only tolerated, but deemed of little account in man.

He has endeavored, in every way that he could, to destroy her confidence in her own powers, to lessen her self-respect, and to make her willing to lead a dependent and abject life.

Now, in view of this entire disfranchisement of one-half the people of this country, their social and religious degradation—in view of the unjust laws above mentioned, and because women do feel themselves aggrieved, oppressed, and fraudulently deprived of their most sacred rights, we insist that they have immediate admission to all the rights and privileges which belong to them as citizens of the United States. . . .

Declaration of Sentiments of the American Anti-Slavery Society (1833)

The convention assembled in the city of Philadelphia, to organize a National Anti-Slavery Society, promptly seize the opportunity to promulgate the following Declaration of Sentiments, as cherished by them in relation to the enslavement of one-sixth portion of the American people.

More than fifty-seven years have elapsed since a band of patriots convened in this place to devise measures for the deliverance of this country from a foreign yoke. The cornerstone upon which they founded the Temple of Freedom was broadly this—"that all men are created equal; that they are endowed by their Creator with certain inalienable rights; that among these are life, LIBERTY, and the pursuit of happiness." . . .

We have met together for the achievement of an enterprise, without which that of our fathers is incomplete; and which, for its magnitude, solemnity, and probable results upon the destiny of the world, as far transcends theirs as moral truth does physical force.

In purity of motive, in earnestness of zeal, in decision of purpose, in intrepidity of action, in steadfastness of faith, in sincerity of spirit, we would not be inferior to them. . . .

Their grievances, great as they were, were trifling in comparison with the wrongs and sufferings of those for whom we plead. Our fathers were never slaves—never bought and sold like cattle—never shut out from the light of knowledge and religion—never subjected to the lash of brutal taskmasters.

But those for whose emancipation we are striving—constituting at the present time at least one-sixth part of our countrymen—are recognized by law, and treated by their fellow-beings, as brute beasts; are plundered daily of the fruits of their toil without redress; really enjoy no constitutional nor legal protection from licentious and murderous outrages upon their persons; and are ruthlessly torn asunder—the tender babe from the arms of its frantic mother—the heartbroken wife from her weeping husband—at the caprice or pleasure of irresponsible tyrants. For the crime of having a dark complexion, they suffer the pangs of hunger, the infliction of stripes, the ignominy of brutal servitude. They are kept in heathenish darkness by laws expressly enacted to make their instruction a criminal offense.

These are the prominent circumstances in the condition of more than two million people, the proof of which may be found in thousands of indisputable facts, and in the laws of the slave-holding States.

Hence we maintain—that, in view of the civil and religious privileges of this nation, the guilt of its oppression is unequalled by any other on the face of the earth, and, therefore, that it is bound to repent instantly, to undo the heavy burdens, and to let the oppressed go free.

We further maintain—that no man has a right to enslave or imbrute his brother—to hold or acknowledge him, for one moment, as a piece of merchandise—to keep back his hire by fraud—or to brutalize his mind, by denying him the means of intellectual, social and moral improvement.

The right to enjoy liberty is inalienable. . . .

Therefore we believe and affirm—that there is no difference, in principle, between the African slave trade and American slavery:

That every American citizen, who detains a human being in involuntary bondage as his property, is, according to Scripture, a man-stealer:

That the slaves ought instantly to be set free, and brought under the protection of law:

That if they had lived from the time of Pharaoh down to the present period, and had been entailed through successive generations, their right to be free could never have been alienated, but their claims would have constantly risen in solemnity:

That all those laws which are not in force, admitting the right of slavery, are therefore, before God, utterly null and void; being an audacious usurpation of the Divine prerogative, a daring infringement on the law of nature, a base overthrow of the very foundations of the social compact, a complete extinction of all the relations, endearments and obligations of mankind, and a presumptuous transgression of all the holy commandments; and that therefore they ought instantly to be abrogated.

We further believe and affirm—that all persons of color, who possess the qualification which are demanded of others, ought to be admitted forwith to the enjoyment of the same privileges, and the exercise of the same prerogatives, as others; and that the paths of preferment, of wealth and of intelligence, should be opened as widely to them as to persons of a white complexion.

We maintain that no compensation should be given to the planters emancipating their slaves:

Because it would be a surrender of the great fundamental principle, that man cannot hold property in man;

Because slavery is a crime, and therefore is not an article to be sold;

Because the holders of slaves are not the just proprietors of what they claim; freeing the slave is not depriving them of property, but restoring it to its rightful owner; it is not wronging the master, but righting the slave—restoring him to himself;

Because immediate and general emancipation would only destroy nominal, not real property; it would not amputate a limb or break a bone of the slaves, but by infusing motives into their breasts, would make them doubly valuable to the masters as free laborers; and

Because, if compensation is to be given at all, it should be given to the outraged and guiltless slaves, and not to those who have plundered and abused them.

We regard as delusive, cruel and dangerous, any scheme of expatriation which pretends to aid, either directly or indirectly, in the emancipation of the slaves, or to be a substitute for the immediate and total abolition of slavery.

We fully and unanimously recognize the sovereignty of each State, to legislate exclusively on the subject of the slavery which is tolerated within its limits; we concede that Congress, under the present national compact, has no right to interfere with any of the slave States, in relation to this momentous subject:

But we maintain that Congress has a right, and is solemnly bound, to suppress the domestic slave trade between the several

States, and to abolish slavery in those portions of our territory which the Constitution has placed under its exclusive jurisdiction.

We also maintain that there are, at the present time, the highest obligations resting upon the people of the free States to remove slavery by moral and political action, as prescribed in the Constitution of the United States. They are now living under a pledge of their tremendous physical force, to fasten the galling fetters of tyranny upon the limbs of millions in the Southern States; they are liable to be called at any moment to suppress a general insurrection of the slaves; they authorize the slave owner to vote for three-fifths of his slaves as property, and thus enable him to perpetuate his oppression; they support a standing army at the South for its protection; and they seize the slave, who has escaped into their territories, and send him back to be tortured by an enraged master or a brutal driver. This relation to slavery is criminal, and full of danger: IT MUST BE BROKEN UP.

These are our views and principles—these our designs and measures. With entire confidence in the overruling justice of God, we plant ourselves upon the Declaration of our Independence and the truths of Divine Revelation, as upon the Everlasting Rock. . . .

Part VI:
Civil War and Reconstruction

A War That Never Goes Away

James M. McPherson

Americans just can't get enough of the Civil War." So says a man who should know, Terry Winschel, historian of the Vicksburg National Military Park. Millions of visitors come to Vicksburg and to more than a dozen other Civil War national battlefield and military parks every year. More than forty thousand Civil War reenactors spend hundreds of dollars each on replica weapons, uniforms, and equipment; many of them travel thousands of miles to help restage Civil War battles. Another two hundred and fifty thousand Americans describe themselves as Civil War buffs or "hobbyists" and belong to one of the hundreds of Civil War round tables or societies, subscribe to at least one of the half-dozen magazines devoted to Civil War history, or buy and sell Civil War memorabilia.

Above all, Americans buy books on the Civil War. This has always been true. More than fifty thousand separate books or pamphlets on the war have been published since the guns ceased firing 125 years ago. In recent years some eight hundred titles, many of them reprints of out-of-print works, have come off the presses annually. Nearly every month a new Civil War book is offered by the History Book Club or the Book-of-the-Month Club, often as main selection. Many bookstore owners echo the words of Jim Lawson, general manager of the Book 'N Card shop in Falls Church, Virginia. "For the last two years," he said in 1988, "Civil War books have been flying out of here. It's not [just] the buffs who buy; it's the general public, from high school kids to retired people."

Although we are approaching the end of the 125th-anniversary commemorations of Civil War events, the boom shows no signs of fading. As a beneficiary of this popular interest in the Civil War, I am often asked to explain what accounts for it—in particular, to explain why my own recent contribution to the literature on the war and its causes, *Battle Cry of Freedom*, was on national best-seller lists for several months as a hardcover book in 1988 and again as a paperback in 1989. I have a few answers.

First, for Americans, the human cost of the Civil War was by far the most devastating in our history. The 620,000 Union and Confederate soldiers who lost their lives almost equaled the 680,000 American soldiers who died in all the other wars this country has fought combined. When we add the unknown but probably substantial number of civilian deaths—from disease, malnutrition, exposure, or injury—among the hundreds of thousands of refugees in the Confederacy, the toll of Civil War dead may exceed war deaths in all the rest of American history. Consider two sobering facts about the Battle of Antietam, America's single bloodiest day. The 25,000 casualties there were nearly four times the number of American casualties on D-day, June 6, 1944. The 6,500 men killed and mortally wounded in one day near Sharpsburg were nearly double the number of Americans killed and mortally wounded in combat in all the rest of the country's nineteenth-century wars combined—the War of 1812, the Mexican War, and the Spanish-American War.

This ghastly toll gives the Civil War a kind of horrifying but hypnotic fascination. As Thomas Hardy once put it, "War makes rattling good history; but Peace is poor reading." The sound of drum and trumpet, the call to arms, the clashing of armies have stirred the blood of nations throughout history. As the horrors and the seamy side of a war recede into the misty past, the romance and honor and glory forge into the foreground. Of no war has this been more true than of the Civil War, with its dashing cavaliers, its generals leading infantry charges, its diamond-stacked locomotives and paddle-wheeled steamboats, its larger-than-life figures like Lincoln, Lee, Jackson, Grant, and Sherman, its heroic and romantic women like Clara Barton and "Mother" Bickerdyke and Rose O'Neal Greenhow, its countless real-life heroines and knaves and heroes capable of transmutation into a Scarlett O'Hara, Rhett Butler, or Ashley Wilkes. If romance is the other face of horror in our perception of the Civil War, the poignancy of a brothers' war is the other face of the tragedy of a civil war. In hundreds of individual cases the war did pit brother against brother, cousin against cousin, even father against son. This was especially true in "border" states like Kentucky, where the war divided such famous families as the Clays, Crittendens, and Breckinridges and where seven brothers and brothers-in-law of the wife of the United States President fought for the

Confederate States. But it was also true of states like Virginia, where Jeb Stuart's father-in-law commanded Union cavalry, and even of South Carolina, where Thomas F. Drayton became a brigadier general in the Confederate army and fought against his brother Percival, a captain in the Union navy, at the Battle of Port Royal. Who can resist the painful human interest of stories like these—particularly when they are recounted in the letters and diaries of Civil War protagonists, preserved through generations and published for all to read as a part of the unending stream of Civil War books?

Indeed, the uncensored contemporary descriptions of that war by participants help explain its appeal to modern readers. There is nothing else in history to equal it. Civil War armies were the most literate that ever fought a war up to that time, and twentieth-century armies censored soldiers' mail and discouraged diary keeping. Thus we have an unparalleled view of the Civil War by the people who experienced it. This has kept the image of the war alive in the families of millions of Americans whose ancestors fought in it. When speaking to audiences as diverse as Civil War buffs, Princeton students and alumni, and local literary clubs, I have sometimes asked how many of them are aware of forebears who fought in the Civil War. I have been surprised by the large response, which demonstrates not only a great number of such people but also their consciousness of events that happened so long ago yet seem part of their family lore today.

This consciousness of the war, of the past as part of the present, continues to be more intense in the South than elsewhere. William Faulkner said of his native section that the past isn't dead; it isn't even past. As any reader of Faulkner's novels knows, the Civil War is central to that past that is present; it is the great watershed of Southern history; it is, as Mark Twain put it a century ago after a tour through the South, "what A.D. is elsewhere; they date from it." The symbols of that past-in-present surround Southerners as they grow up, from the Robert Lee Elementary School or Jefferson Davis High School they attend and the Confederate battle flag that flies over their statehouse to the Confederate soldier enshrined in bronze or granite on the town square and the family folklore about victimization by Sherman's bummers. Some of those symbols remain highly controversial and provoke as much passion today as in 1863: the song "Dixie," for example, and the Confederate flag, which for many Southern whites continue to represent courage, honor, or defiance while to blacks they represent racism and oppression.

This suggests the most important reason for the enduring fascination with the Civil War among professional historians as well as the general public: Great issues were at stake, issues about which Americans were willing to fight and die, issues whose resolution profoundly transformed and redefined the United States. The Civil War was a total war in three senses: It mobilized the total human and material resources of both sides; it ended not in a negotiated peace but in total victory by one side and unconditional surrender by the other; it destroyed the economy and social system of the loser and established those of the winner as the norm for the future.

The Civil War was fought mainly by volunteer soldiers who joined the colors before conscription went into effect. In fact, the Union and Confederate armies mobilized as volunteers a larger percentage of their societies' manpower than any other war in American history—probably in world history, with the possible exception of the French Revolution. And Civil War armies, like those of the French Revolution, were highly ideological in motivation. Most of the volunteers knew what they were fighting for, and why. What were they fighting for? If asked to define it in a single word many soldiers on both sides would have answered: liberty. They fought for the heritage of freedom bequeathed to them by the Founding Fathers. North and South alike wrapped themselves in the mantle of 1776. But the two sides interpreted that heritage in opposite ways, and at first neither side included the slaves in the vision of liberty for which it fought. The slaves did, however, and by the time of Lincoln's Gettysburg Address in 1863, the North also fought for "a new birth of freedom. . . ." These multiple meanings of freedom, and how they dissolved and reformed in kaleidoscopic patterns during the war, provide the central meaning of the war for the American experience.

When the "Black Republican" Abraham Lincoln won the Presidency in 1860 on a platform of excluding slavery from the territories, Southerners compared him to George III and declared their independence from "oppressive Yankee rule." "The same spirit of freedom and independence that impelled our Fathers to the separation from the British Government," proclaimed secessionists, would impel the "liberty loving people of the South" to separation from the United States government. A Georgia secessionist declared that Southerners would be "either *slaves in the Union or freemen out of it*." Young men from Texas to Virginia rushed to enlist in this "Holy Cause of Liberty and Independence" and to raise "the standard of liberty and Equality for white men" against "our Abolition enemies who are pledged to prostrate the white freemen of the South down to equality with negroes." From "the high and solemn motive of defending and protecting the right which our fathers bequeathed to us," declared Jefferson Davis at the outset of war, let us "renew such sacrifices as our fathers made to the holy cause of constitutional liberty."

But most Northerners ridiculed these Southern professions to be fighting for the ideals of 1776. That was "a libel upon the whole character and conduct of the men of '76," said the antislavery poet and journalist William Cullen Bryant. The Founding Fathers had fought "to establish the rights of man . . . and principles of universal liberty." The South, insisted Bryant, had seceded "not in the interest of general humanity, but of domestic despotism . . . Their motto is not liberty, but slavery." Northerners did not deny the right of revolution in principle; after all, the United States was founded on that right. But "the right of revolution," wrote Lincoln in 1861, "is never a legal right. . . . At most, it is but a moral right, when exercised for a morally justifiable cause. When exercised without such a cause revolution is no right, but simply a wicked exercise of physical power." In Lincoln's judgment secession was just such a wicked exercise. The event that precipitated it was Lincoln's election by a constitutional majority. As Northerners saw it, the Southern States, having controlled the national government for most of the previous two generations through their domination of the Democratic party, now decided to leave the Union just because they had lost an election.

For Lincoln and the Northern people, it was the Union that represented the ideals of 1776. The republic established by the Founding Fathers as a bulwark of liberty was a fragile experiment in a nineteenth-century world bestridden by kings, emperors, czars, and dictators. Most republics through history had eventually been overthrown. Some Americans still alive in 1861 had seen French republics succumb twice to emperors and once to the restoration of the Bourbon monarchy. Republics in Latin America came and went with bewildering rapidity. The United States in 1861 represented, in Lincoln's words, "the last, best hope" for the survival of republican liberties in the world. Would that hope also collapse? "Our popular government has often been called an experiment," Lincoln told Congress on July 4, 1861. But if the Confederacy succeeded in splitting the country in two, it would set a fatal precedent that would destroy the experiment. By invoking this precedent, a minority in the future might secede from the Union whenever it did not like what the majority stood for, until the United States fragmented into a multitude of petty, squabbling autocracies. "The central idea pervading this struggle," said Lincoln, "is the necessity of proving that popular government is not an absurdity. We must settle this question now, whether, in a free government, the minority have the right to break up the government whenever they choose."

Many soldiers who enlisted in the Union army felt the same way. A Missourian joined up as "a duty I owe my country and to my children to do what I can to preserve this government as I shudder to think what is ahead of them if this government should be overthrown." A New England soldier wrote to his wife on the eve of the First Battle of Bull Run: "I know . . . how great a debt we owe to those who went before us through the blood and sufferings of the Revolution. And I am willing—perfectly willing—to lay down all my joys in this life, to help maintain this government, and to pay that debt."

Freedom for the slaves was not part of the liberty for which the North fought in 1861. That was not because the Lincoln administration supported slavery; quite the contrary. Slavery was "an unqualified evil to the negro, to the white man . . . and to the State," said Lincoln on many occasions in words that expressed the sentiments of a Northern majority. "The monstrous injustice of slavery . . . deprives our republican example of its just influence in the world— enables the enemies of free institutions, with plausibility, to taunt us as hypocrites. . . ." Yet in his first inaugural address, Lincoln declared that he had "no purpose, directly or indirectly, to interfere with . . . slavery in the state where it exists." He reiterated this pledge in his first message to Congress, on July 4, 1861, when the Civil War was nearly three months old.

What explains this apparent inconsistency? The answer lies in the Constitution and in the Northern polity of 1861. Lincoln was bound by a constitution that protected slavery in any state where citizens wanted it. The republic of liberty for whose preservation the North was fighting had been a republic in which slavery was legal everywhere in 1776. That was the great American paradox—a land of freedom based on slavery. Even in 1861 four states that remained loyal to the Union were slave states, and the Democratic minority in free states opposed any move to make the war for the Union a war against slavery.

But as the war went on, the slaves themselves took the first step toward making it a war against slavery. Coming into Union lines by the thousands, they voted with their feet for freedom. As enemy property they could be confiscated by Union forces as "contraband of war." This was the thin edge of the wedge that finally broke apart the American paradox. By 1863 a series of congressional acts plus Lincoln's Emancipation Proclamation had radically enlarged Union war aims. The North henceforth fought not just to restore the old Union, not just to ensure that the nation born in 1776 "shall not perish from the earth," but to give that nation "a new birth of freedom."

Northern victory in the Civil War resolved two fundamental, festering issues left unresolved by the Revolution of 1776: whether this fragile republican experiment called the United States would survive and whether the house divided would continue to endure half slave and half free. Both these issues remained open questions until 1865. Many Americans doubted the Republic's survival; many European conservatives predicted its demise; some Americans advocated the right of secession and periodically threatened to invoke it; eleven states did invoke it in 1860 and 1861. But since 1865 no state or region has seriously threatened secession, not even during the "massive resistance" to desegregation from 1954 to 1964. Before 1865 the United States, land of liberty, was the largest slaveholding country in the world. Since 1865 that particular "monstrous injustice" and "hypocrisy" has existed no more.

In the process of preserving the Union of 1776 while purging it of slavery, the Civil War also transformed it. Before 1861 the words *United States* were a plural noun: "The United States *are* a large country." Since 1865 *United States* has been a singular noun. The North went to war to preserve the *Union*; it ended by creating a *nation*. This transformation can be traced in Lincoln's most important wartime addresses. The first inaugural address contained the word *Union* twenty times and the word *nation* not once. In Lincoln's first message to Congress, on July 4, 1861, he used *Union* forty-nine times and *nation* only three times. In his famous public letter to Horace Greeley of August 22, 1862, concerning slavery and the war, Lincoln spoke of the Union nine times and the nation not at all. But in the Gettysburg Address fifteen months later, he did not refer to the Union at all but used the word *nation* five times. And in the second inaugural address, looking back over the past four years, Lincoln spoke of one side's seeking to dissolve the Union in 1861 and the other side's accepting the challenge of war to preserve the nation. The old decentralized Republic, in which the post office was the only agency of national government that touched the average citizen, was transformed by the crucible of war into a centralized polity that taxed people directly and created an internal revenue bureau to collect the taxes, expanded the jurisdiction of federal courts, created a national currency and a federally chartered banking system, drafted men into the Army, and created the Freedman's Bureau as the first national agency for social welfare. Eleven of the first twelve amendments to the Constitution had limited the powers of the national government; six of the next seven, starting with the Thirteenth Amendment in 1865, radically expanded those powers at the expense of the states. The first three of these amendments converted four million slaves into citizens and voters within five years, the most rapid and fundamental social transformation in American history—even if the nation did backslide on part of this commitment for three generations after 1877.

From 1789 to 1861 a Southern slaveholder was President of the United States two-thirds of the time, and two-thirds of the Speakers of the House and presidents pro tem of the Senate had also been Southerners. Twenty of the thirty-five Supreme Court justices during that period were from the South, which always had a majority on the Court before 1861. After the Civil War a century passed before another resident of a Southern state was elected President. For half a century after the war hardly any Southerners served as Speaker of the House or president pro tem of the Senate, and only nine of the thirty Supreme Court justices appointed during that half-century were Southerners. The institutions and ideology of a plantation society and a caste system that had dominated half of the country before 1861 and sought to dominate more went down with a great crash in 1865 and were replaced by the institutions and ideology of free-labor entrepreneurial capitalism. For better or for worse, the flames of Civil War forged the framework of modern America.

So even if the veneer of romance and myth that has attracted so many of the current Civil War camp followers were stripped away, leaving only the trauma of violence and suffering, the Civil

War would remain the most dramatic and crucial experience in American history. That fact will ensure the persistence of its popularity and its importance as a historical subject so long as there is a United States.

The Wilmot Proviso 1847

But, sir, the issue now presented is not whether slavery shall exist unmolested where it now is, but whether it shall be carried to new and distant regions, now free, where the footprint of a slave cannot be found. This is the issue. Upon it I take my stand, and from it I cannot be frightened or driven by idle charges of abolitionism.

I ask not that slavery be abolished. I demand that this government preserve the integrity of free territory against the aggressions of slavery—against its wrongful usurpations.

Sir, I was in favor of the annexation of Texas. . . . The Democracy [Democratic Party] of the North, almost to a man, went for annexation. Yes, sir, here was an empire larger than France given up to slavery. Shall further concessions be made by the North? Shall we give up free territory, the inheritance of free labor? Must we yield this also? Never, sir, never, until we ourselves are fit to be slaves. . . .

But, sir, we are told that the joint blood and treasure of the whole country being expended in this acquisition, therefore it should be divided, and slavery allowed to take its share. Sir, the South has her share already; the instalment for slavery was paid in advance. We are fighting this war for Texas and for the South. I affirm it—every intelligent man knows it—Texas is the primary cause of this war. For this, sir, Northern treasure is being exhausted, and Northern blood poured upon the plains of Mexico. We are fighting this war cheerfully, not reluctantly—cheerfully fighting this war for Texas; and yet we seek not to change the character of her institutions. Slavery is there; there let it remain. . . .

Now, sir, we are told that California is ours, that New Mexico is ours—won by the valor of our arms. They are free. Shall they remain free? Shall these fair provinces be the inheritance and homes of the white labor of freemen or the black labor of slaves? This, sir, is the issue—this the question. The North has the right, and her representatives here have the power. . . .

But the South contend that, in their emigration to this free territory, they have the right to take and hold slaves, the same as other property. Unless the amendment I have offered be adopted, or other early legislation is had upon this subject, they will do so. Indeed, they unitedly, as one man, have declared their right and purpose so to do, and the work has already begun.

Slavery follows in the rear of our armies. Shall the war power of our government be exerted to produce such a result? Shall this government depart from its neutrality on this question, and lend its power and influence to plant slavery in these territories?

There is no question of abolition here, sir. Shall the South be permitted, by aggression, by invasion of the right, by subduing free territory and planting slavery upon it, to wrest these provinces from Northern freemen, and turn them to the accomplishment of their own sectional purposes and schemes?

This is the question. Men of the North, answer. Shall it be so? Shall we of the North submit to it? If we do, we are coward slaves, and deserve to have the manacles fastened upon our own limbs.

Mississippi Resolutions On Secession (1860)

Whereas, the Constitutional Union was formed by the several States in their separate sovereign capacity for the purpose of mutual advantage and protection;

That the several States are distinct sovereignties, whose supremacy is limited so far only as the same has been delegated by voluntary compact to a Federal Government, and when it fails to accomplish the ends for which it was established, the parties to the compact have the right to resume, each State for itself, such delegated powers;

That the institution of slavery existed prior to the formation of the Federal Constitution, and is recognized by its letter, and all efforts to impair its value or lessen its duration by Congress, or any of the free States, is a violation of the compact of Union and is destructive of the ends for which it was ordained, but in defiance of the principles of the Union thus established, the people of the Northern States have assumed a revolutionary position toward the Southern States;

That they have set at defiance that provision of the Constitution which was intended to secure domestic tranquillity among the States and promote their general welfare, namely: "No person held to service or labor in one State, under the laws thereof, escaping into another, shall, in consequence of any law or regulation therein, be discharged from such service or labor, but shall be delivered up on claim of the party to whom such service or labor may be due;"

That they have by voluntary associations, individual agencies and State legislation interfered with slavery as it prevails in the slave-holding States;

That they have enticed our slaves from us, and by State intervention obstructed and prevented their rendition under the fugitive slave law;

That they continue their system of agitation obviously for the purpose of encouraging other slaves to escape from service, to weaken the institution in the slave-holding States by rendering the holding of such property insecure, and as a consequence its ultimate abolition certain;

That they claim the right and demand its execution by Congress to exclude slavery from the Territories but claim the right of protection for every species of property owned by themselves;

That they declare in every manner in which pubic opinion is expressed their unalterable determination to exclude from admittance into the Union any new State that tolerates slavery in its Constitution, and thereby force Congress to a condemnation of that species of property;

That they thus seek by an increase of abolition States "to acquire two-thirds of both houses" for the purpose of preparing an amendment to the Constitution of the United States, abolishing slavery in the States, and so continue the agitation that the proposed amendment shall be ratified by the Legislatures of three-fourths of the States;

That they have in violation of the comity of all civilized nations, and in violation of the comity established by the Constitution of the United States, insulted and outraged our citizens when travelling among them for pleasure, health or business, by taking their servants and liberating the same, under the forms of State laws, and subjecting their owners to degrading and ignominious punishment;

That to encourage the stealing of our property they have put at defiance that provision of the Constitution which declares that fugitives from justice (escaping) into another State, on demand of the Executive authority of that State from which he fled, shall be delivered up;

That they have sought to create domestic discord in the Southern States by incendiary publications;

That they encouraged a hostile invasion of a Southern State to excite insurrection, murder and rapine;

That they have deprived Southern citizens of their property and continue an unfriendly agitation of their domestic institutions, claiming for themselves perfect immunity from external interference with their domestic policy. . . .

That they have elected a majority of Electors for President and Vice-President on the ground that there exists an irreconciliable conflict between the two sections of the Confederacy in reference to their respective systems of labor and in pursuance of their hostility to us and our institutions, thus declaring to the civilized world that the powers of this Government are to be used for the dishonor and overthrow of the Southern Section of this great Confederacy. Therefore,

Be it resolved by the Legislature of the State of Mississippi, That in the opinion of those who now constitute the said Legislature, the secession of each aggrieved State is the proper remedy for these injuries.

Hayfoot, Strawfoot!

Bruce Catton

The volunteer soldier in the American Civil War used a clumsy muzzle-loading rifle, lived chiefly on salt pork and hardtack, and retained to the very end a loose-jointed, informal attitude toward the army with which he had cast his lot. But despite all the surface differences, he was at bottom blood brother to the G.I. Joe of modern days.

Which is to say that he was basically, and incurably, a civilian in arms. A volunteer, he was still a soldier because he had to be one, and he lived for the day when he could leave the army forever. His attitude toward discipline, toward his officers, and toward the whole spit-and-polish concept of military existence was essentially one of careless tolerance. He refused to hate his enemies—indeed, he often got along with them much better than with some of his own comrades—and his indoctrination was often so imperfect that what was sometimes despairingly said of the American soldier in World War II would apply equally to him: he seemed to be fighting chiefly so that he could some day get back to Mom's cooking.

What really set the Civil War soldier apart was the fact that he came from a less sophisticated society. He was no starry-eyed innocent, to be sure—or, if he was, the army quickly took care of that—but the America of 1860's was less highly developed than modern America. It lacked the ineffable advantages of radio, television, and moving pictures. It was still essentially a rural nation; it had growing cities, but they were smaller and somehow less urban than today's cities; a much greater percentage of the population lived on farms or in country towns and villages than is the case now, and there was more of a backwoods, hay-seed-in-the-hair flavor to the people who came from them.

For example: every war finds some ardent youngsters who want to enlist despite the fact that they are under the military age limit of eighteen. Such a lad today simply goes to the recruiting station, swears that he is eighteen, and signs up. The lad of the 1860's saw it a little differently. He could not swear that he was eighteen when he was only sixteen; in his innocent way, he felt that to lie to his own government was just plain wrong. But he worked out a little dodge that got him into the army anyway. He would take a bit of paper, scribble the number *18* on it, and put it in the sole of his shoe. Then, when the recruiting officer asked him how old he was, he could truthfully say: "I am *over* eighteen." That was a common happening, early in the Civil War; one cannot possibly imagine it being tried today.

Similarly, the drill sergeants repeatedly found that among the raw recruits there were men so abysmally untaught that they did not know left from right, and hence could not step off on the left foot as all soldiers should. To teach these lads how to march, the sergeants would tie a wisp of hay to the left foot and a wisp of straw to the right; then, setting the men to march, they would chant, "Hay-foot, straw-foot, hay-foot, straw-foot"—and so on, until everybody had caught on. A common name for a green recruit in those days was "strawfoot."

On the drill field, when a squad was getting basic training, the men were as likely as not to intone a little rhythm chant as they tramped across the sod—thus:

March! March! March old soldier march!
Hayfoot, strawfoot,
Belly-full of bean soup—
March old soldier march!

Because of his unsophistication, the ordinary soldier in the Civil War, North and South alike, usually joined up with very romantic ideas about soldiering. Army life rubbed the romance off just as rapidly then as it does now, but at the start every volunteer went into the army thinking that he was heading off to high adventure. Under everything else, he enlisted because he thought army life was going to be fun, and usually it took quite a few weeks in camp to disabuse him of this strange notion. Right at the start, soldiering had an almost idyllic quality; if this quality faded rapidly, the memory of it remained through all the rest of life.

Early days in camp simply cemented the idea. An Illinois recruit, writing home from training camp, confessed: "It is fun to lie around, face unwashed, hair uncombed, shirt unbuttoned and everything un-everythinged. It sure beats clerking." Another Illinois boy confessed: "I don't see why people will stay at home when they can get to soldiering. A year of it is worth getting shot for to any man." And a Massachusetts boy, recalling the early days of army life, wrote that "Our drill, as I remember it, consisted largely of running around the Old Westbury town hall, yelling like Devils and firing at an imaginary foe." One of the commonest discoveries that comes from a reading of Civil War diaries is that the chief worry, in training camp, was a fear that the war would be over before the ardent young recruits could get into it. It is only fair to say that most of the diarists looked back on this innocent worry, a year or so afterward, with rueful amusement.

There was a regiment recruited in northern Pennsylvania in 1861—13th Pennsylvania Reserves officially, known to the rest of the Union Army as the Bucktails because the rookies decorated their camp—and in mid-spring these youthful soldiers were ordered to rendezvous at Harrisburg. So they marched crosscountry (along a road known today as the Bucktail Trail) to the north branch of the Susquehanna, where they built rafts. One raft, for the colonel, was made oversized with a stable; the colonel's horse had to ride too. Then the Bucktails floated down the river, singing and firing their muskets and having a gay old time, camping out along the bank at night, and finally they got to Harrisburg; and they served through the worst of the war, getting badly shot up and losing most of their men to Confederate bullets, but they never forgot the picnic air of those first days of army life, when they drifted down a river through the forests, with a song in the air and the bright light of adventure shining just ahead. Men do not go to war that way nowadays.

Discipline in those early regiments was pretty sketchy. The big catch was that most regiments were recruited locally—in one town, or one county, or in one part of a city—and everybody more or less knew everybody else. Particularly, the privates knew their officers—most of whom were elected to their jobs by the enlisted men—and they never saw any sense in being formal with them. Within reasonable limits, the Civil War private was willing to do what his company commander told him to do, but he saw little point in carrying it to extremes.

So an Indiana Soldier wrote: "We had enlisted to put down the Rebellion, and had no patience with the red-tape tomfoolery of the regular service. The boys recognized no superiors, except in the line of legitimate duty. Shoulder straps waived, a private was ready at the drop of a hat to thrash his commander—a thing that occurred more than once." A New York regiment, drilling on a hot parade ground, heard a private address his company commander thus— "Say, Tom, let's quit this darn foolin' around and go over to the sutler's and get a drink." There was very little of the "Captain, sir" business in those armies. If a company or regimental officer got anything especial in the way of obedience, he got it because the enlisted men recognized him as a natural leader and superior and not just because he had a commission signed by Abraham Lincoln.

Odd rivalries developed between regiments. (It should be noted that the Civil War soldier's first loyalty went usually to his regiment, just as a navy man's loyalty goes to his ship; he liked to believe that his regiment was better than all others, and he would fight for it, any time and anywhere.) The army legends of those days tell of a Manhattan regiment, camped near Washington, whose nearest neighbor was a regiment from Brooklyn, with which the Manhattanites nursed a deep rivalry. Neither regiment had a chaplain; and there came to the Manhattan colonel one day a minister, who volunteered to hold religious services for the men in the ranks.

The colonel doubted that this would be a good idea. His men, he said, were rather irreligious, not to say godless, and he feared they would not give the reverend gentleman a respectful hearing. But the minister said he would take his chances; after all, he had just held services with the Brooklyn regiment, and the men there had been very quiet and devout. That was enough for the colonel. What the Brooklyn regiment could do, his regiment could do. He ordered the men paraded for divine worship, announcing that any man who talked, laughed, or even coughed would be summarily court-martialed.

So the clergyman held services, and everyone was attentive. At the end of the sermon, the minister asked if any of his hearers would care to step forward and make public profession of faith; in the Brooklyn regiment, he said, fourteen men had done this. Instantly the New York colonel was on his feet.

"Adjutant!" he bellowed. "We're not going to let that damn Brooklyn regiment beat us at anything. Detail twenty men and have them baptized at once!"

Each regiment seemed to have its own mythology, tales which may have been false but which, by their mere existence, reflected faithfully certain aspects of army life. The 48th New York, for instance, was said to have an unusually large number of ministers in its ranks, serving not as chaplains but as combat soldiers. The 48th, fairly early in the war, found itself posted in a swamp along the South Carolina coast, toiling mightily in semitropical heat, amid clouds of mosquitoes, to build fortifications, and it was noted that all hands became excessively profane, including the one-time clergymen. A visiting general, watching the regiment at work one day, recalled the legend and asked the regiment's lieutenant colonel if he himself was a minister in private life.

"Well, no, General," said the officer apologetically. "I can't say that I was a regularly ordained minister. I was just one of these ______ ______ local preachers."

Another story was hung on this same 48th New York. A Confederate ironclad gunboat was supposed to be ready to steam through channels in the swamp and attack the 48th's outposts, and elaborate plans were made to trap it with obstruction in the channel, a tangle of ropes to snarl the propellers, and so on. But it occurred to the colonel that even if the gunboat was trapped the soldiers could not get into it; it was sheathed in iron, all its ports would be closed, and men with axes could never chop their way into it. Then the colonel had an inspiration. Remembering that many of his men had been recruited from the less savory districts of New York City, he paraded the regiment and (according to legend) announced:

"Now men, you've been in this cursed swamp for two weeks—up to your ears in mud, no fun, no glory and blessed poor pay. Here's a chance. Let every man who has had experience as a cracksman or a safeblower step to the front." To the last man, the regiment marched forward four paces and came expectantly to attention.

Not unlike this was the reputation of the 6th New York, which contained so many bowery toughs that the rest of the army said a man had to be able to show that he had done time in prison in order to get into the regiment. It was about to leave for the South, and the colonel gave his men an inspirational talk. They were going, he said to a land of wealthy plantation owners, where each Southerner had riches of which he could be despoiled; and he took out his own gold watch and held it up for all to see, remarking that any deserving soldier could easily get one like it, once they got down to plantation-land. Half an hour later, wishing to see what time it was, he felt for his watch . . . and it was gone.

If the Civil War army spun queer tales about itself, it had to face a reality which, in all of its aspects, was singularly unpleasant. One of the worst aspects had to do with food.

From first to last, the Civil War armies enlisted no men as cooks, and there were no cooks' and bakers' schools to help matters. Often enough, when in camp, a company would simply be issued a quantity of provisions—flour, pork, beans, potatoes, and so on—and invited to prepare the stuff as best it could. Half a dozen men would form a mess, members would take turns with the cooking, and everybody had to eat what these amateurs prepared or go hungry. Later in the war, each company commander would usually detail two men to act as cooks for the company, and if either of the two happened to know anything about cooking the company was in luck. One army legend held that company officers usually detailed the least valuable soldiers to this job, on the theory that they would do less harm in the cook shack than anywhere else. One soldier, writing after the war, asserted flatly: "A company cook is a most peculiar being; he generally knows less about cooking than any other man in the company. Not being able to learn the drill, and too dirty to appear on inspection, he is sent to the cook house to get him out of the ranks."

When an army was on the march, the ration issue usually consisted of salt pork, hardtack, and coffee. (In the Confederate Army the coffee was often missing, and the hardtack was frequently replaced by corn bread; often enough the meal was not sifted, and stray bits of cob would appear in it.) The hardtack was good enough, if fresh, which was not always the case; with age it usually got infested with weevils, and veterans remarked that is was better to eat it in the dark.

In the Union Army, most of the time, the soldier could supplement his rations (if he had money) by buying extras from the sutler—the latter being a civilian merchant licensed to accompany the army, functioning somewhat as the regular post exchange functions nowadays. The sutler charged high prices and specialized in indigestibles like pies, canned lobster salad, and so on; and it was noted that men who patronized him regularly came down with stomach upsets. The Confederate Army had few sutlers, which helps to explain why the hungry Confederates were so delighted when they could capture a Yankee camp: to seize a sutler's tent meant high living for the captors, and the men in Lee's army were furious when, in the 1864 campaign, they learned that General Grant had ordered the Union Army to move without sutlers. Johnny Reb felt that Grant was really taking an unfair advantage by cutting off this possible source of supply.

If Civil War cooking arrangements were impromptu and imperfect, the same applied to its hospital system. The surgeons, usually, were good men by the standards of the day—which were low since no one on earth knew anything about germs or about how wounds became infected, and antisepsis in the operating room was a concept that had not yet come into existence; it is common to read of a surgeon whetting his scalpel on the sole of his shoe just before operating. But the hospital attendants, stretcher-bearers, and the like were chosen just as the company cooks were chosen; that is, they were detailed from the ranks, and the average officer selected the most worthless men he had simply because he wanted to get rid of men who could not be counted on in combat. As a result, sick or wounded men often got atrocious care.

A result of all of this—coupled with the fact that many men enlisted without being given any medical examinations—was that every Civil War regiment suffered a constant wastage from sickness. On paper, a regiment was supposed to have a strength ranging between 960 and 1,040 men; actually, no regiment ever got to the battlefield with anything like that strength, and since there was no established system for sending in replacements a veteran regiment that could muster 350 enlisted men present for duty was considered pretty solid. From first to last, approximately twice as many Civil War soldiers died of disease—typhoid, dysentery, and pneumonia were the great killers—as died in action; and in addition to those who died a great many more got medical discharges.

In its wisdom, the Northern government set up a number of base hospitals in Northern states, far from the battle fronts, on the theory that a man recovering from wounds or sickness would recuperate better back home. Unfortunately, the hospitals thus established were under local control, and the men in them were no longer under the orders of their own regiments or armies. As a result, thousands of men who were sent north for convalescence never returned to the army. Many were detailed for light work at the hospitals, and in these details they stayed because nobody had the authority to extract them and send them back to duty. Others, recovering their health, simply went home and stayed there. They were answerable to the hospital authorities, not to the army command, and the hospital authorities rarely cared very much whether they returned to duty or not. The whole system was ideally designed to make desertion easy.

On top of all of this, many men had very little understanding of the requirements of military discipline. A homesick boy often saw nothing wrong in leaving the army and going home to see the folks for a time. A man from a farm might slip off to go home and put in a crop. In neither case would the man look on himself as a deserter; he meant to return, he figured he would get back in time for any fighting that would take place, and in his own mind he was innocent of any wrongdoing. But in many cases the date of return would be postponed from week to week; the man might end as a deserter, even though he had not intended to be one when he left.

This merely reflected the loose discipline that prevailed in Civil War armies, which in turn reflected the underlying civilian-mindedness that pervaded the rank and file. The behavior of Northern armies on the march in Southern territory reflected the same thing—and, in the end, had a profound effect on the institution of chattel slavery.

Armies of occupation always tend to bear down hard on civilian property in enemy territory. Union armies in the Civil War, being imperfectly disciplined to begin with—and suffering, furthermore, from a highly defective rationing system—bore down with especial fervor. Chickens, hams, cornfields, anything edible that might be found on a Southern plantation, looked like fair game, and the loose fringe of stragglers that always trailed around the edges of a moving Union army looted with a fine disregard for civilian property rights.

This was made all the more pointed by the fact that the average Northern soldier, poorly indoctrinated though he was, had strong feelings about the evils of secession. To his mind, the Southerners who sought to set up a nation of their own were in rebellion against the best government mankind had ever known. Being rebels, they had forfeited their rights; if evil things happened to them, that (as the average Northern soldier saw it) was no more than just retribution. This meant that even when the army command tried earnestly to prevent looting and individual foraging, the officers at company and regimental levels seldom tried very hard to carry out the high command's orders.

William Tecumseh Sherman has come down in history as the very archetype of the Northern soldier who believed in pillage and looting; yet during the first years of the was Sherman resorted to all manner of ferocious punishments to keep his men from despoiling Southern property. He had looters tied up by the thumbs, ordered courts-martial, issued any number of stern orders—and all to very little effect. Long before he adopted the practice of commandeering or destroying Southern property as a war measure, his soldiers were practicing it against his will, partly because discipline was poor and partly because they saw nothing wrong with it.

It was common for a Union colonel, as his regiment made camp in a Southern state, to address his men, pointing to a nearby farm, and say: "Now, boys, that barn is full of nice fat pigs and chickens. I don't want to see any of you take any of them"—whereupon he would fold his arms and look sternly in the opposite direction. It was also common for a regimental commander to read, on parade, some ukase from higher authority forbidding foraging, and then to wink solemnly—a clear hint that he did not expect anyone to take the order seriously. One colonel, punishing some men who had robbed a chicken house, said angrily: "Boys, I want you to understand that I am not punishing you for stealing but for getting caught at it."

It is nearly a century since that war was fought, and things look a little different now than they looked at the time. At this distance, it may be possible to look indulgently on the wholesale foraging in which Union armies indulged; to the Southern farmers who bore the brunt of it, the business looked very ugly indeed. Many a Southern family saw the foodstuffs needed for the winter swept away in an hour by grinning hoodlums who did not need and could not use a quarter of what they took. Among the foragers there were many lawless characters who took watches, jewels, and any other valuables they could find; it is recorded that a squad would now and then carry a piano out to the lawn, take it apart, and use the wires to hang pots and pans over the campfire. . . . The Civil War was really romantic only at a considerable distance.

Underneath his feeling that it was good to add chickens and hams to the army ration, and his belief that civilians in a state of secession could expect no better fate, the Union soldier also came to believe that to destroy Southern property was to help win the war. Under orders, he tore up railroads and burned warehouses; it was not long before he realized that anything that damaged the Confederate economy weakened the Confederate war effort, so he rationalized his looting and foraging by arguing that it was a step in breaking the Southern will to resist. It is at this point that the institution of human slavery enters the picture.

Most Northern soldiers had very little feeling against slavery as such, and very little sympathy for the Negro himself. They thought they were fighting to save the Union, not to end slavery, and except for New England troops most Union regiments contained very little abolition sentiment. Nevertheless, the soldiers moved energetically and effectively to destroy slavery, not because they especially intended to but simply because they were out to do all the damage they could do. They were operating against Southern property—and the most obvious, important, and easily removable property of all was the slave. To help the slaves get away from the plantation was, clearly, to weaken Southern productive capacity, which in turn weakened Confederate armies. Hence the Union soldier, wherever he went, took the peculiar institution apart, chattel by chattel.

As a result, slavery had been fatally weakened long before the war itself came to an end. The mere act of fighting the war killed it. Of all institutions on earth, the institution of human slavery was the one least adapted to survive a war. It could not survive the presence of loose-jointed, heavy-handed armies of occupation. It may hardly be too much to say that the mere act of taking up arms in slavery's defense doomed slavery.

Above and beyond everything else, of course, the business of the Civil War soldier was to fight. He fought with weapons that look very crude to modern eyes, and he moved by an outmoded system of tactics, but the price he paid when he got into action was just as high as the price modern soldiers pay despite the almost infinite development of firepower since the 1860's.

Standard infantry weapon in the Civil War was the rifled Springfield—a muzzle-loader firing a conical lead bullet, usually of .54 caliber.

To load was rather laborious, and it took a good man to get off more than two shots a minute. The weapon had a range of nearly a mile, and its "effective range"—that is, the range at which it would hit often enough to make infantry fire truly effective—was figured at about 250 yards. Compared with a modern Garand, the old muzzle-loader is no better than a museum piece; but compared with all previous weapons—the weapons on which infantry tactics in the

1860's were still based—it was a fearfully destructive and efficient piece.

For the infantry of that day still moved and fought in forma tions dictated in the old days of smoothbore muskets, whose effective range was no more than 100 yards and which were wildly inaccurate at any distance. Armies using those weapons attacked in solid mass formations, the men standing, literally, elbow to elbow. They could get from effective range to hand-to-hand fighting in a very short time, and if they had a proper numerical advantage over the defensive line they could come to grips without losing too many men along the way. But in the Civil War the conditions had changed radically; men would be hit while the rival lines were still half a mile apart, and to advance in mass was simply to invite wholesale destruction. Tactics had not yet been adjusted to the new rifles; as a result, Civil War attacks could be fearfully costly, and when the defenders dug entrenchments and got some protection—as the men learned to do, very quickly—a direct frontal assault could be little better than a form of mass suicide.

It took the high command a long time to revise tactics to meet this changed situation, and Civil War battles ran up dreadful casualty lists. For an army to lose 25 per cent of its numbers in a major battle was by no means uncommon, and in some fights—the Confederate army at Gettysburg is an outstanding example—the percentage of loss ran close to one-third of the total number engaged. Individual units were sometimes nearly wiped out. Some of the Union and Confederate regiments that fought at Gettysburg lost up to 80 per cent of their numbers; a regiment with such losses was usually wrecked, as an effective fighting force, for the rest of the war.

The point of all of which is that the discipline which took the Civil War soldier into action, while it may have been very sketchy by modern standards, was nevertheless highly effective on the field of battle. Any armies that could go through such battles as Antietam, Stone's River, Franklin or Chickamauga and come back for more had very little to learn about the business of fighting.

Perhaps the Confederate General D. H. Hill said it, once and for all. The battle of Malvern Hill, fought on the Virginia peninsula early in the summer of 1862, finished the famous Seven Days campaign, in which George B. McClellan's Army of the Potomac was driven back from in front of Richmond by Robert E. Lee's Army of Northern Virginia. At Malvern Hill, McClellan's men fought a rear-guard action—a bitter, confused fight which came at the end of a solid week of wearing, costly battles and forced marches. Federal artillery wrecked the Confederate assault columns, and at the end of the day Hill looked out over the battlefield, strewn with dead and wounded boys. Shaking his head, and reflecting on the valor in attack and in defense which the two armies had displayed, Hill never forgot about this. Looking back on it, long after the war was over, he declared, in substance:

"Give me Confederate infantry and Yankee artillery and I'll whip the world!"

Second Inaugural Address (1865)

Abraham Lincoln

*F*ellow-Countrymen:

At this second appearing to take the oath of the Presidential office there is less occasion for an extended address than there was at the first. Then a statement somewhat in detail of a course to be pursued seemed fitting and proper. Now, at the expiration of four years, during which public declarations have been constantly called forth on every point and phase of the great contest which still absorbs the attention and engrosses the energies of the nation, little that is new could be presented. The progress of our arms, upon which all else chiefly depends, is as well known to the public as to myself, and it is, I trust, reasonably satisfactory and encouraging to all. With high hope for the future, no prediction in regard to it is ventured.

On the occasion corresponding to this four years ago all thoughts were anxiously directed to an impending civil war. All dreaded it, all sought to avert it. While the inaugural address was being delivered from this place, devoted altogether to saving the Union without war, insurgent agents were in the city seeking to destroy it without war—seeking to dissolve the Union and divide effects by negotiation. Both parties deprecated war, but one of them would make war rather than let the nation survive, and the other would accept war rather than let it perish, and the war came.

One-eighth of the whole population were colored slaves, not distributed generally over the Union, but localized in the southern part of it. These slaves constituted a peculiar and powerful interest. All knew that this interest was somehow the cause of the war. To strengthen, perpetuate, and extend this interest was the object for which the insurgents would rend the Union even by war, while the Government claimed no right to do more than to restrict the territorial enlargement of it. Neither party expected for the war the magnitude or the duration which it has already attained. Neither anticipated that the cause of the conflict might cease with or even before the conflict itself should cease. Each looked for an easier triumph, and a result less fundamental and astounding. Both read the same Bible and pray to the same God, and each invokes His aid against the other. It may seem strange that any men should dare to ask a just God's assistance in wringing their bread from the sweat of other men's faces, but let us judge not, that we be not judged. The prayers of both could not be answered. That of neither has been answered fully. The Almighty has His own purposes. "Woe unto the world because of offenses; for it must needs be that offenses come, but woe to that man by whom the offense cometh." If we shall suppose that American slavery is one of those offenses which, in the providence of God, must needs come, but which, having continued through His appointed time, He now wills to remove, and that He gives to both North and South this terrible war as the woe due to those by whom the offense came, shall we discern therein any departure from those divine attributes which the believers in a living God always ascribe to Him? Fondly do we hope, fervently do we pray, that this mighty scourge of war may speedily pass away. Yet, if God wills that it continue until all the wealth piled by the bondsman's two hundred and fifty years of unrequited toil shall be sunk, and until every drop of blood drawn with the lash shall be paid by another drawn with the sword, as was said three thousand years ago, so still it must be said "the judgments of the Lord are true and righteous altogether."

With malice toward none, with charity for all, with firmness in the right as God gives us to see the right, let us strive on to finish the work we are in, to bind up the nation's wounds, to care for him who shall have borne the battle and for his widow and his orphan, to do all which may achieve and cherish a just and lasting peace among ourselves and with all nations.

The Mississippi "Black Code" (1865)

Be it enacted. . . . That all freedmen, free negroes, and mulattoes may sue and be sued, implead and be impleaded, in all the courts of law and equity of this State, and may acquire personal property, and choses in action, by descent or purchase, and may dispose of the same in the same manner and to the same extent that white persons may: . . .

All freedmen, free negroes, and mulattoes may intermarry with each other, in the same manner and under the same regulations that are provided by law for white persons; . . .

All freedmen, free negroes, or mulattoes who do now and have herebefore lived and cohabited together as husband and wife shall be taken and held in law as legally married, and the issue shall be taken and held as legitimate for all purposes; that it shall not be lawful for any freedman, free negro, or mulatto to intermarry with any white person; nor for any white person to intermarry with any freedman, free negro, or mulatto; and any person who shall so intermarry, shall be deemed guilty of felony, and on conviction thereof shall be confined in the State penitentiary for life; . . .

All contracts for labor made with freedmen, free negroes, and mulattoes for a longer period than one month shall be in writing, and in duplicate, attested and read to said freedman, free negro, or mulatto by a beat, city or county officer, or two disinterested white persons of the county in which the labor is to be performed, of which each party shall have one; and said contracts shall be taken and held as entire contracts, and if the laborer shall quit the service of the employer before the expiration of his term of service, without good cause, he shall forfeit his wages for that year up to the time of quitting.

Every civil officer shall, and every person may, arrest and carry back to his or her legal employer any freedman, free negro, or mulatto who shall have quit the service of his or her employer before the expiration of his or her term of service without good cause; . . .

It shall be the duty of all sheriffs, justices of the peace, and other civil officers of the several counties in this State, to report to the probate courts of their respective counties semi-annually, . . . all freedmen, free negroes, and mulattoes, under the age of eighteen, in their respective counties, beats, or districts, who are orphans, or whose parent or parents have not the means or who refuse to provide for and support said minors; and thereupon it shall be the duty of said probate court to order the clerk of said court to apprentice said minors to some competent and suitable person, on such terms as the court may direct, having a particular care to the interest of said minor: *Provided*, that the former owner of said minors shall have the preference when, in the opinion of the court, he or she shall be a suitable person for that purpose.

The said court shall be fully satisfied that the person or persons to whom said minor shall be apprenticed shall be a suitable person to have the charge and care of said minor, and fully to protect the interest of said minor. The said court shall require the said master or mistress to . . . furnish said minor with sufficient food and clothing; to treat said minor humanely; furnish medical attention in case of sickness; teach, or cause to be taught, him or her to read and write, if under fifteen years old. . . .

In the management and control of said apprentices, said master or mistress shall have the power to inflict such moderate corporal chastisement as a father or guardian is allowed to inflict on his or her child or ward at common law; *Provided*, that in no case shall cruel or inhuman punishment be inflicted.

All freedmen, free negroes and mulattoes in this State, over the age of eighteen years, found on the second Monday in January, 1866, or thereafter, with no lawful employment or business, or found unlawfully assembling themselves together, either in the day or night time, and all white persons so assembling themselves with freedmen, free negroes or mulattoes, or usually associating with freedmen, free negroes or mulattoes, on terms of equality or living in adultery or fornication with a freed woman, free negro or mulatto, shall be deemed vagrants, and on conviction thereof shall be fined and imprisoned at the discretion of the court. . . .

No freedman, free negro or mulatto, not in the military service of the United States government, and not licensed so to do by the board of police of his or her county, shall keep or carry fire-arms of any kind, or any ammunition, dirk or bowie knife, and on conviction thereof in the county court shall be punished by fine, . . . and all such arms or ammunition shall be forfeited to the informer; . . .

Any freedman, free negro, or mulatto committing riots, routs, affrays, trespasses, malicious mischief, cruel treatment to animals, seditious speeches, insulting gestures, language, or acts, or assaults on any person, disturbance of the peace, exercising the function of a minister of the Gospel without a license from some regularly organized church, vending spirituous or intoxicating liquors, or committing any other misdemeanor, the punishment of which is not specifically provided for by law, shall, upon conviction thereof in the county court, be fined. . . . and may be imprisoned at the discretion of the court, not exceeding thirty days.